# Word 2007 for Starters

## THE MISSING MANUAL

# Word 2007 for Starters

## THE MISSING MANUAL

### Your best friend for answers

## Chris Grover

**POGUE PRESS™**
**O'REILLY®**

Beijing · Cambridge · Farnham · Köln · Paris · Sebastopol · Taipei · Tokyo

# Word 2007 for Starters: THE MISSING MANUAL

by Chris Grover

Copyright © 2007 O'Reilly Media, Inc. All rights reserved.
Printed in the United States of America.

Published by O'Reilly Media, Inc., 1005 Gravenstein Highway North, Sebastopol, CA 95472.

O'Reilly books may be purchased for educational, business, or sales promotional use. Online editions are also available for most titles (*safari.oreilly.com*). For more information, contact our corporate/institutional sales department: (800) 998-9938 or *corporate@oreilly.com*.

**Printing History:**
January 2007:          First Edition.

RepKover™
This book uses RepKover,™ a durable and flexible lay-flat binding.

ISBN-10: 0-596-52830-2
ISBN-13: 978-0-596-52830-0
[M]

# TABLE OF CONTENTS

# PART TWO: CREATING LONGER AND MORE COMPLEX DOCUMENTS

# THE MISSING CREDITS

## About the Author

 **Chris Grover** got his first computer in 1982 when he realized it was easier to write on a computer than an IBM Selectric. He never looked back. Chris has worked as a technical writer, advertising copywriter, and product publicist for more than 25 years. He is the coauthor of *Digital Photography: The Missing Manual.* In addition to computer topics, he's written book reviews, software reviews, and articles on subjects ranging from home remodeling to video recorder repairs. His latest project is the launching of Bolinas Road Creative (*www.bolinasroad.com*), an agency that helps small businesses promote their products and services. Chris lives in Fairfax, California with his wife and two daughters who have learned to tolerate his computer and gadget obsessions.

## About the Creative Team

**Nan Barber** (editor) has worked with the Missing Manual series since its inception—long enough to remember booting up her computer from a floppy disk. Email: *nanbarber@oreilly.com.*

**Peter Meyers** (editor) works as an editor at O'Reilly on the Missing Manual series. He lives with his wife and cats in New York City. Email: *peter.meyers@gmail.com.*

**Colleen Gorman** (editor) is making a cameo appearance in O'Reilly's Missing Manual series. She lives in Boston with her dictionary. Email: *colleen@oreilly.com.*

**Michele Filshie** (editor, indexer) is O'Reilly's assistant editor for Missing Manuals and editor of *Dont Get Burned on eBay.* Before turning to the world of computer-related books, Michele spent many happy years at Black Sparrow Press. She lives in Sebastopol. Email: *mfilshie@oreilly.com*.

**Dawn Mann** (technical reviewer) has been with O'Reilly for over three years and is currently an editorial assistant. When not working, she likes rock climbing, playing soccer, and generally getting into trouble. Email: *dawn@oreilly.com*.

**Greg Guntle** (technical reviewer) is a Windows veteran covering Office, Programming, Networks and Operating Systems. He's been providing technical editing services for the past 20 years.

**Rick Jewell** (technical reviewer) has been in the technical industry since 1995. He's now a Beta Support Engineer for Microsoft. Since Microsoft acquired Groove in April of 2005, he's been a technical support engineer supporting the Groove product suite, which will be incorporated into the Premium edition of Microsoft Office 2007 when it's released.

**Jill Steinberg** (copy editor) is a freelance writer and editor based in Seattle, and has produced content for O'Reilly, Intel, Microsoft, and the University of Washington. Jill was educated at Brandeis University, Williams College, and Stanford University. Email: *saysjill@mac.com*

## Acknowledgements

Many thanks to the whole Missing Manuals creative team, especially to Nan Barber, who had her work cut out for her making my prose readable. Peter Meyers helped shape the book and gently kept us all on track. Dawn Mann, Greg Guntle, and Rick Jewell checked and double-checked the technical details. Thanks to Michele Filshie for copyediting, indexing, and working weekends.

As always, thanks to my beautiful wife Joyce, my collaborator in that other project—life. And hugs for Mary and Amy who help me approach everything I do with fresh enthusiasm and a bundle of questions.

—*Chris Grover*

## The Missing Manual Series

Missing Manuals are witty, superbly written guides to computer products that don't come with printed manuals (which is just about all of them). Each book features a handcrafted index and RepKover™, a detached-spine binding that lets the book lie perfectly flat without the assistance of weights or cinder blocks.

Recent and upcoming titles include:

*Access 2003 for Starters: The Missing Manual* by Kate Chase and Scott Palmer

*Access 2007 for Starters: The Missing Manual* by Matthew MacDonald

*Access 2007: The Missing Manual* by Matthew MacDonald

*Digital Photography: The Missing Manual* by Chris Grover and Barbara Brundage

*Excel 2003 for Starters: The Missing Manual* by Matthew MacDonald

*Excel 2003: The Missing Manual* by Matthew MacDonald

*Excel 2007: The Missing Manual* by Matthew MacDonald

*Excel 2007 for Starters: The Missing Manual* by Matthew MacDonald

*Google: The Missing Manual*, Second Edition by Sarah Milstein, J.D. Biersdorfer, and Matthew MacDonald

*iMovie 6 & iDVD: The Missing Manual* by David Pogue

*iPhoto 6: The Missing Manual* by David Pogue

*iPod: The Missing Manual*, Fifth Edition by J.D. Biersdorfer

*PCs: The Missing Manual* by Andy Rathbone

*Photoshop Elements 5: The Missing Manual* by Barbara Brundage

*PowerPoint 2007 for Starters: The Missing Manual* by E.A. Vander Veer

*PowerPoint 2007: The Missing Manual* by E.A. Vander Veer

*Quicken for Starters: The Missing Manual* by Bonnie Biafore

*The Internet: The Missing Manual* by David Pogue and J.D. Biersdorfer

*Windows XP for Starters: The Missing Manual* by David Pogue

*Windows XP Home Edition: The Missing Manual*, Second Edition by David Pogue

*Windows XP Pro: The Missing Manual*, Second Edition by David Pogue, Craig Zacker, and Linda Zacker

*Windows Vista: The Missing Manual* by David Pogue

*Windows Vista for Starters: The Missing Manual* by David Pogue

*Word 2007: The Missing Manual* by Chris Grover

# INTRODUCTION

**WORD.** Microsoft Word has been the world's most popular word processor for so long, it needs only one name—like Oprah or Madonna. Unlike certain celebrities, though, Word has undergone a makeover that goes well beyond cosmetic. Microsoft has redesigned the way you interact with the program and has redefined the underlying document format (don't worry; your old Word documents will still work).

Some things haven't changed: Word 2007 still makes it easy to create professional-looking letters, business reports, and novels. But Microsoft has loaded the program with new features to make designing and formatting attractive documents easier than ever. So even if you're well acquainted with its predecessors, Word 2007 needs an introduction and a new book too. Some of the commands that are old favorites—like Cut and Paste—are in new places.

# What Word Does

You type words, and they appear onscreen, what else? Well, maybe in the first version of Word. But in Word 2007, the program does a whole lot more. Word's designers knew what kinds of documents folks are likely to create, and stocked the program with predesigned templates that have all the important elements in place—headings, signature line, text boxes, and so on. You don't even have to worry about making it look nice: Word comes with attractive, built-in color schemes—called themes—that you can apply with a single click. Here are just some of the things you can create:

▶ Letters, lists, notecards, and other personal documents. You can even print your own greeting cards and invitations.

▶ Programs, menus, and booklets. Some of Word's templates are multipage affairs, letting you create scrapbooks, catalogs, playbills, and more.

▶ Brochures, reports, business cards, and other business documents. Word even has a feature that lets you create tables, so you don't have to use a spreadsheet program like Excel for simple tables. Word's are better looking, too.

To create all these documents, all you have to do is type the words. But even there, Word takes some of the work off your hands. It has tools that help you check your spelling and grammar, and look up facts and definitions. Word's AutoText feature even does some of the typing for you. And if you need an illustration, Word gives you a slew of pictures you can plunk right onto the page—no drawing skills required.

## The New Word

In the past, when Microsoft introduced new versions of Word, it seemed as if the developers had simply tacked new features on top of the old program wherever they'd fit. Sometimes the result was sort of like putting fins on a Volkswagen beetle. With Word 2007, however, Microsoft listened to the critics who complained about Word's maze of menus and dialog boxes. There were also legitimate complaints about illogically placed commands and important tools that were buried. With Word 2007, all the commands have been reorganized according to task and function. Is the new system going to put a smile on everyone's face? No, probably not. Is it an improvement that makes Word easier to use for most people? Yes.

Another concern was security. Microsoft has made major changes in Word's file formats to minimize the chance that you'll open a document containing a virus. It would be naïve to think these steps will eliminate virus threats, but they'll certainly help.

So c'mon, pop the hood, kick the tires, and take a look at Word's new chassis.

▶ **Meet the ribbon.** The first thing you notice when you fire up Word 2007 is that it looks different from other Windows programs you've used. The old menus are gone and so are the toolbars. In their place you have the ribbon, which is sort of a hybrid of the two, as shown in Figure I-1. Where you used to see menu names, you see the names on tabs. Click a tab, and you see a ribbon full of buttons, tools, and commands. Unlike Word's previous toolbars, these buttons and tools are big, visual, and often include labels. Buttons clearly state what they do with both words and pictures, and if you see a down arrow, you can be assured it opens a menu of closely related commands.

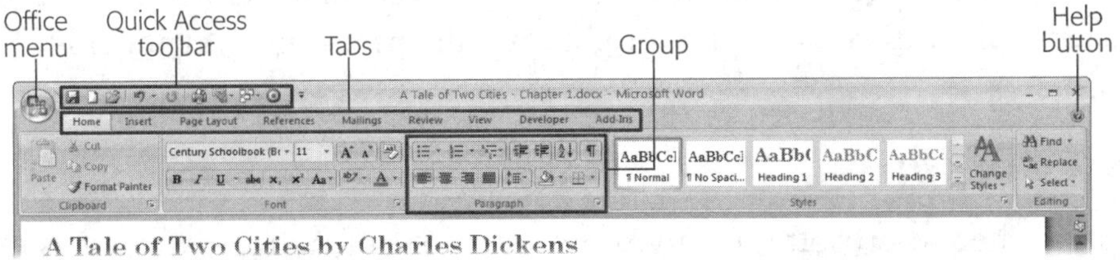

**Figure I-1.** That big round button in the upper-left corner is the Office button, where you find the commands that used to live in the File menu. When you click one of the tabs along the top of the ribbon, you see buttons and drop-down menus arranged by task. You can customize the Quick Access Toolbar by adding the commands you use most frequently. The Help button—a circle with a question mark—is always available in the upper-right corner of the main window and the dialog boxes.

___ **TIP** _____

Word's new ribbon is one of those features that's easier to understand when you see it in action. You can see a *screencast* (onscreen demonstration) of the ribbon over on the Missing Manuals Web site. Head over to the Missing CD page at www.missingmanuals.com. Look for other screencasts throughout this book.

▶ **Building Blocks for better docs.** Word 2007's Building Blocks save time and stress if you consider yourself a writer (or a doctor, or a manager), not a designer. Building Blocks are predesigned, preformatted elements that you can easily drop into your document. Microsoft has thrown in dozens of things like headers, footers, tables of contents, and fax cover pages. Choose a Building Block with the look you want, and then pop it into your document, knowing it will look good and include any of the pertinent details, like page number, document title, even your name.

▶ **Instant gratification with Live Preview.** Have you ever paused with your mouse over a command or a formatting option and wondered what it would do to your document? Those days are over. Live Preview is a new feature in Word 2007. Now when you hold your mouse over a formatting style, Building Block, or color, you see a preview right within your document. If you like the look, click your mouse button. If you don't, move your mouse away from the button or menu option, and your document snaps back to its previous appearance. And, of course, you can preview some more options.

▶ **More art for the masses.** Each version of Word includes more of everything, and Word 2007 is no different in that respect: more clip art; more charts and graphs; and more lines, shapes, and arrows. There's even a new type of artwork called SmartArt. Developed for business presentations, SmartArt makes it a breeze to create flow charts, organizational charts, and other graphics that combine words and pictures. You provide the words, and SmartArt takes care of all the sizing and formatting.

▶ **Help! Get me security.** That was the cry of many Word users when they opened a document only to let loose a virus on their poor, unsuspecting computer. Microsoft has tackled security problems from several different directions. For example, Word 2007 has a new file format that makes it easier to ferret out documents that may contain virus-infected programs. (When it comes to Word viruses, the main culprits are Visual Basic for Applications and the tools it creates, called ActiveX controls.) In Word 2007, it's also easier than ever to add digital signatures to documents to make sure files come from a trusted source and haven't been tampered with.

▶ **File this way, please.** The groans are audible any time an industry standard like Microsoft Word makes major changes to its "file format." The file format is the way a program writes information to a computer disc. As mentioned earlier, Microsoft is switching to a new file format for the best of reasons—to make all our computers safer from viruses. The downside of a new file format is that you can't open the new documents with older versions of Word unless you install a compatibility pack for the older programs. (You can read all the gory details on page 484.)

# About This Book

Microsoft expects you to get all the information you need about Word from the Help button in the upper-left corner of the window. Word's help system contains a wealth of information, and it's great in a pinch. But the helps screens are a little long on computer geek-speak and short on useful tips and explanations that make sense to the rest of us. In fact, some of the help screens are on Microsoft's Web site, so you can't even read them without an Internet connection. If you're on the road and can't afford a hotel with a wireless connection, you're out of luck.

This book is the manual you need but Microsoft didn't give you. You'll even find some things in here that Microsoft would never say. If a feature isn't up to snuff, you'll read about it in these pages. What's more, *Word for Starters 2007: The Missing Manual* is designed to accommodate readers at every technical level. You won't be lost even if you've never used any version of Microsoft Word. Look for the sidebars called Up To Speed if you feel like you need to catch up on a topic. For the advanced beginner and intermediate readers, there are plenty of details. Word's a humongous program, and this book pokes into all the nooks and crannies. You'll find examples and step-by-step instructions for many of Word's more complicated features and functions. For even more detail on the advanced topics, look for the Power Users' Clinic sidebars.

## About the Outline

*Word 2007 for Starters: The Missing Manual* is divided into three parts, each containing several chapters:

▶ Part 1 starts at the very beginning and gets you up and running fast, whether you're a Word veteran or a newcomer. This part covers creating, opening, and saving documents—complete with a description of Word's new file formats. You'll learn how to view your Word documents as outlines, Web pages, and in special print preview and reading modes.

You'll find chapters devoted to editing text and setting up new documents with custom margins, headers, and footers. You'll learn how to use Word's templates and themes—special tools that make it easy for you to create professional-looking documents. You probably know that Word includes reference tools that check your spelling and help you find the right word, but have you ever used Word's language translation tools or created a custom dictionary of your own technical terms? Now's your chance to learn how it's done. Part 1 wraps up with a complete discussion about printing Word documents.

▶ Part 2 helps you when you graduate to the next level of Word creations. When you work with long documents, it's more important than ever to plan ahead, so outlines are covered first. These chapters also cover the elements you're likely to add to longer and more complex documents, like tables and pictures.

▶ At the end of this book, an appendix explains how to find your way around Word's built-in and online help pages. It also shows you how to get assistance from a vast online community of fans and experts.

**NOTE**

This book is based on *Word 2007: The Missing Manual* (O'Reilly). That book is a truly complete reference for Word 2007, covering every feature, including geeky stuff like creating indexes and tables of contents in Word, collaborating with other writers in the same document, and running off form letters by merging Word with a list of names and addresses. If you get really deep into Word and want to learn more, *Word 2007: The Missing Manual* can be your trusted guide.

## About These Arrows

Throughout this book, and throughout the Missing Manual series, you'll find sentences like this one: "Click Start → All Programs → Microsoft Office → Microsoft Office Word 2007." That's shorthand for a much longer instruction that directs you to click the Start button to open the Start menu, and then choose All Programs. From there, click the Microsoft Office folder, and then click Word's icon to launch the program.

Similarly, this kind of arrow shorthand helps to simply the business of choosing commands and menus, as shown in Figure I-2.

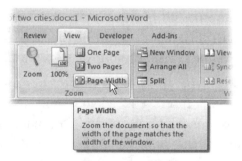

**Figure I-2.** In this book, arrow notations help to simplify Word's ribbon structure and commands. For example, "Choose View → Zoom → Page Width" is a more compact way of saying: "Click the View tab, and then go to the Zoom group and click Page Width," as shown here.

## The Very Basics

If your fingers have ever graced a computer keyboard, you're probably familiar with the following: Press the keys on your keyboard, and text appears in your document. Hold the Shift key down to type capitals or to enter the various punctuation marks you see above the numbers keys (!@#$*&^). Press Caps Lock, and your keyboard types only capital letters, but the numbers and other symbols continue to work as usual. To correct an error you've just made, you can use the Backspace key. Press it down once, and the cursor moves backward one space, erasing the last character you typed. If you continue to hold it down, it will keep on going, eating up your work like a starving man at a smorgasbord. The Delete (or Del) key, usually on or near the numerical keypad, does the same thing but for the character in *front* of the insertion point.

If you've got that under your belt, then you're ready for the rest of *Word 2007: The Missing Manual*. This book assumes you're familiar with just a few other terms and concepts:

▶ **Clicking.** This book gives you three kinds of instructions that require you to use your computer's mouse or trackpad. To *click* means to point the arrow cursor at something on the screen, and then—without moving the cursor at all—to press and release the clicker button on the mouse (or laptop trackpad). To *right-click* means to do the same thing, but with the right mouse button. To *double-click*, of course, means to click twice in rapid succession, again without moving the cursor at all. And to *drag* means to move the cursor while pressing the button.

▶ **Shift-clicking.** Here's another bit of shorthand. *Shift-click* means to hold down the Shift key, and then to click before releasing the key. If you understand that much, then instructions like Ctrl-click and Alt-click should be clear.

▶ **The ribbon.** Like the older menu system, Word's ribbon shows names across the top of the window—Home, Insert, Page Layout, and so on. In this book, these names are referred to as *tabs*. The buttons and commands on the ribbon change when you click each tab, as shown in Figure I-3. The ribbon organizes buttons and commands in *groups*; the name of each group appears along the bottom of the ribbon. For example, the Insert tab has groups called Pages, Tables, Illustrations, Links, and so on.

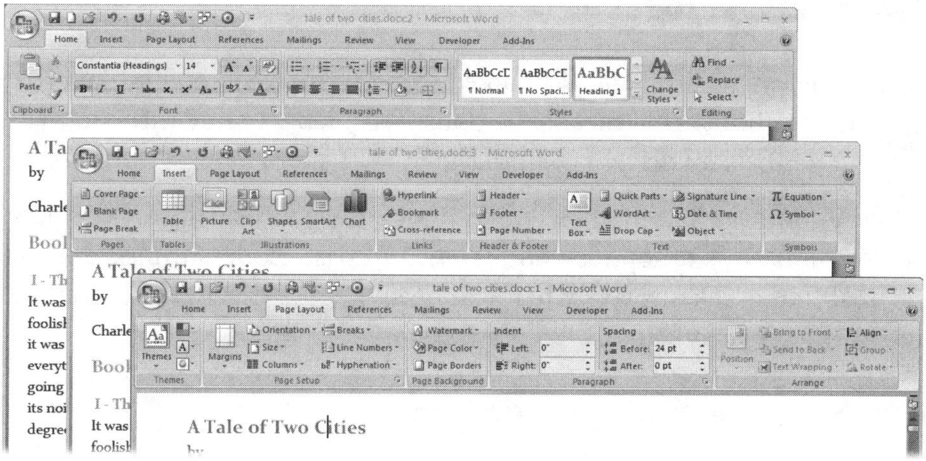

**Figure I-3.** The tools on the ribbon change when you click different tabs. From top to bottom, these examples show the Home tab, the Insert tab, and the Page Layout tab.

▶ **Keyboard shortcuts.** If you're typing along in a burst of creative energy, it's sometimes disruptive to take your hand off the keyboard, grab the mouse, and then travel all the way up to the top of the screen to, say, save your document. That's why many computer mavens prefer to trigger commands by pressing certain combinations on the keyboard. For example, in most programs you can press Ctrl+S to save the file you're currently working on. When you read an instruction like "press Ctrl+S," start by pressing the Ctrl key; while it's down, type the letter S, and then release both keys.

## About MissingManuals.com

At the *www.missingmauals.com* Web site, click the "Missing CD" link to reveal a neat, organized, chapter-by-chapter list of the downloadable practice files mentioned in this book. The Web site also offers corrections and updates to the book (to see them, click the book's title, and then click Errata). In fact, you're invited and encouraged to submit such corrections and updates yourself. In an effort to keep the book as up to date and accurate as possible, each time we print more copies of this book, we incorporate any confirmed corrections you've suggested. We also note such changes on the Web site, so you can mark corrections in your own copy of the book, if you like.

# Safari® Enabled

 When you see a Safari® Enabled icon on the cover of your favorite technology book, that means the book is available online through the O'Reilly Network Safari Bookshelf.

Safari offers a solution that's better than e-books. It's a virtual library that lets you easily search thousands of top tech books, cut and paste code samples, download chapters, and find quick answers when you need the most accurate, current information. Try it for free at *http://safari.oreilly.com*.

# PART ONE: WORD BASICS FOR SIMPLE DOCUMENTS

# CREATING, OPENING, AND SAVING DOCUMENTS

1

- ▶ Launching Word
- ▶ Creating a New Document
- ▶ Opening an Existing Document
- ▶ Your Different Document View Views
- ▶ Saving and Closing Documents

EVERY WORD PROJECT YOU CREATE—whether it's a personal letter, a TV sitcom script, or a thesis in microbiology—begins and ends the same way. You start by creating a document, and you end by saving your work. Sounds simple, but to manage your Word documents effectively, you need to know these basics and beyond. This chapter shows you all the different ways to create a new Word document—like starting from an existing document or adding text to a predesigned template—and how to choose the best one for your particular project.

You'll also learn how to work faster and smarter by changing your view of your document. If you want, you can use Word's Outline view when you're brainstorming, and then switch to Print view when you're ready for hard copy. This chapter gets you up and running with these fundamental tools so you can focus on the important stuff—your words.

---
**TIP**

If you've used Word before, then you're probably familiar with opening and saving documents. Still, you may want to skim this chapter to catch up on the differences between this version of Word and the ghosts of Word past. You'll grasp some of the big changes just by examining the figures. For more detail, check out the gray boxes and the notes and tips—like this one!

---

# Launching Word

The first time you launch Word after installation, the program asks you to confirm your name and initials. This isn't Microsoft's nefarious plan to pin you down: Word uses this information to identify documents that you create and modify. Word uses your initials to mark your edits when you review and add comments to Word documents that other people send to you.

You have three popular ways to fire up Word, so use whichever method you find quickest:

▶ **Start menu.** The Start button in the lower-left corner of your screen gives you access to all programs on your PC—Word included. To start Word, choose Start → All Programs → Microsoft Office → Microsoft Office Word.

▶ **Quick Launch toolbar.** The Quick Launch toolbar at the bottom of your screen (just to the right of the Start menu) is a great place to start programs you use frequently. Microsoft modestly assumes that you'll be using Word a lot, so it usually installs the Word icon in the Quick Launch toolbar. To start using Word, just click the W icon, and voila!

> **TIP**
>
> When you don't see the Quick Launch toolbar, here's how to display it: On the bar at the bottom of your screen, right-click an empty spot. From the menu that pops up, choose Toolbars → Quick Launch. When you're done, icons for some of your programs appear in the bottom bar. A single click fires up the program.

▶ **Opening a Word document.** Once you've created some Word documents, this method is fastest of all, since you don't have to start Word as a separate step. Just open an existing Word document, and Word starts itself. Try going to Start → My Recent Documents, and then, from the list of files, choose a Word document. You can also double-click the document's icon on the desktop or wherever it lives on your PC.

> **TIP**
>
> If you need to get familiar with the Start menu, Quick Launch toolbar, and other Windows features, then pick up a copy of *Windows XP: The Missing Manual, Second Edition* or *Windows Vista: The Missing Manual.*

So, what happens once you've got Word's motor running? If you're a newcomer, you're probably just staring with curiosity. If you're familiar with previous versions of Word, though, you may be doing a double take (Figure 1-1). In Word 2007, Microsoft combined all the old menus and toolbars into a new feature called the ribbon. Click one of the tabs above the ribbon, and you see the command buttons change below. The ribbon commands are organized into groups, with the name of each group listed at the bottom.

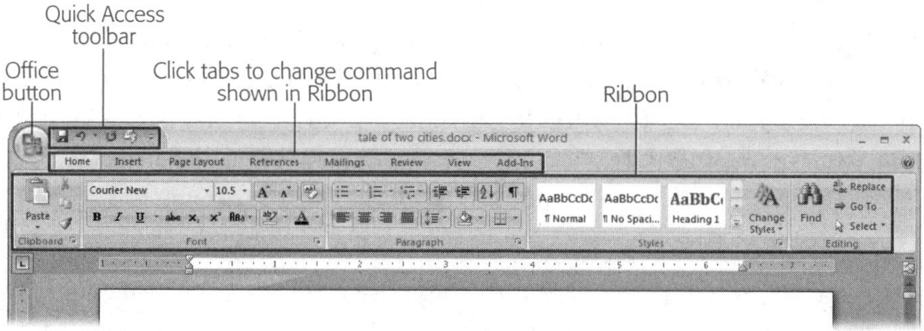

Quick Access toolbar

Office button

Click tabs to change command shown in Ribbon

Ribbon

**Figure 1-1.** When you start Word 2007 for the first time, it may look a little top-heavy. The ribbon takes up more real estate than the old menus and toolbars. This change may not matter if you have a nice big monitor. But if you want to reclaim some of that space, you can hide the ribbon by double-clicking the active tab. Later, when you need to see the ribbon commands, just click a tab

# Creating a New Document

When you start Word without opening an existing document, the program gives you an empty one to work in. If you're eager to put words to page, then type away.

Sooner or later, though, you'll want to start *another* new document. Word gives you three ways to do so:

▶ **Creating a new blank document.** When you're preparing a simple document—like a two-page essay, a note for the babysitter, or a press release—a plain, unadorned page is fine. Or, when you're just brainstorming and you're not sure what you want the final document to look like, you probably want to start with a blank slate or use one of Word's templates (more on that in a moment) to provide structure for your text.

▶ **Creating a document from an existing document.** For letters, resumes, and other documents that require more formatting, why reinvent the wheel? You can save time by using an existing document as a starting point. When you have a letter format that you like, you can use it over and over by editing the contents.

▶ **Creating a document from a template** (page 170). Use a template when you need a professional design for a complex document, like a newsletter, a contract, or meeting minutes. Templates are a lot like forms—the margins, formatting, and graphics are already in place. All you do is fill in your text.

___ TIP ___

Microsoft provides a mind-boggling number of templates with Word, but they're not the only source. You can find loads more on the Internet, as described on page 22. Your employer may even provide official templates for company documents.

To start your document in any of the above ways, click the Windows logo in the upper-left corner of the screen. That's Office 2007's new *Office button*. Click it, and a drop-down menu opens, revealing commands for creating, opening, and saving documents. Next to these commands, you see a list of your Word documents. This list includes documents that are open, as well as those that you've recently opened. The Office button is also where you go to print and email your documents (Figure 1-2).

**Figure 1-2.** The phrase most frequently uttered by experienced Word fans the first time they start Word 2007 is, "Okay, where's my File menu?" Never fear, the equivalent of the File menu is still there—it's just camouflaged a bit. Clicking the Office button (the one that looks like a Windows logo) reveals the commands you use to create, open, and save Word documents.

## Creating a New Blank Document

Say you want a new blank document, just like the one Word shows you when you start the program. No problem—here are the steps:

1. **Choose Office button → New.**

   The New Document dialog box appears.

2. **In the upper-left corner of the large "Create a new Word document" panel, click "Blank document" (Figure 1-3).**

   The New Document box presents a seemingly endless number of options, but don't panic. The "Blank document" option you want is on the left side of the first line.

3. **At the bottom of the New Document dialog box, click Create.**

   The dialog box disappears, and you're gazing at the blank page of a new Word document.

Better get to work.

## Creating a New Document from an Existing Document

A blank Word document is sort of like a shapeless lump of clay. With some work, you can mold it to become just about anything. Often, however, you can save time by opening an existing document that's similar to the one you want to create. Imagine that you write the minutes for the monthly meetings of the Chief Executive Officer's Surfing Association (CEOSA). When it's time to write up the June minutes, it's a lot faster to open the minutes from May. You keep the boilerplate text and all the formatting, but you delete the text that's specific to the previous month. Now all you have to do is enter the text for June and save the document with a new name: *JuneMinutes.docx.*

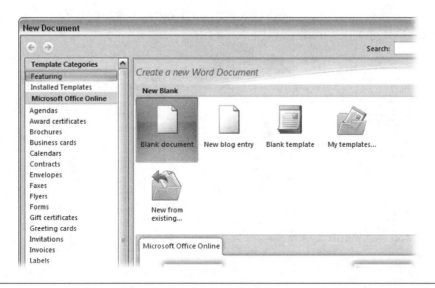

**Figure 1-3.** Open the New Document box (Office button → New, or Alt+F, N), and Word gives you several ways to create a new document. Click "Blank document" to open an empty document, similar to the one Word shows when you first start the program. Or you can click "New from existing" to open a document that you previously created under a new name.

---

**NOTE**

The .docx extension on the end of the filename is Word 2007's new version of .doc. The switch from three-letter to four-letter filename extensions indicates a change in the way Word stores documents. (If you need to share documents with folks using earlier versions of Word, choose Office button → Save As → Word 97-2003 document when you save the file. See the box on page 22 for details.)

---

Word gives you a "New from existing" document-creation option to satisfy your desire to spend more time surfing and less time writing meeting minutes. Here's how to create a new document from an existing document:

1.  **Choose Office button → New (Alt+F, N) to open the New Document window. Then click "New from existing…" (it sits directly below the "Blank document" button).**

    The three dots at the end of the button's title tell you that there's another dialog box to come. And sure enough, when you click "New from existing…", it opens another box, appropriately titled New from Existing Document (Figure 1-4).

This box looks—and works—like a standard Windows Open File box. It lets you navigate to a specific folder and open a file.

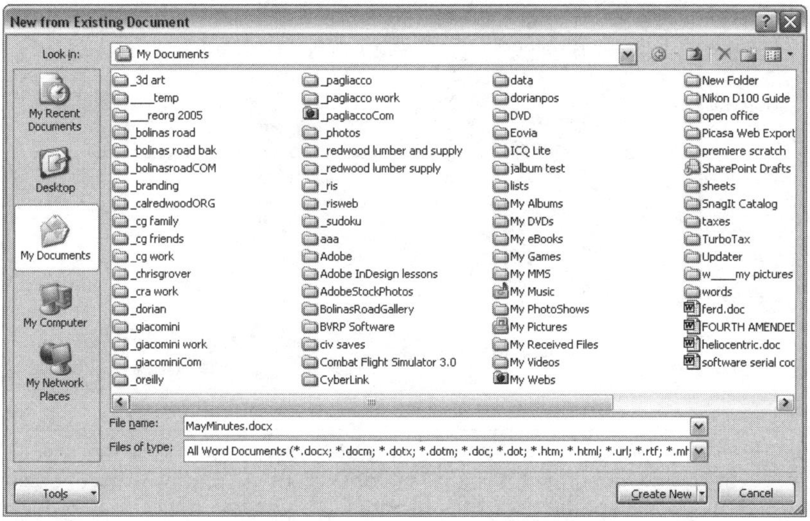

**Figure 1-4.** Use the New from Existing Document box to find an existing Word document that you'd like to open as a model for your new document. When you click Create New at bottom-right, Word opens a new copy of the document, leaving the original untouched. You can modify the copy to your heart's content and save it under a different file name.

2. **On your computer, find the existing document you're using for a model.**

   You can use the bar on the left to change the folder view. Word starts you in your My Documents folder, but you can switch to your desktop or your My Computer icon by clicking the icons on the left. Double-click folder icons in the large window to open them and see their contents.

3. **Click to select the file, and then click Create New (in the lower-right corner). (Alternatively, just double-click the file's icon to open it. This trick works in all Open File boxes.)**

   Instead of the usual Open button at the bottom of the box, the button in the New from Existing Document box reads Create New—your clue that this box behaves differently in one important respect: Instead of opening an existing file, you're making a *copy* of an existing file. Once open, the file's name is something like *Document2.docx* instead of the original name. This way, when you save the file, you don't overwrite the original document. (Still, it's best to save it with a new descriptive name right away.)

**TIP**

Windows' Open File boxes, like New from Existing Document, let you do a lot more than just find files. In fact, they let you do just about anything you can do in Windows Explorer. Using keyboard shortcuts, you can cut (Ctrl+X), copy (Ctrl+C), and paste (Ctrl+V) files. A right-click displays a shortcut menu with even more commands, letting you rename files, view Properties dialog boxes, and much more. You can even drag and drop to move files and folders.

## Creating a New Document from a Template

Say you're creating meeting minutes for the first time. You don't have an existing document to give you a leg up, but you do want to end up with handsome, properly formatted minutes. Word is at your service—with *templates.* Microsoft provides dozens upon dozens of prebuilt templates for everything from newsletters to postcards. Remember all the busy stuff in the New Document box in Figure 1-3? About 90 percent of the items in there are templates.

In the previous example, where you use an existing document to create the meeting minutes for the Chief Executive Officer's Surfing Association (CEOSA), each month you open the minutes from the previous month. You delete the information that pertains to the previous month and enter the current month's minutes. A template works pretty much the same way, except it's a generic document, designed to be adaptable to lots of different situations. You just open it and add your text. The structure, formatting, graphics, colors, and other doodads are already in place.

**NOTE**

The subject of Word templates is a lengthy one, especially when it comes to creating your own, so there's a whole chapter devoted to that topic in *Word 2007: The Missing Manual.*

# Word's New File Formats: .docx and .docm

With Office 2007, Microsoft took the drastic step of changing its file formats in hopes of improving your computer's security. Malicious programmers were using Office's macros to do nasty things to unsuspecting computers. The *.docx* format, the new standard for Word files, doesn't permit macros, making it safe from those threats. The *.docm* format indicates that a document contains macros or other bits of programming code. When opening one of these files, play it safe: If you don't know who created the .docm file, then don't open it.

The downside of the new file formats is that older versions of Word don't know how to open these .docx and .docm documents. To open Word 2007 files with an older version (even Word 2003), you need to install the Microsoft Office Compatibility Pack.

This software fix gives pre-2007 versions of Word the power to open documents in the new formats. Even then, you may not be able to use or edit parts of the file that use new Word features (like themes, equations, and content controls). To download the free compatibility pack, go to *www.office.microsoft.com* and type *office 2007 compatibility* into the search box at the top of the page.

Also, if you're preparing a Word document for someone who's using an older Word version, then you have to save it in a compatible format, as described in the tip on page 19. (Fortunately, the compatibility issue doesn't go both ways: Word 2007 can open old .doc docs just fine.)

---

Here's how to get some help from one of Microsoft's templates for meeting minutes:

1. **Choose Office button → New (Alt+F, N) to open the New Document window.**

   On the left of the New Document box is a Template Categories list. The top entry on this list is Installed Templates—the ones Word has installed on your computer.

   You could use any of these, but you also have a world of choice waiting for you online. On its Web site Microsoft offers hundreds of templates for all sorts of documents, and you can access them right from the New Document box. If you have a fast Internet connection, then it's just as quick and easy to use an online template as it is using the ones stored on your computer. In fact, you'll use an online template for this example.

If you can't connect to the Internet right now, then simply choose one of the installed templates instead. Click Create, and then skip to step 4.

2. **Scroll down the Template Categories list to the Microsoft Office Online heading. Under this heading, select Minutes.**

In the center pane, you'll see all different types of minutes templates, from PTA minutes to Annual shareholder's meeting minutes (Figure 1-5). When you click a template's icon, a preview appears in the pane on the right.

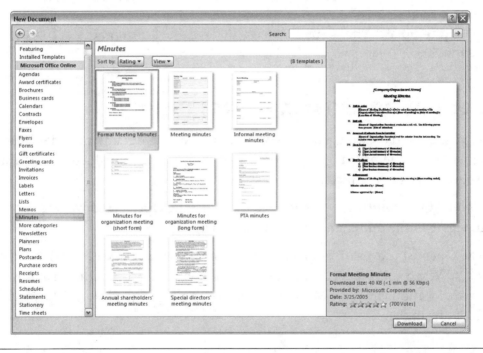

**Figure 1-5.** The New Document box lists prebuilt templates that live at Microsoft Office Online in categories like Agendas, Brochures, Calendars, and Minutes. Below the thumbnail you see an estimate of how long it takes to download the template from the Microsoft Office Online Web site. A rating, from 0 to 5 stars, tells you what other people think of the template (the rating system is kind of like the one at Amazon.com).

3. **When you're done perusing the various styles, click the Formal Meeting Minutes icon. (After all, CEOSA is a very formal organization.) Then click Download.**

   Word downloads and opens the document.

4. **Start writing up the minutes for the CEO Surfers.**

   To follow the template's structure, replace all the words in square brackets ([ ]) with text relevant to CEOSA.

   ___ **TIP** _____

   If you'd rather not download the Formal Meeting Minutes template every time you use it, then you can save the file on your computer as a Word template. The steps for saving files are just around the corner on page 39.

   _____

# Opening an Existing Document

If you've mastered creating a document from an existing document and creating a document from a template, you'll find that opening an existing document is a snap. The steps are nearly identical.

1. **Choose Office button → Open (Alt+F, O). In the Open window (Figure 1-6), navigate to the folder and file you want to open.**

   The Open window starts out showing your My Documents folder, since that's where Word suggests you save your files. When your document's in a more exotic location, click the My Computer icon, and then navigate to the proper folder from there.

   ___ **TIP** _____

   When you open a document you've used recently, you may see its name right on the Office button → Recent Documents menu. If so, simply click to open it without a trip to the Open dialog box.

   _____

2. **With the file selected, click Open in the lower-right corner.**

   The Open box goes away and your document opens in Word. You're all set to get to work. Just remember, when you save this document (Alt+F, S or Ctrl+S), you write over the previous file. Essentially, you create a new, improved, and only copy of the file you just opened. If you don't want to write over the existing document, use the Save As command (Alt+F, A), and then type a new name in the File Name text box.

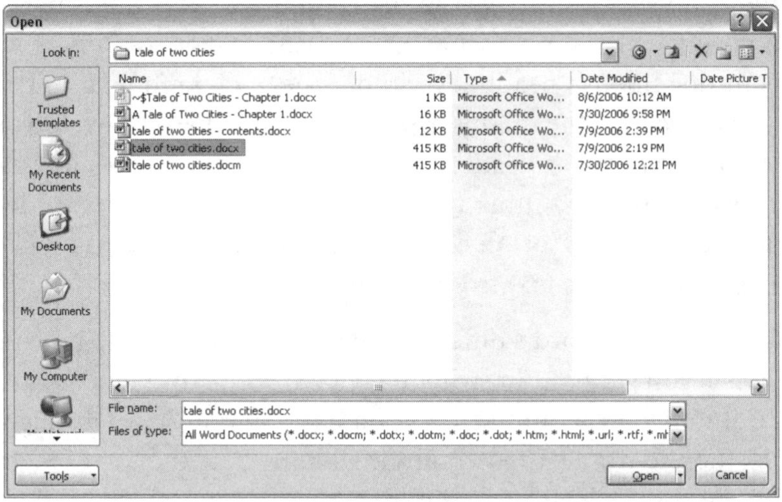

**Figure 1-6.** This Open dialog box shows the contents of the tale of two cities folder, according to the "Look in" box at the top. As you can see in the "File name box" at the bottom of the window, the file tale of two cities.docx is selected, a. By clicking Open, Mr. Dickens is ready to go to work.

___ TIP ___

Opening a file in Word doesn't mean you're limited to documents *created* in Word. You can choose documents created in other programs from the Files of Type drop-down menu at the bottom of the Open dialog box. Word then shows you that type of document in the main part of the window. You can open Outlook messages (.msg), Web pages (.htm or .html), or files from other word processors (.rtf, .mcw, .wps).

# Your Different Document View Views

Now that you know a handful of ways to create and open Word documents, it's time to take a look around the establishment. You may think a document's a document—just look at it straight on and get your work done. It's surprising, though, how changing your view of the page can help you work faster and smarter. When you're working with a very long document, you can change to Outline view and peruse just your document's headlines without the paragraph text. In Outline view, you get a better feeling for the manuscript as a whole. Likewise, when you're working on a document that's headed for the Web, it makes sense to view the page as it will appear in a browser. Other times, you may want to have two documents open on your screen at once (or on each of your two monitors, you lucky dog), to make it easy to cut and paste text from one to the other.

The key to working with Word's different view options is to match the view to the job at hand. Once you get used to switching views, you'll find lots of reasons to change your point of view. Find the tools you need on the View tab (Figure 1-7). To get there, click the View tab (Alt+W) on the ribbon (near the top of Word's window). The tab divides the view commands into four groups:

▶ **Document Views.** These commands change the big picture. For the most part, use these when you want to view a document in a dramatically different way: two pages side by side, Outline view, Web layout view, and so on.

▶ **Show/Hide.** The Show/Hide commands display and conceal Word tools like rulers and gridlines. These tools don't show when you print your document; they're just visual aids that help you when you're working in Word.

▶ **Zoom.** As you can guess, the Zoom tools let you choose between a close-up and a long shot of your document. Getting in close makes your words easier to read and helps prevent eyestrain. But zooming out makes scrolling faster and helps you keep your eye on the big picture.

> **TIP**
>
> In addition to the Zoom tools on the ribbon, handy Zoom tools are available in the window's lower-right corner. Check out the + (Zoom In) and - (Zoom Out) buttons and the slider in between them. See page 32 for the details on using them.

▶ **Window.** In the Window group, you'll find creative ways to organize document windows on your screen—like split views of a single document or side-by-side views of two different documents.

All the commands in the View tab's four groups are covered in the following pages.

___ **NOTE** _____

As you can see in this section, Word gives you a wealth of different ways to look at a document. If you'd like to adjust how you vuiew your Word documents even further, there's a whole chapter devoted to customizing Word in *Word 2007: The Missing Manual*.

**Figure 1-7.** The View tab is your document-viewing control center. Look closely, and you see it's divided into four groups with names at the bottom of the ribbon: Document Views, Show/Hide, Zoom, and Window. To apply a view command, just click the button or label.

## Document Views: Five Ways to Look at Your Manuscript

Word gives you five basic document views. To select a view, go to the View tab (Alt+W) and choose one of the Document Views on the left side of the ribbon (Figure 1-8). You have another great option for switching from one view to another that's always available in the lower-right corner of Word's window. Click one of the five small buttons to the left of the slider to jump between Print Layout, Full Screen Reading, Web Layout, Outline, and Draft views. Each view has a special purpose, and you can modify them even more using the other commands on the View tab.

___ **NOTE** _____

Changing your view in no way affects the document itself—you're just looking at the same document from a different perspective.

▶ **Print Layout (Alt+W, P).** The most frequently used view in Word, Print Layout is the one you see when you first start the program or create a new blank document.

**Figure 1-8.** On the left side of the View tab, you find the five basic document views: Print Layout, Full Screen Reading, Web Layout, Outline, and Draft. You can edit your document in any of the views, although they come with different tools for different purposes. Outline view provides a menu that lets you show or hide headings at different outline levels.

In this view, the page you see on your computer screen looks much as it does when you print it. This view's handy for letters, reports, and most documents headed for the printer.

▶ **Full Screen Reading (Alt+W, F).** If you'd like to get rid of the clutter of menus, ribbons, and all the rest of the word-processing gadgetry, then use Full Screen Reading view. As the name implies, this view's designed primarily for reading documents. It includes options you don't find in the other views, like a command that temporarily decreases or increases the text size. In the upper-right corner you see some document-proofing tools (like a text highlighter and an insert comment command), but when you want to change or edit your document, you must first use the View Options → Allow Typing command.

▶ **Web Layout (Alt+W, L).** This view shows your document as if it were a single Web page loaded in a browser. You don't see any page breaks in this view. Along with your text, you see any photos or videos that you've placed in the document—just like a Web page.

▶ **Outline (Alt+W, U).** For lots of writers, an outline is the first step in creating a manuscript. Once they've created a framework of chapters and headings, they dive in and fill out the document with text. If you like to work this way, then you'll love Outline view. It's easy to jump back and forth between Outline view and Print Layout view or Draft view, so you can bounce back and forth between a macro and a micro view of your epic. (For more details on using Word's Outline view, see page 28.)

▶ **Draft (Alt+W, V).** Here's the no-nonsense, roll-up-your-sleeves view of your work (Figure 1-9). You see most formatting as it appears on the printed page, except for headers and footers. Page breaks are indicated by a thin dotted line. In this view, it's as if your document is on one single roll of paper that scrolls through your computer screen. This view's a good choice for longer documents and those moments when you want to focus on the words without being distracted by page breaks and other formatting niceties.

**Figure 1-9.** In Draft view, you see most text and paragraph formatting, but headers, footers, and other distracting page formatting features are hidden. Your text appears as a continuous scroll, with the margins hidden. Page breaks appear as dotted lines.

## Show and Hide Window Tools

Word gives you some visual aids that make it easier to work with your documents. Tools like rulers and gridlines don't show up when you print your document, but they help you line up the elements on the page. Use the ruler to set page margins and to create tabs for your documents. Checkboxes on the View tab let you show or hide tools, but some tools aren't available in all the views, so they're grayed out. You can't, for example, display page rulers in Outline or Full Screen Reading views.

Use the checkboxes in the Show/Hide group of the View tab (Figure 1-10) to turn these tools on and off:

- **Ruler.** Use the ruler to adjust margins, set tabs, and position items on your page. For more detail on formatting text and paragraphs, see page 83.

- **Gridlines.** When you click the Gridlines box, it looks like you created your document on a piece of graph paper. This effect isn't too helpful for an all-text document, but it sure comes in handy if you're trying to line up photos on a page.

- **Message Bar.** The Message Bar resides directly under the ribbon, and it's where you see alerts about a document's behavior. For example, when a document is trying to run a macro and your Word settings prohibit macros, an alert appears in the Message Bar. Click the checkbox to show or hide the Message Bar.

- **Document Map.** If you work with long documents, you'll like the Document Map. This useful tool appears to the left of your text (you can see it in Figure 1-10), showing the document's headings at various levels. Click the little + and − buttons next to a heading to expand or collapse the outline. Click a heading, and you jump to that location in your document.

- **Thumbnails.** Select the Thumbnails option, and you see little icons of your document's pages in the bar on the left. Click a thumbnail to go to that page. In general, thumbnails are more useful for shorter documents and for pages that are visually distinctive. For longer documents, you'll find the Document Map easier to use for navigation.

## Zooming Your View In and Out

When you're working, do you ever find that you sometimes hold pages at arm's length to get a complete view, and then, at other times, you stick your nose close to the page to examine the details? Word's Zoom options (Figure 1-11) let you do the same thing with your screen—but without looking nearly as silly.

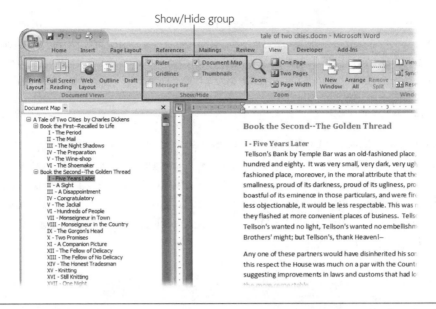

Show/Hide group

**Figure 1-10.** Use the Show/Hide group on the View tab to display or conceal Word tools. The Ruler gives you a quick and easy way to set tabs and margins. The Document Map is particularly helpful when you work with longer documents because it displays headings in the bar on the left of the screen. In the left pane, you can see that Mr. Dickens wrote more than his fair share of chapters.

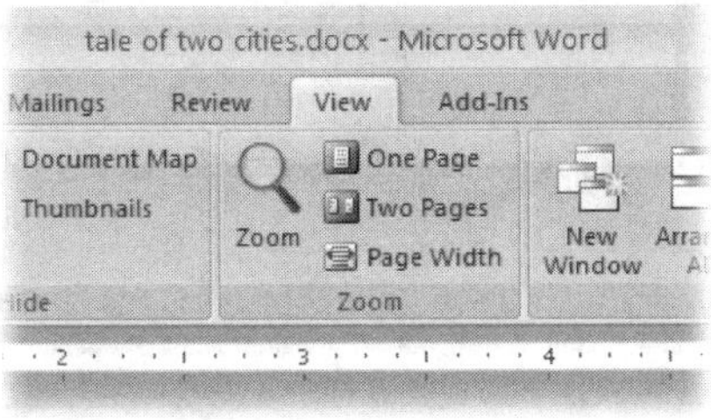

**Figure 1-11.** The Zoom group of options lets you view your document close up or at a distance. The big magnifying glass opens the Zoom dialog box with more controls for fine-tuning your zoom level. For quick changes, click one of the three buttons on the right: One Page, Two Pages, or Page Width.

___ NOTE ___

Even though the text appears to get bigger and smaller when you zoom, you're not actually changing the document in any way. Zoom is similar to bringing a page closer so you can read the fine print. If you want to actually change the font size, then use the formatting options on the Home tab (Alt+H, FS).

On the View tab, click the big magnifying glass to open the Zoom dialog box (Figure 1-12). Depending on your current Document View (see page 27), you can adjust your view by percentage or relative to the page and text (more on that in a moment). The options change slightly depending on which Document View you're using. The Page options don't really apply to Web layouts, so they're grayed out and inactive if you're in the Web Layout view.

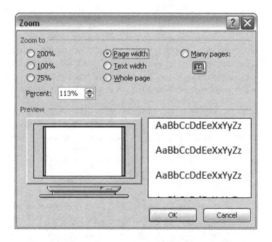

**Figure 1-12.** The Zoom dialog box lets you choose from a variety of views. Just click one of the option buttons, and then click OK. The monitor and text sample at the bottom of the Zoom box provide visual clues as you change the settings.

## Zooming by percentage

In the box's upper-left corner, you find controls to zoom in and out of your document by percentage. The view varies depending on your computer screen and settings, but in general, 100% is a respectable, middle-of-the-road view of your document. The higher the percentage, the more zoomed in you are, and the bigger everything looks—vice versa with a lower percentage.

The three radio buttons (200%, 100%, and 75%) give you quick access to some standard settings. For in-between percentages (like 145%), type a number in the box below the buttons, or use the up-down arrows to change the value. For a quick way to zoom in and out without opening a dialog box, use the Zoom slider (Figure 1-13) in the lower-right corner of your window. Drag the slider to the right to zoom in on your document, and drag it to the left to zoom out. The percentage changes as you drag.

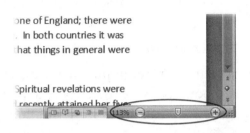

**Figure 1-13.** The Zoom slider at the bottom of the document window gives you a quick and easy way to change your perspective. Drag the slider to the right to zoom in on your document, and drag it to the left to zoom out. To the left of the slider are five View buttons: Print Layout, Full Screen Reading, Web Layout, Outline, and Draft (page 27).

## Zooming relative to page or text

Not everyone's a number person. (That's especially true of writers.) So you may prefer to zoom without worrying about percentage figures. The Zoom dialog box (on the View tab, click the magnifying-glass icon) gives you four radio buttons with plain-English zoom settings:

**Page width.** Click this button, and the page resizes to fill the screen from one side to the other. It's the fastest way to zoom to a text size that most people find comfortable to read. (You may have to scroll, though, to read the page from top to bottom.)

**Text width.** This button zooms in even farther, because it ignores the margins of your page. Use this one if you have a high-resolution monitor (or you've misplaced your reading glasses).

**Whole page.** When you want to see an entire page from top to bottom and left to right, click this button. It's great for getting an overview of how your headings and paragraphs look on the page.

**Many pages.** This view is the equivalent of spreading your document out on the floor, and then viewing it from the top of a ladder. You can use it to see how close you are to finishing that five-page paper, or to inspect the layout of a multi-page newsletter.

> **WARNING**
>
> When you're zoomed out to Whole or "Many pages" view, watch those fingers on the keyboard. You can still make changes to your text in these views, even though you can't see what you're doing.

### Changing page view from the ribbon

The ribbon offers radio buttons for three popular page views. (You can see them back in Figure 1-11, to the Zoom tool's right.) They're a quick and dirty way to change the number of pages you see onscreen without fiddling with zoom controls.

▶ **One Page.** This view shows the entire page in Word's document window. If your screen is large enough, you can read and edit text in this view.

▶ **Two Pages.** In this view, you see two pages side by side. This view's handy when you're working with documents that have two-page spreads, like booklets.

▶ **Page Width.** This button does the exact same thing as the "Page Width" button in the Zoom dialog box (page 31). It's more readable than the One Page and Two Page options, because the page fills the screen from edge to edge, making the text appear larger.

## The Window Group: Doing the Splits

Back when dinosaurs roamed the earth and people used typewriters (or very early word processors), you could work on only one document at a time—the one right in front of you. Although Word 2007 has more options for viewing multiple documents and multiple windows than ever, some folks forget to use them. Big mistake. If you ever find yourself comparing two documents or borrowing extensively from some other text, then having two or more documents visible on your screen can double or triple your work speed.

The commands for managing multiple documents, views, and windows are in the View tab's Window group (Figure 1-14).

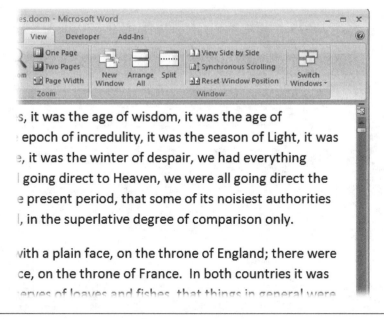

**Figure 1-14.** In the Window group, the three commands—New Window, Arrange All, and Split—let you open and view your work from multiple vantage points. The commands View Side by Side, Synchronous Scrolling, and Reset Window Position are helpful when reviewing and comparing documents. The big Switch Windows button lets you hop from one document to another.

▶ **New Window (Alt+W, N).** When you're working on a long document, sometimes you want to see two different parts of the document at the same time, as if they were two separate documents. You may want to keep referring to what you said in the Introduction while you're working on Chapter 5. Or perhaps you want to keep an Outline view open while editing in Draft view. That's where the New Window command comes in. When you click this button (or hit this keystroke), you've got your document open in two windows that you can scroll independently. Make a change to one window, and it immediately appears in the other.

▶ **Arrange All (Alt+W, A).** Great—now you've got documents open in two or more windows, but it takes a heck of a lot of mousing around and window resizing to get them lined up on your screen at the same time. Click Arrange All and, like magic, your open Word document windows are sharing the screen, making it easy to work on one and then the other. Word takes an egalitarian approach to screen real estate, giving all windows an equal amount of property (Figure 1-15).

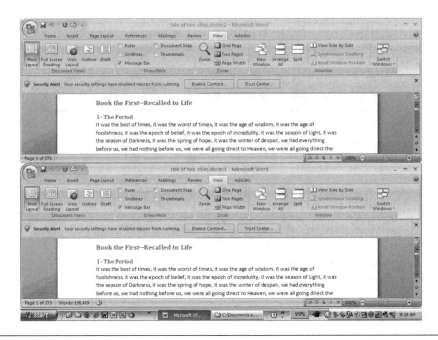

**Figure 1-15.** One downside of Office 2007's ribbon: It takes up more space on your computer's screen than menus or even the older button bars. When you open a couple of windows, you're not left with much space to do your work, especially when you're working on an ultra-portable laptop or a computer with a small screen. You can double-click the active tab to hide the ribbon, but in most cases, you're better off working with a split screen, as shown in Figure 1-16.

▶ **Split (Alt+W, S).** The Split button divides a single window so you can see two different parts of the same document—particularly handy if you're copying text from one part of a document to another. The other advantage of the Split command is that it gives you more room to work than using Arrange All for multiple windows because it doesn't duplicate the ribbon, ruler, and other Word tools (Figure 1-16).

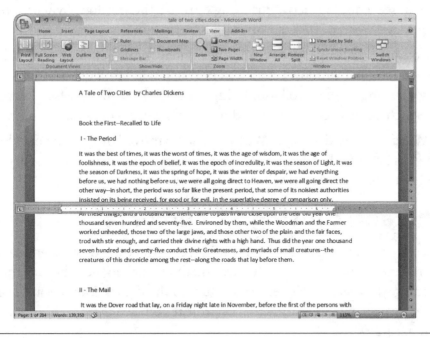

**Figure 1-16.** When you're viewing two different parts of a single document, use the Split command; it leaves you more room to work than two separate windows, as shown in Figure 1-15. Each section of the split window has a scroll bar, so you can independently control different parts of your document. If you want to fine-tune your split, just drag the middle bar exactly where you want it. When you're done, click Remove Split to return to a single screen view.

## Viewing multiple windows

One common reason for wanting to see two documents or more on your screen at once is so you can make line-by-line comparisons. Imagine you have two Word documents that are almost identical, but you have to find the spots where there are differences. A great way to make those differences jump out is to put both versions on your screen side by side and scroll through them. As you scroll, you can see differences in the paragraph lengths and the line lengths. Here are the commands to help you with the process:

▶ **View Side by Side (Alt+W, B).** Click the View Side by Side command and Word arranges two windows vertically side by side. As you work with side-by-side documents, you can rearrange windows on your screen by dragging the very top of the Window frame. You can resize the windows by pointing to any edge of the frame.

When you see a double arrow, just drag to resize the window. Synchronous Scrolling (described next) is automatically turned on.

▶ **Synchronous Scrolling (Alt+W, Y).** The Synchronous Scrolling feature keeps multiple document windows in lock step. When you scroll one window, the other windows automatically scroll too. Using the same button or keystroke, you can toggle Synchronous Scrolling on and off as you work with your documents.

▶ **Reset Windows Position (Alt+W, T).** If you've moved or resized your document windows as described earlier under View Side by Side, then you can click this button to reset your view so the windows share the screen equally.

# Saving and Closing Documents

From the earliest days of personal computing, the watchword has been "save early, save often." There's nothing more frustrating than working half the day and then having the Great American Novel evaporate into the digital ether because your power goes out. So, here are some tips to protect your work from disasters human-made and natural:

▶ Name and save your document shortly after you first create it. You'll see the steps to do so later in this section.

▶ Get in the habit of doing a quick save with Alt+F, S (think *File Save*) when you pause to think or get up to go to the kitchen for a snack. (Note for old-timers: Ctrl+S still works for a quick save too.)

▶ If you're leaving your computer for an extended period of time, save and close your document with Alt+F, C (think *File Close*).

## The Many Ways to Save Documents

It's the Microsoft Way to give you multiple ways to do most everything. Whether that's because the company's programmers believe in giving you lots of choices, or because they can't make up their minds about the best way to do something is a question best left to the philosophers. But the point is, you do have a choice. You don't have to memorize every keystroke, button, and command. Especially with saving, the important thing is to find a way you like and stick with it. The next section gives some ways you can save the document you're working on.

# Where Are My Keyboard Shortcuts?

Ribbons, buttons, and menus are all well and good when you're doing something new or complicated. But when you know where you're going, a good keyboard shortcut can save time. Word 2007 has dozens of keyboard shortcuts. If you don't have your favorites memorized, use the Alt key to reveal them.

Press the Alt key, and you see small badges with letters and numbers pop up next to menus and buttons. These are your shortcuts. If you're looking for the keyboard shortcut to close your document, follow these steps:

1. Press and release the Alt key to show the keyboard shortcut badges.

   When you do this, the badges appear over menu items and ribbon buttons. (The Alt key acts as a toggle. If you change your mind and don't want to use a shortcut, then press the Alt key again and you're back in normal typing mode.)

2. Press F to open the Office menu.

   Pressing F (which used to stand for File menu) does the same thing as clicking the button with your mouse, except that now it sports little keyboard shortcut badges.

3. Press C to close your document.

   Looking at the bottom of the Office menu, you see the Close command. A small C badge indicates that pressing C closes your document.

As you can guess, most keyboard shortcuts are based on the initial letter of the actual command words. This doesn't always work out for popular letters. As a result, you have cases like the References tab, which has the keyboard shortcut S.

Even if you don't deliberately work to memorize the keyboard shortcuts, you'll find that you begin to learn your favorites as you use them. Before long, your fingers will tap them out automatically.

If a substantial portion of your brain is occupied by keyboard shortcuts from previous versions of Word, never fear. Most of those old commands still work—including Ctrl+B for Bold, Ctrl+N for new document, and F7 for spell checking.

### Saving by keyboard shortcut

▶ **Ctrl+S.** If you're an old hand at Word, this keyboard shortcut may already be burned in your brain. It still works with Word and other Office programs. This command quickly saves the document and lets you get back to work.

▶ **Alt+F, S.** This keyboard shortcut does the exact same thing as Ctrl+S. Unlike Ctrl+S, though, you get visual reminders of which keys to press when you press the Alt key. See the box on page 39.

### Saving by menu command

▶ **Office button → Save.** If you don't want to use keyboard shortcuts, you can mouse your way to the same place using menus. Like the options above, this command saves your file with its current name.

▶ **Office button → Save As.** The Save As option lets you save your file with a new name (Figure 1-17). When you use this command, you create a new document with a new name that includes any changes you've made. (The individual steps are described in the next section.)

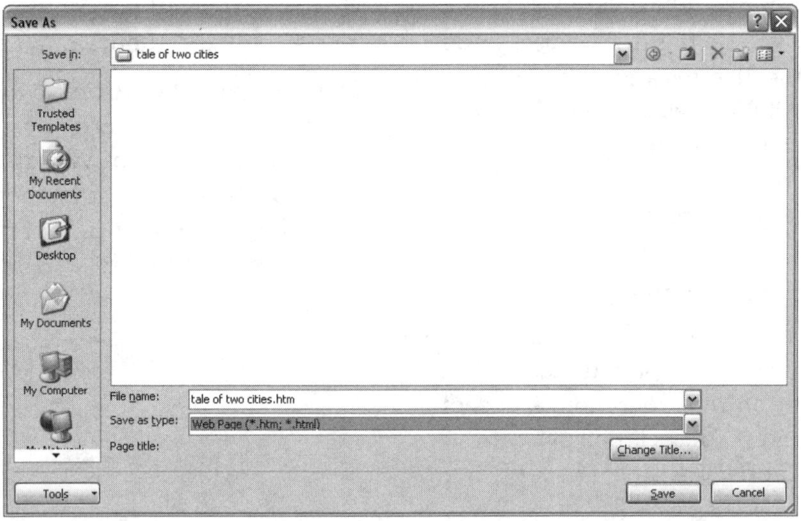

**Figure 1-17.** Use Office button → Save As to save your file with a new name or in a different file format. In this example, the Word file tale of two cities is being saved as an HTML type file—a format used for Web pages.

▶ **Office button** → **Close.** When you close a document, Word checks to see if you made any changes to the file. When you've made changes, Word always asks whether you'd like to save the document (Figure 1-18).

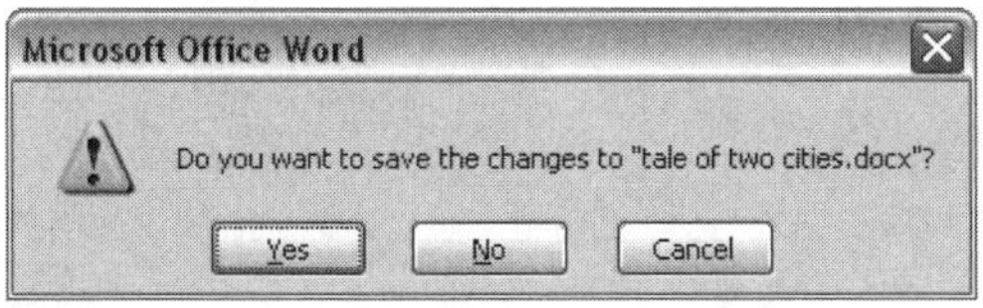

**Figure 1-18.** When you see this message box, you have three choices: Yes saves your document before closing it; No closes your document without saving it; Cancel leaves your document open without saving it.

# Preventing and Recovering from Disaster

Lightning strikes. Children trip over power cords. Computers crash. Saving your work frequently and keeping backup copies of your documents are important safeguards. You can have Word save backup copies every time you save a document, so you always have the last two versions of your work stored on your computer. Word doesn't automatically save backup copies of your files, but it's easy enough to change this setting. Click the Office button, and then click Word Options at the bottom of the box.

After the Word Options dialog box opens, scroll down to the Save group, and turn on the "Always create backup copy" checkbox. Choose Office button → Open to find and open your backup file (Figure 1-19).

When disaster strikes in spite of your meticulous preventive measures, Word can help too. Word's new file formats have been designed to be easier to recover and repair. In many cases, if a picture or a table is corrupted in the file, you can still retrieve everything else (Figure 1-20).

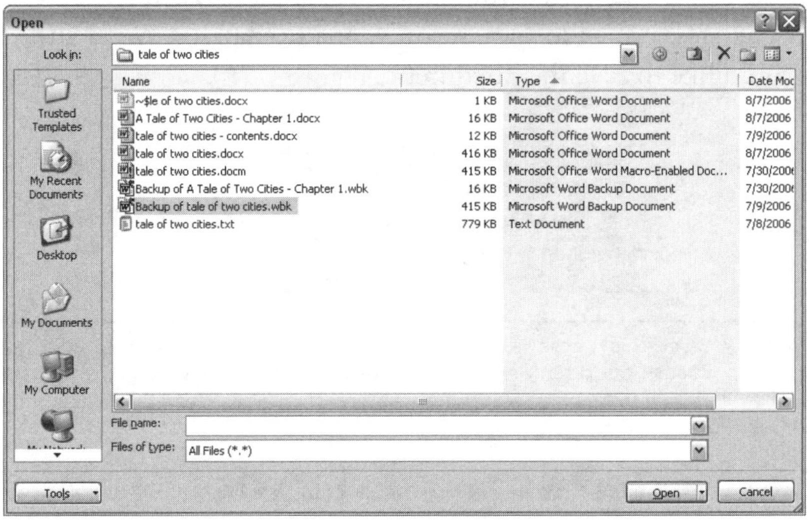

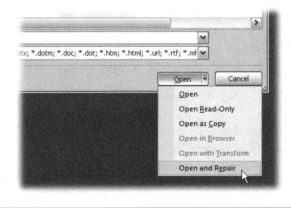

**Figure 1-19.** To open a backup file, choose All Files (*.*) in the "Files of type" drop-down menu at the bottom of the Open dialog box. Look for a file that begins with the words "Backup of." Double-click to open the file.

**Figure 1-20.** When you can't open a file with a normal Open command, click the arrow to the right of the Open button, and choose Open and Repair from the drop-down menu. Some parts of your file may still be damaged, but you can usually recover most of your work.

## Saving with a new name

When you save a new document or save a document with a new name (Save As), you've got three things to consider: a filename, a file location, and a file format.

Here are the steps for saving a file, complete with a new name:

1. **Choose Office button → Save As to open the Save As box.**

   You use the Save As command when you're saving a file with a new name. Word also displays the Save As box the first time you save a new document.

2. **Use the "Save in" drop-down list or double-click to open folders in the window to find a location to store your file.**

   The buttons in the upper-right corner can also help you navigate. See the details in Figure 1-21. Word doesn't care where you save your files, so you can choose your desktop or any folder on your computer.

**Figure 1-21.** The Save As dialog box has all the controls you need to navigate to any location on your computer—including five nifty buttons in the upper-right corner. From left to right: The left arrow button steps you backward through your past locations (just like the back button in a Web browser). The up arrow takes you out to the folder enclosing the one you're in now. The X button deletes folders and files—be careful with it. Click the folder with the star in the corner to create a new folder.

---

**TIP**

The more files you save on your computer, the more helpful it is to have a logical folder and file system. If you keep hundreds of Word documents, you may want to have different folders named: letters, memos, reports, and newsletters.

3. **At the bottom of the Save As dialog box, type a name in the File name box.**

   Word accepts long names, so you don't need to skimp. Use a descriptive name that will help you identify the file two weeks or two years from now. A good name saves you time in the long run.

4. **Use the "Save as type" box to choose a file type.**

   In most cases you don't need to change the file type. Word automatically selects either *.docx* or *.docm* depending on the contents of your file, but Word can save files in over a dozen different formats. If you're sharing the file with someone who's using an older version of Word, then choose Word 97-2003 Document to save the document in .doc format. If you're sharing with someone who uses a Mac or Linux computer, then you may want to use the more universal Rich Text Format (.rtf).

   ___ TIP _____

   If you want to use your document as a template in the future, then choose Word Template (dotx).

   _____

   Unless you're sharing your file with someone using an older version of Word or a different operating system or making a template, stick with the new standard Word file types .docx (for normal Word files) and .docm (for files that run macros). See the box on page 22 for a complete rundown.

5. **Click Save.**

   Word does the rest. All you need to do is remember where you saved your work.

# Understanding Word File Types

When you save your first file in Word 2007, you'll find a bewildering array of file types. Don't sweat it—you'll use some new file types on the list frequently, but you'll probably ignore a lot of types. The two you'll use most often are .docx and .docm.

* **.docx.** New format for most Word documents. Pre-2007 versions of Word can't open these documents without the help of the Office Compatibility Pack, as described in the box on page 22.

* **.docm.** New format for Word documents containing macros. (Microsoft is making an effort to increase computer security by reining in Office macros.)

* **.dotx.** New format for templates (page 22).

* **.dotm.** New format for templates containing macros.

* **.doc.** Format for all the previous versions of Word including: Word 6.0, Word 95, and Word 97-2003.

* **.dot.** The template format for previous versions of Word.

* **.xps.** XML Paper specification. This format is Microsoft's answer to PDF for creating documents that anyone can open on any computer.

* **.pdf.** Adobe Reader (also known as Acrobat) files. PDF stands for Portable Document Format.

* **.mhtm, .mhtml.** Single file Web page. In other words, all the files that make up a Web page (including images) are contained in one single file. (There's no difference between .mhtm and .mhtml files; they're just 4-letter and 5-letter versions of the same filename extension.)

* **htm, .html.** Standard Web page format. This format is for the Web pages you see on the Internet. When the page includes photos or other files, links on the page point to those external files. (There's no difference between .htm and .html; both mean the same thing.)

* **.rtf.** Rich Text Format, a file format used to exchange files with other word processors and other types of computers like Macs and Linux computers.

* **.txt.** This plain text format doesn't have a lot of the formatting you can do in Word. It makes for a nice, small file size, and you can open it on any computer, but it's not pretty.

* **.xml.** eXtensible Markup Language is a standard language for describing many different types of data.

* **.wps.** This format indicates a document created in Office's little sibling, Microsoft Works.

# ENTERING AND EDITING TEXT

▶ Typing in Word

▶ Selecting Text

▶ Moving Around Your Document

▶ Cutting, Copying, and Pasting

▶ Finding and Replacing Text

▶ Saving Keystrokes with Quick Parts

DESPITE ADVANCED FEATURES like grammar checking, indexing, and image editing, Word is still, at heart, a word processor. You probably spend most of your time entering text and massaging it into shape. Amidst all the slick graphics and gee-whiz automation, Word 2007 makes it faster and easier than ever for you to enter and edit your text. A quick read through this chapter will reveal timesaving techniques that'll help you spend less time hunting, pecking, and clicking, so you can move on to the important stuff—polishing your prose and sharing it with the world.

This chapter starts with a quick review of the basics—putting words on the page and moving around your document. You'll also learn how to cut, copy, paste, and generally put text exactly where you want it. To top it off, you'll explore the Find and Replace features and learn how to save keystrokes using Word's Quick Parts.

# Typing in Word

Whenever you're entering text into Word, the *insertion point* is where all the action takes place (Figure 2-1). It's that vertical, blinking bar that's a little taller than a capital letter. When you press a key, a letter appears at the insertion point, and the blinking bar moves a space to the right. To type in a different spot, just click somewhere in your text, and the insertion point moves to that location.

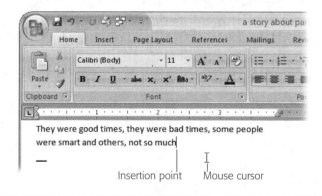

**Figure 2-1.** As you type, the characters appear at the insertion point. Sometimes people call the insertion point the "cursor," but the insertion point and the mouse cursor are actually two different things. You use the mouse cursor to choose commands from the ribbon, select text, and place the insertion point in your document. The cursor can roam all over the Word window, but the insertion point remains hard at work, blinking patiently, waiting for you to enter the next character.

Press Shift to type capitals or to enter the various punctuation marks you see above the numbers keys (!@#$*&^). When you want to type several words in uppercase letters, press the Caps Lock key. You don't have to keep holding it down. It works like a toggle. Press it once and you're in caps mode. Press it again and you're back to lowercase.

## ChoosingBetween Insert and Overtype Mode

Most of the time, you type in *insert mode*. Put your cursor in the middle of a sentence, start typing, and Word inserts the letters you type at that point. Existing text scoots along to the right to make room.

In the other mode—*overtype mode*—every time you type a character, it *writes over* and erases the next one. Before Word 2007, most people stumbled upon overtype mode by accident. They'd click in the middle of a sentence and start typing—and the letters to the right of the cursor started to disappear! In those earlier versions of Word, pressing the Insert key threw you right into overtype mode. It was an easy mistake to make, since Insert is just above the much-used Delete key (on most keyboards).

Microsoft made overtype mode harder to get to, so people would not accidentally type over all their hard work. Now the Insert key doesn't do anything unless you make a few tweaks to Word's settings.

If you miss that old overtype mode and want to toggle back and forth with the Insert key, follow these steps.

1. Go to Office button → Word Options to open the Word Options dialog box.

2. In the left bar, select Advanced.

3. In the first group of options, called Editing Options, turn on the "Use the Insert Key to control overtype mode" checkbox.

If you want to use overtype mode as your regular text entry mode, turn on the "Use overtype mode" checkbox.

The Backspace key and the Delete key both erase characters, but there's a difference: The Backspace erases the characters behind the insertion point, while the Delete key eliminates characters in front.

> Word's cursor changes its appearance like a chameleon, hinting at what will happen when you click the mouse button. When you move the cursor over the ribbon, it turns into an arrow, indicating that you can point and click a command. Hold it over your text, and it looks like an I-beam, giving you a precise tool for placing the insertion point between characters.

But if all you do with Word is type, you're missing out on 95 percent of its potential. What makes Word a 21st-century tool is the ease with which you can edit text, as described next.

## Click and Type for Quick Formatting

Word's *Click and Type* feature makes it easy to position and align text on a blank spot on the page. It's great for those jobs where you want to position a block of text in an unusual place. Imagine you're putting together a title page for a report and you want the title about a third of the way down on the right side of the page with text aligned to the right. All you have to do is position your mouse cursor where you want the text. Notice, as you move the cursor around the page, sometimes four small lines appear near the I-beam. When the cursor's on the right side of the page, the lines trail off to the left (Figure 2-2).

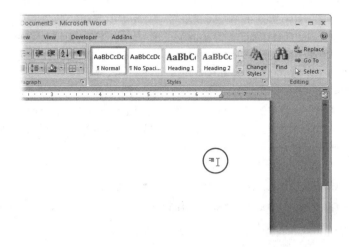

**Figure 2-2.** The Click and Type cursor changes (circled) depending on where it's located on the page. Here the cursor indicates that text will be aligned to the right.

When the cursor's in the center of the page, the lines are centered at the bottom of the I-beam. As usual, the cursor is giving a hint about what will happen next.

If you double-click when the cursor's on the right side of the page (with the lines trailing off to the left), then several things happen. Most noticeable, your insertion point is exactly where you clicked. Behind the scenes, Word makes several other adjustments. If necessary, Word positions the insertion point vertically and horizontally on the page by adding paragraph marks and tabs as needed. Word changes the paragraph alignment setting to Align Right—it's just as if you clicked the button on the ribbon. Fortunately, you don't need to worry about these details; all you have to do is type the text (Figure 2-3).

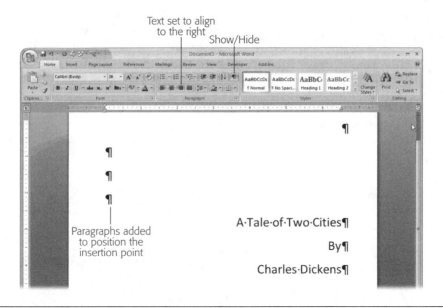

**Figure 2-3.** When you double-click with the Click and Type cursor shown in Figure 2-2, Word adds several paragraph marks to position the insertion point down the page. When you type some text, it's right-aligned—just as the cursor indicated. (To see these usually hidden paragraph marks, click the paragraph mark button on the Home tab.)

# Entering Special Characters

Letters, numbers, and punctuation are the common currency of most documents. Still, you may want to use a bunch of other fairly common characters, like © and ®, that don't show up on your keyboard. And where are all those foreign characters, math symbols, and fractions?

They're waiting for you on the Insert tab. Choose Insert → Symbols → Symbol (Figure 2-4). If the character you need is on the menu, then click to insert it into your text. If you don't see it, click "More symbols" to see a more comprehensive list of characters. The first group—Symbols—gives you access to every character Word can put on the page.

Use the Font box on the left to select your typeface. If you want to use the typeface you're currently using in your document, as is often the case, then leave this set to "(normal text)." Use the Subset drop-down menu to choose a language (like Greek, Cyrillic, or Latin), or choose from other groupings (accented letters, math symbols, and so on). You can also use the scroll bar on the right to visually search for a symbol. Symbols that you've used recently are lined up near the bottom of the dialog box, so you can grab them quickly.

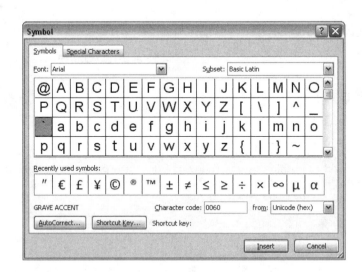

**Figure 2-4.** To insert a character in your text, either double-click the character or single-click it, and then click Insert. The right-hand tab—Special Characters—contains a list of specialized punctuation marks like dashes and nonbreaking hyphens.

# Selecting Text

Even among the best writers, the first draft needs a lot of editing before it's ready for public viewing. You'll need to change words, delete boring parts, and move sentences (or even whole paragraphs) to reorganize your text.

In Word, as in most programs, you have to *select* something before you can do anything to it. Say you want to change the word "good" to "awesome": Select "good," and then type your new, improved adjective in its place. To delete or move a block of text, first select it, and then use the mouse, keyboard, or ribbon commands to do the deed. Since selection is such a fundamental editing skill, Word gives you many different and new ways to do it, including the Mini toolbar (see Figure 2-5). If you've been dragging your mouse around for the past 20 years, you're lagging behind. This section shows you some timesaving selection techniques—with and without the mouse.

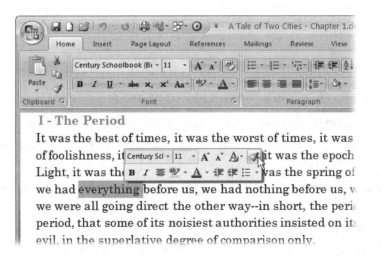

**Figure 2-5.** As you make selections, you'll notice the Mini Toolbar pops up occasionally. It's faint at first, but when you move the mouse toward the toolbar, it comes into focus, giving you easy access to the most often used formatting commands, including the format painter.

## Selecting with the Mouse

The mouse is an easy, visual, intuitive way to make selections. It's the first way most people learn, and besides, it's right there on your desktop. Here's how to select various document parts using your mouse:

▶ **Select individual characters.** Click to place the insertion point at the beginning of the text you want to select. Press and hold the left mouse button and drag over the characters. As you drag, the characters you select are highlighted to indicate they're part of the selection (Figure 2-6).

---
**TIP**

> Word doesn't care if you move forward or backward as you select text. It simply uses the point where you click as either the beginning or the ending point of the selection. These examples describe how to select text moving forward, but most of the techniques, including the keyboard techniques, work going backward too. Don't be afraid to experiment. Before you know it, you'll be proficient selecting text with both the mouse and the keyboard.
---

▶ **Select a word.** Double-click the word. The entire word's highlighted.

▶ **Select a sentence.** Ctrl-click the sentence. The entire sentence is highlighted.

▶ **Select a line of text.** Move the cursor into the left margin. The cursor changes to an arrow. Click right next to the line you want to select. The line's highlighted, showing that it's selected.

▶ **Select a whole paragraph.** Move the cursor into the left margin. When it changes into an arrow, double-click next to the paragraph. The entire paragraph is highlighted. To add more paragraphs, keep your finger on the mouse button and drag until the cursor points at another paragraph, and another…

▶ **Select a block of text.** Click to place the insertion point at the beginning of the block you want to select. (No need to keep pressing the mouse button.) Hold the Shift key down, and then click at the other end of the selection. The block of text is highlighted, and your wrist is happy. Everybody wins.

▶ **Select an entire document.** Move the cursor into the left margin, so that it changes into an arrow. Click the left mouse button three times. Your entire document's highlighted. (In other words, do the same thing as for selecting a paragraph, except you triple-click instead of double-click.)

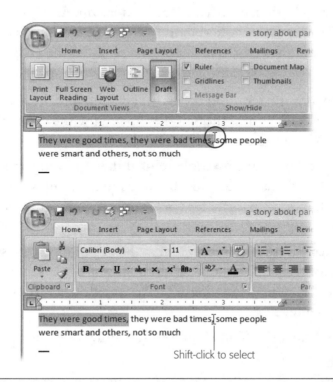

**Figure 2-6.** Top: To select text with your mouse, drag your cursor (circled) over the text. The selected text is highlighted to show you what's included in the selection.

Bottom: Or use the Shift-click trick. Shift-clicking at the end of "bad times" extends the selection to include both phrases: "They were good times, they were bad times," As you can see, Dickens still has some wordsmithing to do.

**TIP**

This section focuses on selecting text, but the same techniques apply to tables and pictures, which Word handles as parts of your text. You'll learn all the details when you encounter these features in later chapters.

## Selecting with the Keyboard

When it comes to selecting fine details, like a single letter, the mouse can make you feel like you're trying to thread a needle with mittens on. And if you're a fast typist, taking your hands away from the keyboard to grasp the mouse causes a needless loss of time. Word nerds, in fact, do as much as possible from the keyboard, even selecting. If you've never selected text using the keyboard before, prepare to be amazed:

▶ **Select individual characters.** Tap the arrow keys to place the insertion point on one end of the selection. Press the Shift key as you use the left or right arrow keys to highlight the characters you want to select.

▶ **Select a word.** Start with the insertion point at the beginning or end of the word. Press Ctrl+Shift+right arrow to select the word to the right or Ctrl+Shift+left arrow to select the word to the left. To select more words, just keep hitting the arrow key.

▶ **Select a sentence.** Put the insertion point at the beginning of the sentence. Press Shift+right arrow repeatedly until you reach the end of the sentence. (OK, so this method is a workaround. Word doesn't have a single keyboard command to select an entire sentence.)

▶ **Select to end of line.** Press Shift+End. Word highlights all the text from the insertion point to the end of line.

▶ **Select to beginning of line.** Press Shift+Home to select text from the insertion point to the beginning of the line.**Select a paragraph.** Place the insertion point at the beginning of the paragraph and press Ctrl+Shift+down arrow.

▶ **Select a block of text.** Click to place the insertion point at the beginning of your selection. Hold the Shift key down and use any of the arrow keys (up, down, left, and right) or navigation keys (Home, End, Page Up, and Page Down) to mark your selection.

▶ **Select an entire document.** Press Ctrl+A. (Think select All). Word highlights the entire document. You can also select the entire document by pressing the F8 key repeatedly. See the box on page 58.

# Extending a Selection

What if you've selected some text and then realize you'd like to add a little bit more to your selection? You have a couple of options. The most common method: Extend your selection by Shift-clicking in your text, as shown previously in Figure 2-6. Word highlights the text between the previous selection and your Shift-click and includes it in the new selection.

A similar, but even more elegant way to extend a selection is with the F8 key. Pressing F8 sets one end of your selection at the insertion point. Click either forward or backward in your document, and everything in between the insertion point and your click is instantly highlighted and selected. F8 has several other surprising selection powers. See the box on page 58 for all the details.

# Selecting Multiple Chunks of Text in Different Places

If you're into efficiency and multitasking, Word's multiple selection feature was made for you. Multiple selections save you time by applying formatting to similar, but disconnected elements. Say you have several paragraphs of text and you decide you'd like to make the first sentence in each paragraph bold (Figure 2-7) for emphasis. After you select the sentences, you can format them all at once. You can also collect items from several locations and then copy and paste them into a new spot. See page 66 for more on cutting and pasting.

To make a multiple selection, simply make your first selection and then press the Ctrl key while you make another. The areas you select don't need to be connected.

> **TIP**
> You can also use just about any of the selection techniques mentioned earlier in this section to add to the multiple selection. For example, when you want to add an entire paragraph to your selection, press Ctrl while you double-click in the left margin next to the paragraph.

So, here are the steps to follow for the example in Figure 2-7:

1. **Drag to select the first sentence in the first paragraph.**

   Word highlights the sentence to indicate it's selected.

# F8—The Selection Superhero

For an unassuming function key sitting there almost unused at the top of your keyboard, the F8 key has surprisingly powerful text selection skills. Pressing it helps you select much more than you can with any other single keystroke or mouse click.

* **Sticky selection end point.** Pressing F8 at the beginning of your intended selection makes any selection method you use stay "on" without your having to press any keys. Here's how it works: Put your insertion point at the beginning of where you want to start a selection. Press F8 once (don't hold it down), and then use the mouse or arrow keys to complete the selection. Look ma, no hands! Word makes the selection just as if you were pressing the Shift key while navigating to a new point.

* **Select a word.** Press F8 twice to select a whole word. Used this way, F8 works just like double-clicking the word.

* **Select a sentence.** Press F8 three times to select a sentence.

* **Select a paragraph.** Press F8 four times to select all the text in a paragraph.

* **Select an entire document.** Press F8 five times. Voila! The whole document is selected.

The F8 key with its sticky behavior keeps selecting text left and right until you turn it off. Press the Esc key to deactivate the F8 key's selection proclivities. Then you can once again move the insertion point without selecting text.

---

2. **Press Ctrl, and keep holding it as you drag to select the first sentence in the *next* paragraph.**

   Word highlights each sentence you select but nothing in between. Repeat this step for each sentence you want to select.

3. **Press Ctrl+B.**

   Word makes the selected sentences bold and leaves them highlighted. You can enter another command if you want—bold italics, anyone?

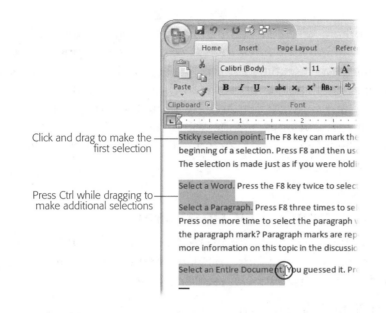

Click and drag to make the first selection

Press Ctrl while dragging to make additional selections

**Figure 2-7.** By making multiple selections with the Ctrl key, you can do cool things like apply the same formatting to several disconnected words at once. For example, you can Ctrl-drag to select the first sentence in each paragraph, as shown here. The mouse cursor (circled) shows where the last drag ended. You can then make the sentences bold (Ctrl+B) for emphasis. (Find more on typeface formatting in Chapter 3.)

# Moving Around Your Document

Using that nice blue scrollbar on the right side of your document is the most obvious way to navigate your document. And if your mouse has a wheel on it, then using it to scroll is pretty speedy too. But when your document's more than a few pages long, trying to scroll to the exact point you're looking for is just plain inefficient.

Word's most powerful ways of boogieing around your document don't involve scrolling at all. You can use the keyboard to hop from place to place. For really long documents, as with long journeys, the best way to get around is by using landmarks. For example, you can check all the graphics in a document by jumping directly from one to the next. Or you can go directly to a specific heading in a 400-page business report by telling Word to find it for you. You can even create your own landmarks using Word's bookmarking feature. Word's got the tools, and this section tells you how to use 'em.

___ TIP _____

> If you're working with a large document, then Word has some other great ways to find your way around. You can use Outline view (View → Documents View → Outline) to easily navigate between chapter and section headings. The Document Map (View → Documents View → Document Map) shows a similar view in the bar along the left side of your document. If your pages include distinctive graphics, then the Thumbnail View (View → Show/Hide → Thumbnails) can help you find the spot you want by eye.

## Keyboarding Around Your Document

You've heard it before: You lose time every time you take your hands off the keyboard to fumble for the mouse. For short jaunts especially, get in the habit of using these keyboard commands to move the insertion point:

▶ **Move left or right.** Left/right arrow keys.

▶ **Move to the beginning or the end of a line.** Home/End. (On most keyboards, these keys are just above the arrow keys. On most laptops, the Home and End keys are either along the right side or in the top-right corner.)

▶ **Move up or down a line.** Up/down arrow keys.

▶ **Move up or down a paragraph.** Ctrl+up/down arrow.

▶ **Move up or down one screenful of text.** Page up/down.

▶ **Move to the beginning or the end of a document.** Ctrl+Home/End.

## Using the Scroll Bars

If you've used Word or any of the other Microsoft Office programs in the past, that skinny bar down the right side of your document should look familiar. In the center of the bar is a box that you drag to move up or down your document. The bar also has some arrow buttons at top and bottom for finer control (shown in Figure 2-8). Click the buttons to scroll just a line or two at a time. To cover big distances, click in the bar above or below the box, and the document scrolls one screen at a time.

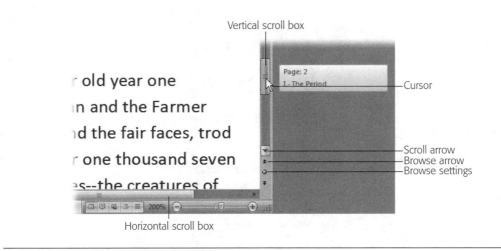

**Figure 2-8.** Drag the scroll box to move rapidly through your document. Click the arrow buttons to scroll a line at a time. The three buttons at the bottom of the scroll bar let you browse your document by page, heading, or graphic.

Easier still, you can scroll without using the scroll bar at all; see Figures 2-9 and 2-10 for instructions.

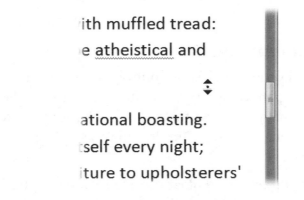

**Figure 2-9.** Click the mouse wheel, and you see the scroll symbol shown here. When this symbol is present, you can scroll your document by moving the mouse cursor away from the symbol. Move your cursor down to start to scroll down. The further you move the cursor down the screen, the faster the document scrolls. Click the wheel button to stop the auto-scrolling.

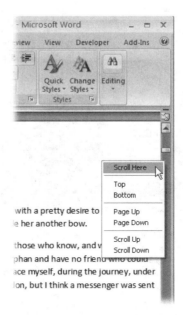

**Figure 2-10.** Right-click the scroll bar, and you see a pop-up menu with navigation shortcuts. At the top of the list is Scroll Here, which is the equivalent of dragging the scroll box to the location you clicked on the scroll bar. (In previous versions of Word, you could Shift-click for the same result.) Other shortcuts take you to the beginning or the end of your document and scroll a line or a screenful at a time.

## Browsing by Headings and Other Objects

For longer documents, the most interesting controls are at the bottom of the scroll bar: two double arrows separated by a round button. What makes these *Browse buttons* so handy is the fact that you can customize their behavior to match your needs. The round button puts you in control. Click it, and you see the Select Browse Settings menu (Figure 2-11).

At first, the icons in the "Browse by" toolbar may seem a little cryptic, but never fear, you can get help. Hold the cursor over the icons, and their function is explained in the text box at the top. The "Open the Go To box" and "Open the Find box" options open the dialog box where you can search for specific text and jump to a certain location in your document, as described later in this chapter (page 76). The rest of the options determine what happens when you click the double-arrow Browse buttons. For example, when you click Browse by Headings, clicking the Browse arrows then takes you forward (or back) through your document, jumping from one head-

**Figure 2-11.** The Browse Settings menu lets you set the behavior of the Browse buttons and perform other useful navigation tasks. For example, you can set the buttons to browse by headings, pages, or even graphics within your document. These settings make the Browse buttons an extremely powerful navigation feature. It's a shame they're overlooked and underused.

ing to the next and skipping everything in between. As you learn to use more advanced features like end notes and comments, described later in this book, you'll find it very convenient to use them as your landmarks, as well.

## Browsing by Bookmark

The bookmarks that slip between the pages of books are elegant in their simplicity, even decorative, but they're kind of primitive. They only do one thing—mark a point between two adjacent pages—and if they fall out, well then they don't do anything at all. Word's electronic bookmarks let you get much more specific. You can use them to mark the exact *word* where you left off. And since there's no limit on how many you can put in a document, you can use them to help organize a long document as you work your way through it. Bookmarks don't show up when you print the document; they're just reference points that let you jump instantly to places you want to return to most often.

### Creating bookmarks

You can create as many bookmarks as you want in a document with just a few mouse clicks. Bookmarks are invisible in your documents, but that's just Word's factory setting. You can change your Word Options to show bookmarks in your text. (Maybe Microsoft turns them off because the bookmarks are sort of unattractive—they appear as brackets around the bookmarked text.)

To see bookmarks in your text, choose Office button → Word Options → Advanced. (The Word Options button is at the bottom of the Office menu, near the Exit button.) Scroll down to the options under "Show document content," and then turn on the "Show bookmarks" checkbox.

Here's how to insert a bookmark in your Word document:

1. **Select the text you want to bookmark.**

   The selected text is the location of the bookmark. If the text moves as you edit, the bookmark stays with the text.

   You can also create a bookmark without selecting text: Word simply places the bookmark at the insertion point. However, it's a little easier to keep track of your bookmarks if you select text.

2. **Go to Insert → Links → Bookmark.**

   The Bookmark dialog box opens (Figure 2-12).

3. **In the "Bookmark name" box, type a name for the bookmark.**

   Use a descriptive name, one that describes the location in the text, or perhaps the work you need to do at that spot. For example, if you're marking a place to come back and add something about guillotines, name it LaGuillotine.

   > **NOTE**
   >
   > For its own computerish reasons, Word doesn't let you use spaces in your bookmark name. To separate words, you can use dashes or under-scores instead.

4. **Click Add.**

   When you click Add, the dialog box disappears, and your bookmark is set and ready for use.

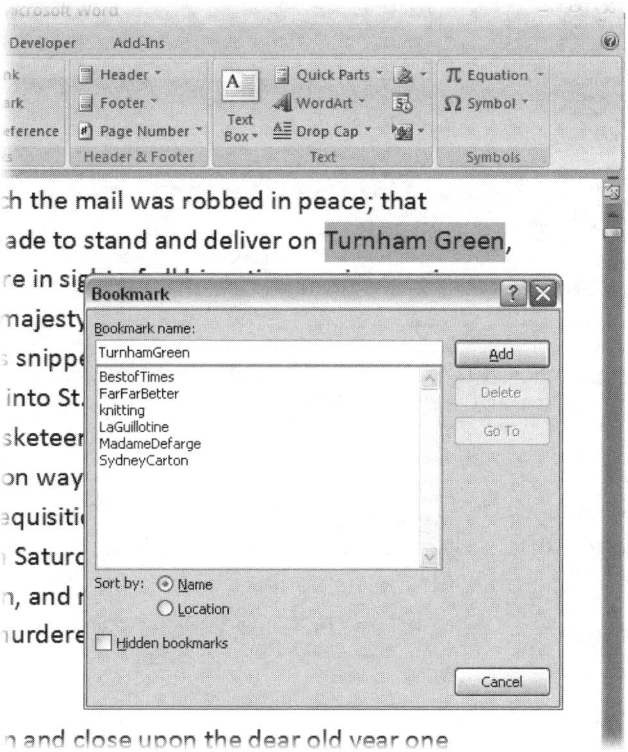

**Figure 2-12.** The Bookmark dialog box is easy to use. Use the text box at the top to name your bookmarks. The list below shows all the bookmarks in your document. The two radio buttons at the bottom sort the list alphabetically by name or by their order of appearance (Location) in your document. Use the buttons on the right to create (Add), delete, and jump to (Go To) your bookmarks.

### Jumping to bookmarks

Using bookmarks is even easier than creating them. The quickest way to use a bookmark is to hit F5 key to bring up the Go To dialog box (Figure 2-13). From the "Go to what" list, select Bookmark. When you've done that, the drop-down list at right shows all the bookmarks in your document. Select one, and then click the Go To button. Your document scrolls to put the highlighted, bookmarked text at the top of your screen. Click Close to hide the dialog box. After you've searched for a bookmark, you can use the Browse buttons below the scroll bar to jump to other bookmarks.

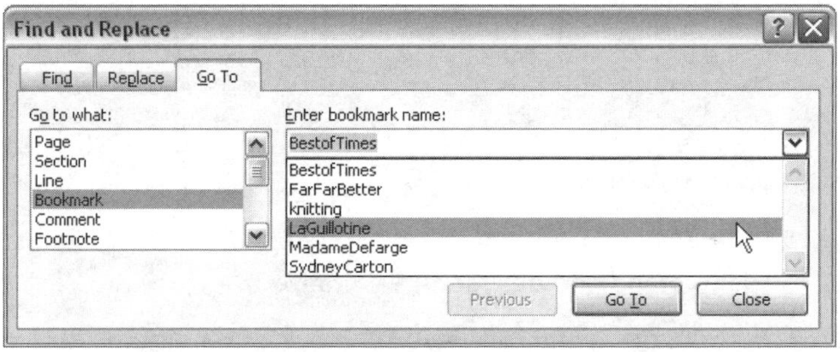

**Figure 2-13.** Bookmarks are useful if you need to jump back and forth between different locations. To move to a bookmark, open the Go To dialog box (F5), and then select Bookmark from the list at left. The drop-down list at right lists all the bookmarks in your document. Simply choose one from the list.

— **TIP**

The Find, Replace, and Go To dialog boxes have memory. While you're working in a document, it remembers the tab and list items you last used. So, if earlier you found a particular bookmark, then the next time you click Go To (or press F5), Word finds that same bookmark.

### Deleting bookmarks

About the only reason you'd want to delete a bookmark is if your list's getting cluttered and it's hard to find the bookmark you want. In any case, it's easy to delete bookmarks using the same dialog box you use to create them (Figure 2-12). Just pick the soon-to-be-terminated bookmark from the list and click Delete. It's a goner.

# Cutting, Copying, and Pasting

When it comes time to edit your text and shape it into a masterpiece of communication, the job is all about cutting, copying, and pasting. Compared to actually using scissors and paste (which is what writers and editors did in the pre-PC era), Word makes manipulating text almost effortless. You're free to experiment, moving words, sentences, and paragraphs around until you've got everything just right.

# The Many Paths to Go To

The Go To, Find, and Replace dialog boxes are actually three different tabs in the same window. You either open the dialog box directly to one of the tabs, or, if it's already open, then just click a tab at the top of the box. As usual, Microsoft provides many ways to open this particular box:

* **Home → Editing → Find.** Opens the Find tab.

* **Home → Editing → Replace.** Opens the Replace tab.

* **Home → Editing → Go To.** Opens the Go To tab.

* **Browse Settings button.** Click Browse Settings (the tiny circle in the window's lower-right corner, as shown in Figure 2-8), and then click the Go To (arrow) or Find (binoculars).

* **Ctrl+F.** Opens the Find tab.

* **Ctrl+H.** Opens the Replace tab.

* **Ctrl+G or F5.** Opens the Go To tab.

* **Double-click Status bar.** Double-clicking the status bar in the lower-left corner also opens the Go To tab.

By now, you've probably figured that most Word functions can be done in at least two ways—by keyboard and by mouse. That's certainly the case when it comes to the basic editing functions, as shown in the table. If you're typing away and don't want to take your hands off the keyboard, then you'll probably want to use the keyboard shortcuts, which can all be performed with a flick of your left hand.

| Command | Ribbon Command | Ribbon Icon | Keyboard Shortcut |
| --- | --- | --- | --- |
| **Cut** | Home → Clipboard → Cut | Scissors | Ctrl+X |
| **Copy** | Home → Clipboard → Copy | 2 pages | Ctrl+C |
| **Paste** | Home → Clipboard → Paste | Clipboard | Ctrl+V |

## Editing with the Ribbon

▶ Word's new ribbon is where all the commands live, and it's hardly a surprise that cut, copy, and paste are the first commands on the first tab (Home) in the first group (Clipboard). As you can see in Figure 2-14, these commands are conveniently located right near another place you frequently mouse over to, the Office button.

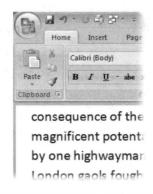

**Figure 2-14.** The basic editing commands Cut, Copy, and Paste are easy to find. Go to Home → Clipboard, and there they are. As always, the first step is to select the text that you want to cut (scissors) or copy (two pages). Then, position the insertion point at the location where you want to paste (clipboard) the text.

Once you've found the commands, here's how to use 'em:

▶ **Cut (Home → Clipboard → Cut).** Just as described on page 53, you need to select text (or an object, like a picture or a table) before you can cut it from your document. When you invoke the Cut command, your selected item disappears, but Cut is very different from a Delete or a Clear command. The Cut command actually stores the cut item on the Office Clipboard, where you can bring it back later using the Paste command. You can actually open this Clipboard and see recently cut and copied items. The Office Clipboard works across all Microsoft Office programs, so you can cut a paragraph from your novel and paste it into an Outlook email or PowerPoint slide.

- **Copy (Home → Clipboard → Copy).** As you may expect, Copy makes a duplicate of the selected text or object and stores it on the Clipboard. It leaves the selection in place in its original location.

- **Paste (Home → Clipboard → Paste).** Before you use the Paste command, you must first cut or copy some text (or a picture or other object). Then, put the insertion point exactly where you want to place the item, and then paste away.

> **NOTE**
>
> See page 73 for more about working with Word's Clipboard.

## Editing with Keyboard Shortcuts

The keyboard shortcuts are the quickest and easiest editing commands to use as you're typing along, because you don't need to take your hands off the keyboard. You can use the Cut, Copy, and Paste commands with only a couple fingers of the left hand. These shortcuts use the Ctrl key in combination with nearby keys on the bottom row—X, C, and V. As an added bonus, the adjacent Z key is used for the Undo command—another oft-used editor's tool. These keys perform the exact same functions as the ones run when you use the ribbon commands using Word's ribbon:

- **Cut.** Ctrl+X.
- **Copy.** Ctrl+C.
- **Paste.** Ctrl+V.
- **Undo.** Ctrl+Z.

## Editing with the Mouse

After Cut, Copy, and Paste, the next great leap forward for writers and editors was the *graphical user interface* (GUI) and the ability to use a mouse to drag and drop text. After all, most of editing is deleting unneeded words and pushing the others around into the most effective positions. With a mouse, you can really see what you're doing: Take *this* and drag it over *there*.

But some people are never satisfied. And lo and behold, Microsoft added a right mouse button. When you right-click, you get a pop-up menu that includes Cut, Copy, Paste, and other commands, right where you need them (Figure 2-15). The pop-up menu contains only the most common commands, to save you a trip all the way up to that ribbon. To get to more advanced commands (like line spacing or alphabetic sorting), you do have to use the ribbon.

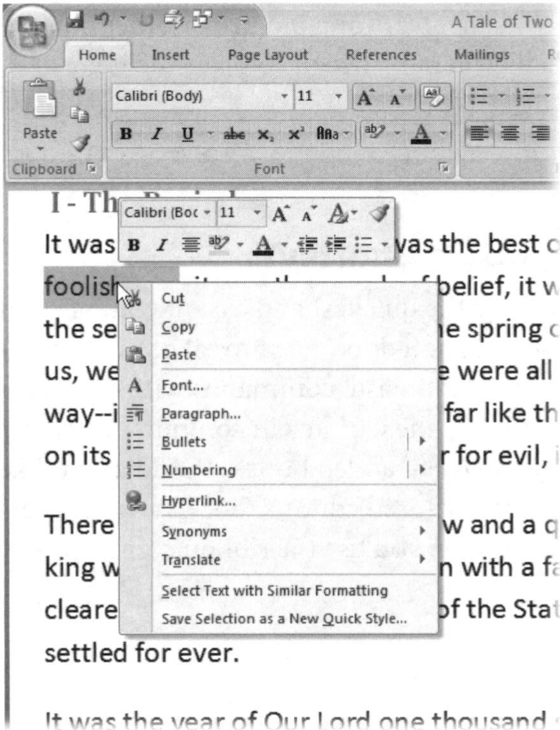

**Figure 2-15.** Right-click in your text to display the Edit shortcut menu. If you've selected text, you can use the Cut and Copy commands. Word 2007 adds a slew of additional commands, including language translation, hyperlink creation, and formatting options. As an added bonus, you see the Mini Toolbar with formatting commands above the edit commands.

It's easy to drag and drop text to a new location using just your mouse. Take your hands off the keyboard, lean back in your chair, grab the mouse, and follow these steps:

1. **Click (the left mouse button) and drag to select the text that you want to relocate.**

   Word highlights the text to show you what you've selected. Let go of the mouse button when you're done.

2. **Click the selected text and, holding down the mouse button, drag the mouse to the new location for the text.**

As shown in Figure 2-16 (top), a little rectangle below the cursor means you're dragging something. As you move the mouse, the insertion point follows, marking where the moved text will appear.

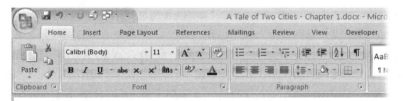

**Figure 2-16.** Gutenberg would be amazed at how easy it is to reset type with Word. Top: Select the text you want to move, and then point to it and click. Continue to hold the left mouse button while you drag the text to a new location.

Bottom: When you release the mouse button, Word plops the text into the new location.

3. **Release the mouse button.**

   Releasing the mouse button finishes the job, placing the moved text at the insertion point, as shown in Figure 2-16 (bottom).

## Moving Text Between Two Documents

Moving text from one document to another isn't much different from moving it from place to place within a document. You can use keyboard or ribbon commands to cut and paste, or you can drag and drop between documents (Figure 2-17). In fact, it's just as easy to move text between documents created by different programs. For example, you can cut or copy text in Word and paste it into documents created in Outlook, PowerPoint, Access, Excel, and many non-Microsoft programs, too. Even the same keyboard shortcuts do the trick: Ctrl+X (Cut), Ctrl+C (Copy), and Ctrl+V (Paste). Of course, you can also use menu commands if you insist.

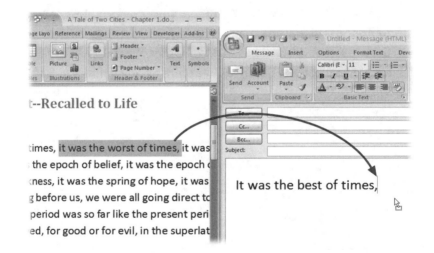

**Figure 2-17.** You can drag and drop text between Word documents and into documents of other programs. Here, text is being dragged from Word into an Outlook email message. The insertion point shows where the text will end up. The small rectangle on the arrow-shaped cursor indicates that the cursor is holding text.

## Viewing and Pasting Clippings

More often than not, when you cut or copy text, a picture, or an object, you want to paste it into a new location right away. But what if you wanted to copy several items and paste them into the same location? Or, what if you want to again paste an item that you copied several edits ago? Enter the Office Clipboard. The Clipboard's nothing new to Microsoft Office programs, but the 2007 version gives this familiar tool a new look (Figure 2-18). As you cut and copy text, graphics, and other objects, Word (or whatever Office program you're in) stashes them here for reuse. The Clipboard lets you view the stored items and lets you paste them into other documents with just a click or two.

**Figure 2-18.** The new Office 2007 Clipboard sports an updated look but provides the same functions as previous versions. Compared to previous versions, the new Clipboard gives you a more generous view of the items it stores. The Options button at the bottom of the Clipboard lets you adjust its appearance, location, and behavior.

# Working With the Clipboard Task Pane

Open the Clipboard task pane by clicking the launcher in the lower-right corner of the Clipboard group (Home → Clipboard). (You find it in exactly the same spot in Access, Excel, and PowerPoint.) With the Clipboard task pane open, you see all the items you recently cut or copied. Click an item to paste it into your Word document at the insertion point. Or, if you want, you can switch to another program (Alt+Tab) and paste it there. Point to an item on the Clipboard, and you see a drop-down menu with two options: Paste and Delete. It's easier to simply click to paste an item, but Delete gives you a handy way to clean up the Clipboard contents before you use the Paste All command. The Paste All and Clear All buttons are at the top of the Clipboard task pane.

The Options menu (at bottom) is where you fine-tune the Clipboard's behavior:

✽ **Show Office Clipboard Automatically.** Turn on this option to have the Clipboard appear whenever you copy an item.

✽ **Show Office Clipboard when Ctrl+C Pressed Twice.** This option works easily as you're typing. Press Ctrl+C once to copy selected text; press Ctrl+C a second time, and you see the Clipboard.

✽ **Show Office Clipboard Icon on Taskbar.** With this option selected, the Office Clipboard appears in the Taskbar in the lower-right corner of your screen.

✽ **Show Status Near Taskbar when Copying.** Each time you cut or copy an item, a screen tip appears near the Taskbar detailing how many items are on the Clipboard.

Your most recent cut items or copied items appear at the top of the Clipboard and move down as you add more. When you use the Paste command (Ctrl+V), Word is simply pasting the item at the top of the Clipboard at the insertion point. That's what happens whether the Clipboard is open or closed. To paste a different item instead of the most recent, just place the insertion point where you want it, and then click that item on the Clipboard, as shown in Figure 2-19.

But wait—the Clipboard's coolness is just getting warmed up. Not only can you see multiple pasteable items, you can paste them in bunches too. The Clipboard acts as a collection palette. For example, suppose you've created a dinner menu for your

**Figure 2-19.** Use the Office Clipboard to paste text, graphics, and other objects into your documents. Unlike the Cut and Paste commands, the Clipboard isn't limited to the last item you cut or copied. You can choose from an appetizing menu of words and images that you recently edited. Deleting removes the item from the Clipboard

restaurant in Word, and you want to create a new lunch menu that includes just a few of the items from the dinner menu. Follow these steps to collect and paste those tasty morsels into a new document:

1. **With the source document open in front of you (in this case, the dinner menu), go to Home → Clipboard, and then click the small square next to the Clipboard group label.**

    This square, with an arrow in the lower-right corner, is called the Clipboard *launcher,* and its job is to open and close the Clipboard. Initially, the Clipboard opens in a panel on the left side of the window, but you can drag it from that location and use it like a freestanding palette.

2. **At the top of the Clipboard, click Clear All to remove any previously copied items.**

    If you've been working on other projects, there may be items already on your Clipboard, including those from other Office programs. Since you probably don't want all that stuff on your lunch menu, clear the decks with the Clear All button.

Clippings stay on the Office Clipboard until you clear them—or until you exit all Microsoft Office programs (Word, Outlook, Excel, and PowerPoint).

3. **Copy (Ctrl+C) the entrees, side dishes, and beverages you want to put on the lunch menu.**

   Use any of the methods described in this chapter to find, select, and copy the items. As you copy each item, Word adds it to the clipboard.

4. **Open a new document (Office button → New → Blank) to use as your lunch menu.**

   A new Word window opens, but notice that you still have access to the Clipboard with all your copied menu entries.

5. **Click Paste All.**

   When you click Paste All, the Clipboard's entire contents appear in your new document. (Now all you need to do is figure out the lunch prices.)

# Finding and Replacing Text

Scanning every word of your 400-page novel to find the exact spot where you first mentioned Madame DeFarge is drudgery with a capital D. Fortunately, Word performs this task quickly and without whining or demanding overtime pay. What's more, it's just as easy to find and then replace text. Suppose you decide to change the name of the character from Madame DeFarge to Madame de Stael. Simple—here's how to do a Find and Replace:

1. **Open the Find and Replace dialog box (Figure 2-20). For example, press Ctrl+H.**

   You have many ways to open the Find and Replace dialog box, as explained in the box on page 79. If your hands are on the keyboard, then Ctrl+H is the fastest.

   When the dialog box opens, you see tabs at the top for each of the panels: Find, Replace, and Go To. The controls and options under the Find and Replace tabs are nearly identical. The main difference is that the Replace tab includes *two* text boxes—"Replace with" as well as "Find what."

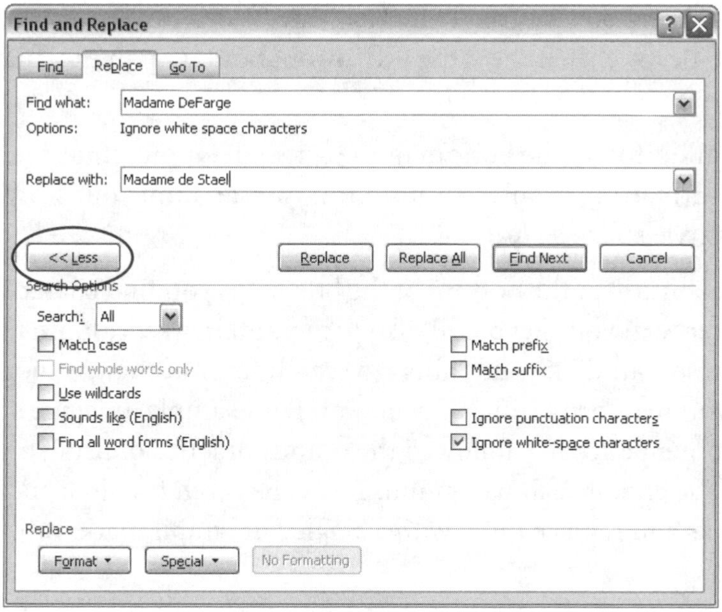

**Figure 2-20.** Initially, the Replace box is pretty simple, but when you click More, you see a number of options for fine-tuning your search. (And the More button turns into a Less button, as shown here.) The box on page 79 explains all the Search options in detail.

2. **In the "Find what" box, type the text you want to find, and, in the "Replace with" box, type the replacement text.**

   For example, type *Madame DeFarge* in "Find what" and *Madame de Stael* in "Replace with."

   ___ NOTE _____

   The "Find what" is a drop-down box that remembers your past searches. So the next time you go to this box, Madame DeFarge will be there waiting for you.

   _____

3. **If you wish, click More to reveal additional Find options.**

When you click More, the box expands, and you see a number of additional controls that can fine-tune your search. For example, if you're searching for "Madame DeFarge" but you don't know how it's capitalized, then make sure the Match Case checkbox is turned off. That way, Word finds every occurrence even if you didn't capitalize it the same way throughout. For an explanation of all the Search options, see the box on page 79.

The Format button at the bottom of the screen lets you refine your search by including formatting details. For instance, you can limit your search to a specific paragraph style such as Heading 1.

The Special button at the bottom of the box helps you find characters that aren't easy to enter with your keyboard, like paragraph marks, column breaks, and em dashes. These sound like odd things to search for, but they're enormously helpful when you're reformatting a document. For example, imagine someone sends you a document and they followed the odious practice of using two carriage returns at the end of each paragraph. You can search for all the double paragraph marks and replace them with a single paragraph mark. Problem solved.

___ TIP _____

A better way to leave extra space between paragraphs is to include it in the paragraph formatting itself. See page 96 for details.

4. **Click Find Next to begin your search and replace mission.**

   The search begins at the insertion point, so if you want to find all the instances of Madame DeFarge, start at the beginning of your document. A quick Ctrl+Home takes you there. Word finds the text and highlights it in the document. If you need a better look at your text, you can click the top edge of the Replace box and drag it to another position.

5. **Examine the text and make sure you want to replace this instance of Madame DeFarge with Madame de Stael. Click Replace, and the text is swapped.**

   Word automatically finds the next instance of your search text.

6. **If you're certain that you want to replace every instance of Madame DeFarge, click Replace All.**

   Word makes all the changes and reports back with the number of replacements it made.

# Search Options Explained

Computers are dumb. They don't know that, if you type *bird* in the Find dialog box, you're looking for flying things, not some Mr. Birdley. So Microsoft gives you the Find and Replace dialog boxes with some options to help you make them smarter. Here's what the options do when you turn on their checkboxes:

* **Match case.** Find shows you only words that exactly match the uppercase and lowercase letters of your search entry. So, DeFarge finds "DeFarge" but not "defarge."

* **Find whole words only.** Find only shows you complete words that match your entry. For example, if you enter some, the search shows you the word "some" but not the word "somewhere."

* **Use wildcards.** Wild cards let you expand your search. For example, ^? is the wildcard that matches any character. A search for ^?ill returns the words "will," "bill," "kill," "dill," and so forth.

* **Sounds like.** Finds words that sound like your entry. (Consider this help for the spelling-impaired.)

If, say, you enter *inglund*, then Word finds "England."

* **Find all word forms.** Type is, and Word finds "was," "were," and "being."

* **Match prefix.** Finds characters at the beginning of a word, so re finds "reason" but not "are." (In this option and the next, Word doesn't consider prefix and suffix in a grammatical sense; it's just looking for the beginning and the ending of words.)

* **Match suffix.** Use this option to find characters at the end of a word. For example, ed finds "mashed" but not "eddy."

* **Ignore punctuation characters.** Word doesn't include periods, commas, hyphens, apostrophes, and other punctuation marks when it makes a match. For example, coachlamps finds coach-lamps.

* **Ignore white-space characters.** Word leaves paragraph marks, spaces, tabs, and other nonprinting, "space" characters out of the search. In this case, *coachlamps* finds "coach lamps."

# Saving Keystrokes with Quick Parts

Suppose your company has an extremely long name and an even longer address (complete with nine-digit Zip code). Now say you type in the name and address about three times an hour. Wouldn't it be great to just type *address* and have Word fill in the whole shebang? That's exactly the kind of magic you can do with Word 2007's Quick Parts feature. You can have Word memorize whole chunks of text, and then spit them back out when you type an abbreviation word followed by the F3 key.

Quick Parts evolved from the AutoText feature found in earlier versions of Word. AutoText was one of the program's most overlooked and underused features. Quick Parts work like this: You store text, graphics, or anything else you've created in Word in a Quick Part and give it a name, preferably something short and memorable. When you want to retrieve the Quick Part, simply type that name, and then press F3. Word replaces the name with the entire contents of the Quick Part. Few keystrokes, mucho text.

Here are step-by-step instructions for creating a new Quick Part:

1. **Select the text you want to save as a Quick Part.**

   Your selection can include text, pictures, and other objects that Office recognizes. There's virtually no size limit. You can even use an entire document as a Quick Part (like a rejection letter that you send out every day).

2. **Use Alt+F3 to open the Create New Building Block dialog box (Figure 2-21).**

   The Alt+F3 keyboard shortcut's the quickest route to creating a new Quick Part Building Block. (And, after all, speed's the name of the Quick Part game.) You see six boxes in the Create New Building Block dialog box, but the first one, Name, is the most important.

3. **Give your Quick Part a Name.**

   Think carefully when you type a name for your Quick Part, because the name is the key you use to retrieve the Quick Part. The name can be as short or as long as you want. For speed's sake, shorter is better, but you don't want to make it so cryptic you can't remember it.

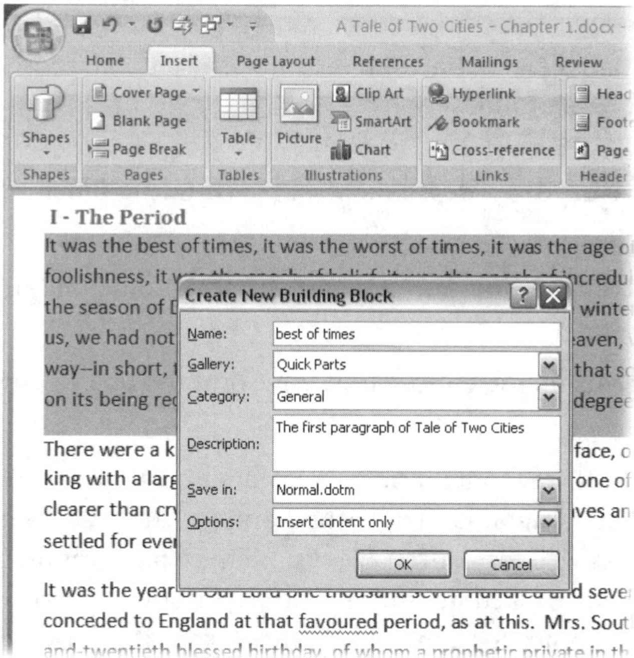

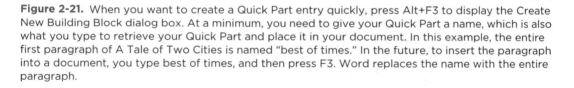

**Figure 2-21.** When you want to create a Quick Part entry quickly, press Alt+F3 to display the Create New Building Block dialog box. At a minimum, you need to give your Quick Part a name, which is also what you type to retrieve your Quick Part and place it in your document. In this example, the entire first paragraph of A Tale of Two Cities is named "best of times." In the future, to insert the paragraph into a document, you type best of times, and then press F3. Word replaces the name with the entire paragraph.

4. **Type a Description and, if you wish, choose a Category for your Quick Part.**

   A description is optional, but it's helpful for other people who use Word, or even for you, a couple of years down the road. And if you create a lot of Quick Parts, then you may find it helpful to store them in different categories as a way to organize them. For example, you can create a Help Desk category with answers to frequently asked questions and a Contracts category with a legal boilerplate.

> You can use the Gallery drop-down menu to store your entry as something other than a Quick Part. For example, you could store it as a Cover Page or as a Bibliography.

5. **Leave the "Save in" drop-down menu set to Building Blocks.dotx.**

   The Quick Part is saved in Building Blocks.dotx, a Word template that's available to any document. You can find more information about using templates on page 170.

6. **From the Options menu, choose how you want the text to appear every time you press F3.**

   The first option, "Insert content only," is a good one to use if you plan to use the Quick Part within paragraphs. The second option, "Insert content in its own paragraph," works well for address blocks or entire paragraphs, such as the answers to frequently asked questions. The last option, "Insert content in its own page," is a logical choice for a memo or other text that rightfully belongs on its own.

# FORMATTING TEXT, PARAGRAPHS, AND HEADINGS

▶ Formatting Basics

▶ Formatting Characters

▶ Formatting Paragraphs

▶ Creating Bulleted and Numbered Lists

▶ Setting Tabs

▶ Using Word's Rulers

▶ Fast Formatting with Format Painter

▶ Formatting with Styles

▶ Modifying Styles

▶ Managing Style Sets

**FORMATTING IS THE FINE ART** of making your documents effective and attractive. Good formatting distinguishes different parts of your text and helps your readers take in your message. You can apply formatting to just about every element of your document, from a single character to entire paragraphs. Body text needs to be readable and easy on the eyes. Headings should be big and bold, and they should also be consistent throughout your document. Important words need to resonate with emphasis. Quotes and references should be set off from the other text.

This chapter starts with the basics: how to format individual characters and words—selecting fonts and making characters bold, italicized, underlined, or capitalized. You learn how to format paragraphs with indents and spacing, and how to control the way Word breaks up the words in a line and the lines in a paragraph. Finally, you find out how to copy and reuse formatting with tools like the Format Painter and style sets.

# Formatting Basics

Word deals with formatting on three levels encompassing small and specific on up to big and broad—through characters, paragraphs, and sections. You apply different types of formatting to each of these parts. Character formatting includes selecting a font, a font size, bold or italics, and so on. At the paragraph level, you apply indents, bullets, and line spacing. For each section of your document (even if there's only one), you set the page size, orientation, and margins, as described in the previous chapter. Sometimes it helps to think of the parts of a document as Russian nesting dolls: Characters go inside paragraphs, which go inside sections, which fit inside your document.

Each type of formatting has its own dialog box, giving you access to all possible settings. You can also apply most types of formatting via the ribbon, the mini-toolbar, or the keyboard shortcut.

▶ **Characters.** Use the Font dialog box (Alt+H, FN) to format characters. Letters, numbers, and punctuation marks are all printable characters and, as such, you can format them. Once you select a character or a group of characters, you can apply any of the formatting commands on the Home tab's Font group (Alt+H). You can choose a font and a size for any character in your document. You can make characters bold, underlined, superscript, or change them to just about any color of the rainbow.

___ **NOTE** _____

Prior to the use of computers, groups of letters, numbers, and punctuation of a certain style, such as Helvetica or Bodoni, were called *typefaces*. The term *font* was more specific, referring to variations within a typeface such as bold, narrow, or italic. Today, the terms are interchangeable. Word uses the term *font*, probably because it's shorter and therefore easier to fit into a dialog box.

▶ **Paragraphs.** Use the Paragraph dialog box (Alt+H, PG) to format paragraphs. You can set formatting for text alignment, indents, line spacing, line breaks, and paragraph breaks. You don't have to select a paragraph to format it; just click to place the insertion point within a paragraph. Because characters are part of paragraphs (remember those Russian nesting dolls), every paragraph includes a basic font description. When you select characters within a paragraph and change the font settings, you override the basic font description in the paragraph's style.

▶ **Sections.** Use the Page Setup dialog box (Alt+P, SP) to format sections. When you change margins, page orientation, page size, and the number of columns per page (all described in Chapter 4), you're formatting the section. Many documents have only one section, so when you make formatting changes to a section, you're actually formatting the entire document.

# Formatting Characters

Every character in your document is formatted. The formatting describes the typeface, the size of the character, the color, and whether or not the character is underlined, bold, or capitalized. It's easy to change the formatting, and Word gives you quite a few different ways to do it. The easiest and most visual way is with the ribbon (Home → Font). You can further fine-tune the font formatting using the Font dialog box (Alt+H, FN).

For quick formatting, you may not need to go any further than the mini-toolbar that pops up when you select text for formatting. And when you get really good, you can do most of your formatting with keyboard shortcuts, never even slowing down long enough to reach for the mouse.

Whichever method you use, formatting is a two-step process. First, tell Word which text you want to format by selecting it. Then format away. Or, you can set up your formatting options first, and then begin to type. Your letters and words will be beautifully formatted from the get-go.

## Formatting with the Ribbon or the Font Dialog Box

Since character formatting is one of the most often used Word features, Microsoft put the most popular settings right on the Home tab. If you don't see what you're looking for there, then you must open the Font dialog box. The good thing about the dialog box is that it puts all your character formatting options in one place so you can quickly make multiple changes. It's one-stop shopping if you want to change the typeface and the size, and add that pink double-underline.

Here are the steps:

1. **Select a group of characters, as shown in Figure 3-1.**

   You can use any of the selection methods described in Chapter 2. You can drag to select a single character. You can double-click to select a word. Or you can move the mouse cursor to the left side of a paragraph, and then double-click to select the whole paragraph.

   Of course, if you haven't typed anything yet, you can always go right to the ribbon and make your formatting choices first. Then type away.

2. **Go to Home → Font or the Font dialog box (click the little launcher button shown in Figure 3-1 or press Alt+H, FN) and make your formatting choices.**

   Many of the buttons in the Font group act like toggles. So, when you select text and click the underline button, Word underlines all the characters in the selection. When you click the underline button again, the underline goes away.

   If you can't find the command you want on the ribbon, or if you want to make several character formatting changes at once, then open the Font box (Figure 3-2).

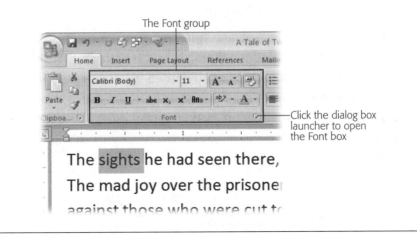

The Font group

Click the dialog box launcher to open the Font box

**Figure 3-1.** The Font group on the Home tab holds most of the common character formatting commands. Choices you make here apply to text you've selected (like the word "sights" in this example). If you don't see the command you need, in the lower-right corner, click the dialog box launcher to open the Font dialog box (Figure 3-2).

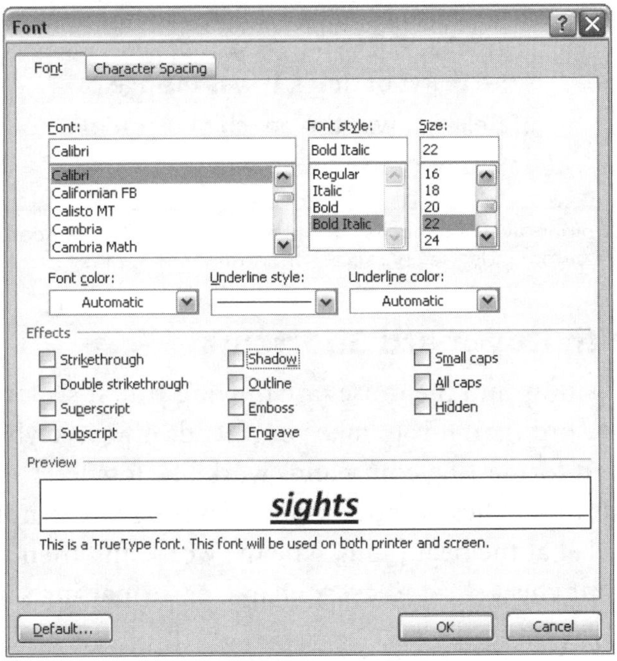

**Figure 3-2.** Open the Font box (Alt+H+FN) to change the typeface, style, size, color, and other effects. Like many dialog boxes, the Font box gives you access to more commands than you find on the ribbon.

## Formatting with the Mini Toolbar

Word's Mini Toolbar isn't quite as much fun as your hotel room's mini-bar, but there are times when you'll be glad it's there. A new feature in Word 2007, the Mini Toolbar pops up after you've selected text (Figure 3-3). It's faint at first, but if you move your mouse toward it, the Mini Toolbar comes into focus showing commands, most of which are character formatting commands. Just click one of the buttons to format your selection (or move your mouse away from the toolbar if you want it to go away).

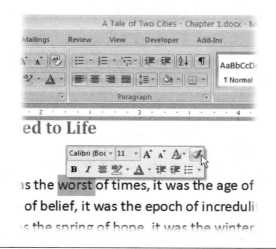

**Figure 3-3.** The mini-toolbar gives you access to the most commonly used commands. It just so happens that most of these commands are character formatting commands.

## Formatting with Keyboard Shortcuts

When you're typing away and the muses are moving you, it's a lot easier to hit Ctrl+I to italicize a word than it is to take your hands off the keyboard and grab a mouse. Because most formatting commands work like toggles, formatting options like bold, underline, and italics become second nature. For example, to italicize a word, just press Ctrl+I at the beginning, type the word, and then press Ctrl+I at the end. Table 3-1 is your cheat sheet to every character formatting shortcut known to Word.

**Table 3-1.** As a result of Word's evolution, most formatting commands have more than one keyboard shortcut. A new set of keyboard shortcuts is part of the reorganization that came up with Word 2007's new ribbon feature. But if commands like Ctrl+B for bold and Ctrl+U for underline are permanently burned into your brain, don't worry: Those commands from previous versions still work just fine.

| Command | Keyboard Shortcut | Old Keyboard Shortcut | Description |
|---------|-------------------|-----------------------|-------------|
| Font | Alt+H, FF, arrow keys, Enter | Ctrl+D, arrow keys, Enter | Alt+H, FF selects the font drop-down menu; use the arrow keys to highlight the font; press Enter to finish the selection. |
| Font Size | Alt+H, FS, arrow keys, Enter | Ctrl+Shift+P, arrow keys, Enter | Alt+H, FS selects the font size drop-down menu; use the arrow keys to highlight the size; press Enter to finish the selection. |
| Increase Font Size | Alt+H, FG | Ctrl+> | Increases font size. |
| Decrease Font Size | Alt+H, FK | Ctrl+< | Decreases font size. |
| Bold | Alt+H,1 | Ctrl+B | Toggles bold on and off. |
| Italic | Alt+H,2 | Ctrl+I | Toggles italics on and off. |
| Underline | Alt+H, 3, Enter | Ctrl+U | Toggles underline on and off. |
| Double underline | Alt+H, 3, down arrow, Enter | Ctrl+Shift+D | Toggles double underline on and off. |
| Underline style | Alt+H, 3, arrow keys | | Alt+H, 3 selects the underline style drop-down menu; use the arrow keys to highlight the style; press Enter to finish the selection. |
| Strikethrough | Alt+H, 4 | | Toggles strikethrough on and off. |
| Subscript | Alt+H, 5 | Ctrl+= | Toggles subscript on and off. |
| Superscript | Alt+H, 6 | Ctrl++ | Toggles superscript on and off. |

| Command | Keyboard Shortcut | Old Keyboard Shortcut | Description |
| --- | --- | --- | --- |
| Change Case | Alt+H, 7, arrow keys | Shift+F3 | Toggles through five case options: sentence case, lowercase, uppercase, capitalize each word, toggle case. |
| Color | Alt+H, FC, arrow keys, Enter | | Alt+H, FS FC selects the font color drop-down menu; use the arrow keys to highlight the color; press Enter to finish the selection. |
| Highlight Text | Alt+H, I, Enter | | Alt+H, I selects the highlight drop-down menu; Enter highlights the selection. |
| Clear formatting | Alt+H, E | Ctrl+Spacebar | Removes text formatting from the selection. |

# Where's the Animated Type?

In what may be an unprecedented move, Microsoft actually *reduced* the number of text formatting options in Word 2007. Fortunately, the defunct feature is something most folks won't miss—animated type. In Word 2003, Alt+O, FX opened the Effects panel on the Font dialog box. There you found such animated effects as Blinking Background, Las Vegas Lights, Marching Black Ants, Marching Red Ants, Shimmer, and Sparkle.

(Microsoft intended these effects for use on Web sites, of course, not on printed documents.) Presumably, the general public had good enough taste to shun these annoying type effects, and Microsoft dropped them due to disuse.

In any case, if you absolutely must have red marching ants dancing around the perimeter of your letters, the only way to enlist them is to cut and paste preformatted text from an older version of Word.

## Changing Capitalization

Any letter can be uppercase or lowercase, but when you get to words and sentences, you find some variations on the theme. It's not unusual to have a heading or a company name where all the letters are capitalized. Sentences start with an initial cap on the first word only, and titles usually have the major words capped. In an effort to automate anything that can possibly be automated, Microsoft provides the Change Case menu (Alt+H, 7) on the ribbon (Figure 3-4).

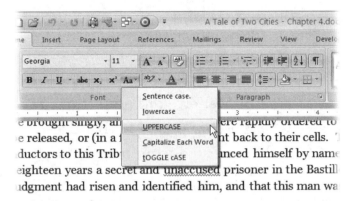

**Figure 3-4.** The Change Case menu gives you five ways to change the case of a selection. To open it, click the button that looks like two letter A's.

The Change Case command defies the usual rules about selecting before you apply character formatting. If you don't select anything, Word assumes you want to apply the Change Case command to an entire word, so the program selects the word at the insertion point. If you've selected text, the command works, as you'd expect, only on the selection.

### Small caps for headers

Small caps (Figure 3-5) are another variation on the capitalization theme. You won't find this option on the Change Case button; for small caps you have to use the Font dialog box, which you find on the right side under Effects (where underline or strikethrough are). Small caps are great for headings and letterhead (especially if you're a lawyer or an accountant), but you wouldn't want to use them for body text. It's difficult to read all capitalized text for an entire paragraph.

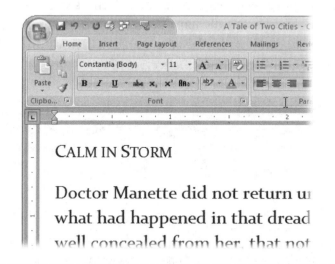

**Figure 3-5.** Small caps are a great way to distinguish a heading or subheading from body text, like the words "Calm in Storm." Initial letters get full-sized capitals while the letters that would normally be lowercase get small capitals.

# Formatting Paragraphs

Formatting a paragraph usually entails changing its shape. You may be squeezing it in with indents or stretching it out with additional line spacing. Other kinds of formatting change a paragraph's very nature, like adding a border or making it part of a numbered or bulleted list. The Paragraph formatting group (Home → Paragraph) is right next door to the Font group (Figure 3-6). You don't need to *select* text to format a paragraph; just make sure the insertion point is in the paragraph you want to format. However, if you want to format several paragraphs at once, select them all before you apply a command.

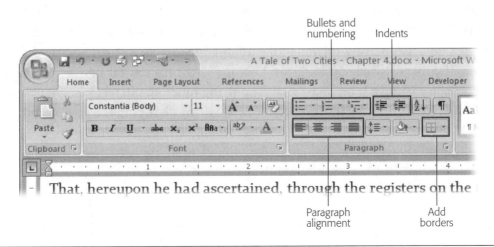

**Figure 3-6.** Paragraph formatting commands are in the Home → Paragraph group. Left to right, from the top, you find buttons to add bullets and numbers, apply indents, sort paragraphs, show the paragraph mark, align paragraphs, adjust line spacing, change the background color, and add borders.

## Aligning Text

It's easy to apply alignment to text. With your insertion point in the paragraph you want to change, click one of the alignment buttons in the Paragraph group on the Home Tab. For example, Home → Paragraph → Left sets the current paragraph's alignment. As shown in Figure 3-7, you have four choices when it comes to aligning your paragraphs:

▸ **Left (Alt+H, AL).** Aligns the lines in the paragraph flush on the left side and ragged on the right. Left alignment is standard for letters, reports, and many business documents.

▸ **Centered (Alt+H, AC).** Centers each line in the paragraph, leaving both left and right margins ragged. This setting is appropriate for headings and short chunks of text, as in invitations and advertisements. Avoid using centered text for long paragraphs, since it's hard for readers' eyes to track from the end of one line to the beginning of the next when the left margin is uneven.

▸ **Right (Alt+H, AR).** Aligns the lines in the paragraph flush on the right side and ragged on the left. This unusual alignment is most often used for setting captions or quotations apart from the main text.

▶ **Justified (Alt+H, AJ).** Adds space between letters and words so that both the left and right sides of the paragraph are straight and flush with the margins. Justified margins give text a more formal look suitable for textbooks or scholarly documents. If your justified text looks odd because big gaps appear between the letters or words, try using a long line—that is, putting more characters per line. You can do this by extending the margins (Alt+P, M) or by changing the size of your font (Alt+H, FS).

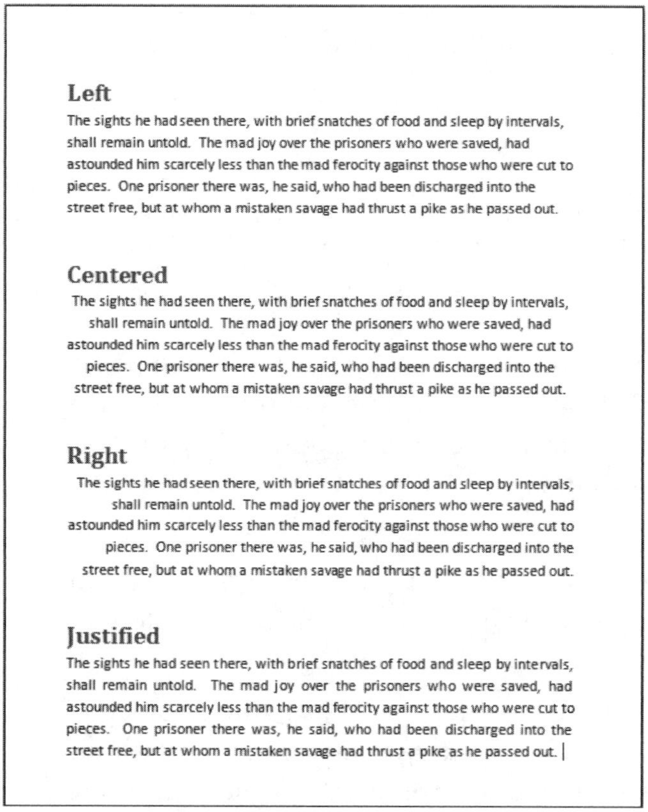

**Left**

The sights he had seen there, with brief snatches of food and sleep by intervals, shall remain untold. The mad joy over the prisoners who were saved, had astounded him scarcely less than the mad ferocity against those who were cut to pieces. One prisoner there was, he said, who had been discharged into the street free, but at whom a mistaken savage had thrust a pike as he passed out.

**Centered**

The sights he had seen there, with brief snatches of food and sleep by intervals, shall remain untold. The mad joy over the prisoners who were saved, had astounded him scarcely less than the mad ferocity against those who were cut to pieces. One prisoner there was, he said, who had been discharged into the street free, but at whom a mistaken savage had thrust a pike as he passed out.

**Right**

The sights he had seen there, with brief snatches of food and sleep by intervals, shall remain untold. The mad joy over the prisoners who were saved, had astounded him scarcely less than the mad ferocity against those who were cut to pieces. One prisoner there was, he said, who had been discharged into the street free, but at whom a mistaken savage had thrust a pike as he passed out.

**Justified**

The sights he had seen there, with brief snatches of food and sleep by intervals, shall remain untold. The mad joy over the prisoners who were saved, had astounded him scarcely less than the mad ferocity against those who were cut to pieces. One prisoner there was, he said, who had been discharged into the street free, but at whom a mistaken savage had thrust a pike as he passed out.

**Figure 3-7.** Set the alignment of your paragraphs using the buttons on the ribbon. Four settings are available: Left, Centered, Right, and Justified.

## Indenting Paragraphs

One of the most common reasons for indenting a paragraph is to set off quoted text from the rest of the document. Usually, you move the paragraph's left edge in about a half inch from the left margin. Word makes it easy to indent text in this way. Just use the Increase Indent button on the ribbon (shown back in Figure 3-6) or the shortcut Alt+H, AI. If you change your mind and want to remove the indent, use the companion command Decrease Indent (Alt+H, AO).

The ribbon buttons handle most everyday indentation chores, but what if you need to customize your indents? To do that, open the Paragraph dialog box to the Indents and Spacing tab (Alt+H, PG), and you see the Indentation tools in the middle of the tab (Figure 3-8).

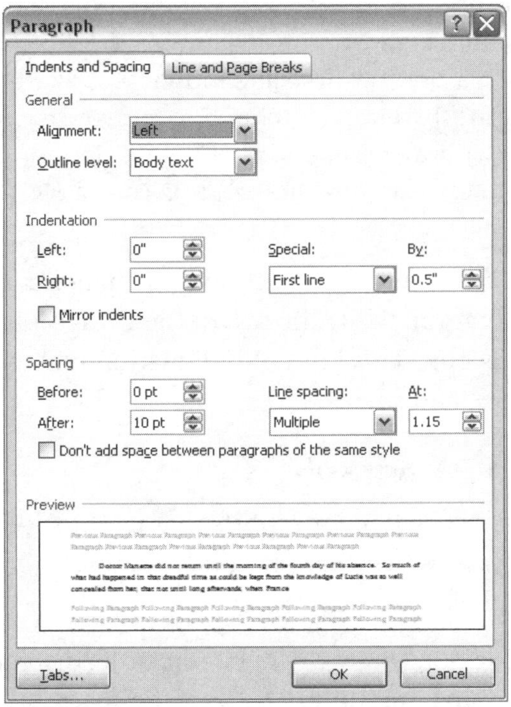

**Figure 3-8.** The Paragraph box is divided into four sections. From the top you see: General, Indentation, Spacing, and Preview. As you adjust your paragraph formatting using tools from the first three groups, you see the changes take place in an example paragraph in the Preview window.

The indentation tools in the Paragraph box let you set indents with much more precision than the simple Increase and Decrease buttons. For one thing, you can indent your paragraph from both margins using the Left and Right text boxes. Type a number in the box or use the arrow buttons to make an adjustment. Look in the Preview window at bottom to get a sense of the changes you're making.

Novels, short stories, and other manuscripts often indent the first line of each paragraph. To set up this format, click the Special drop-down menu, and then choose "First line." Type a number, in inches, in the By box on the right. A quarter inch (.25") is usually an attractive first-line indent.

---

**TIP**

By the way, don't hit Tab to create a first-line indent. For one thing, it creates an amateurish, typewriter-like half-inch indent. And you lose all the benefits of paragraph formatting. For example, when you press Enter to start a new paragraph, Word automatically carries your settings forward, with a perfect first-line indent just like the paragraph above. If you use the Tab key, you have to remember to hit it at the beginning of every paragraph, and there's the danger of messing up your indents if you change the tab settings (page 105).

---

For the reverse of the "First line" indent, choose the hanging indent where the first line extends to the left margin, while the rest of the paragraph is indented the amount shown in the By box. This kind of indentation makes great looking glossaries, bibliographies, and such.

## Spacing Between Paragraphs

For documents like business letters or reports that use block-style paragraphs, there's usually a little space between each. You can adjust this spacing between paragraphs to set off some blocks of text from the rest.

Use the Paragraph dialog box (Figure 3-8) to adjust the distance between paragraphs. On the left, you can enter numbers to set the space before the paragraph and the space after. With body text paragraphs, it's good to set the same, relatively small distance before and after—say, three points. For headers, you may want to put a little extra space before the header to distance it from the preceding text. That space makes it clear that the header is related to the text beneath it. Generally speaking, the more significant the header, the larger the type and the greater the spacing around it.

## Spacing Between Lines

In the Paragraph box, to the right of the paragraph spacing controls, you find the "Line spacing" tools. Use these controls to set the distance between lines *within* paragraphs. You have three presets and three custom settings:

- **Single** keeps the lines close together, with a minimum amount of space between. Single spacing is usually easy to read, and it sure saves paper.

- **1.5 lines** gives your text a little more breathing room, and still offers a nice professional look.

- **Double** is the option preferred by teachers and editors, so there's plenty of room for their helpful comments.

- **At least** is a good option if you have a mix of font sizes or include inline graphics with your text. This option ensures that everything fits, as Figure 3-9 illustrates.

- **Exactly** puts you in control. Type a number in the At box, and Word won't mess with that setting.

- **Multiple** is the oddball of the bunch. Think of Multiple as a percentage of a single line space: 1=100 Percent; .8=80 percent; 1.2=120 Percent; and so on.

## Inserting Page Breaks and Line Breaks

Some things just look wrong, such as a heading at the bottom of a page with no text beneath it. That heading should be at the top of the next page. Sure, you could force it over there with a page break (Ctrl+Enter), but that can cause trouble if you edit your text and things move around. You could end up with a page break in some weird spot. The solution is to adjust your Line and Page Break settings so that headings and paragraphs behave the way you want them to.

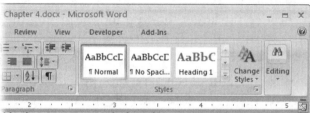

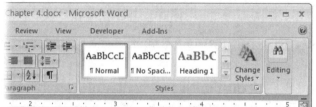

**Figure 3-9.** Line spacing controls the space between lines within a paragraph. These examples show the same paragraph, with two different settings. All the type is set to 11 points except for the word "by," which is 24-point type.

Top: Using the "At least" option with 12 points entered in the At box (see Figure 3-8), this setting adjusts so that the oversized word fits.

Bottom: Selecting Exactly from the "Line spacing" drop-down menu with 12 points in the At box, the b and y get clipped off.

On the Paragraph box's Line and Page Breaks tab (Figure 3-10), you can adjust how paragraphs handle these breaks. The behavior becomes part of the paragraph's formatting and travels with the text no matter where you move the text or breaks. The keyboard shortcut to get there is Alt+H, PG, Alt+P. You can use four settings:

▶ **Widow/Orphan control.** Single lines abandoned at the top (widows) or bottom (orphans) of the page look out of place. Turn on this checkbox, and Word keeps the whole family, er, *paragraph* together.

▶ **Keep with next.** Certain paragraphs, like headings, need to stay attached to the paragraph that comes immediately after them. Choose the "Keep with next" option for your headings, and they always appear above following paragraph.

▶ **Keep lines together.** Sometimes you have a paragraph that shouldn't be split between two pages, like a one-paragraph quote or disclaimer. Use this option to keep the paragraph as one unit.

▶ **Page break before.** Use this command with major headings to make sure new sections of your document start on a new page.

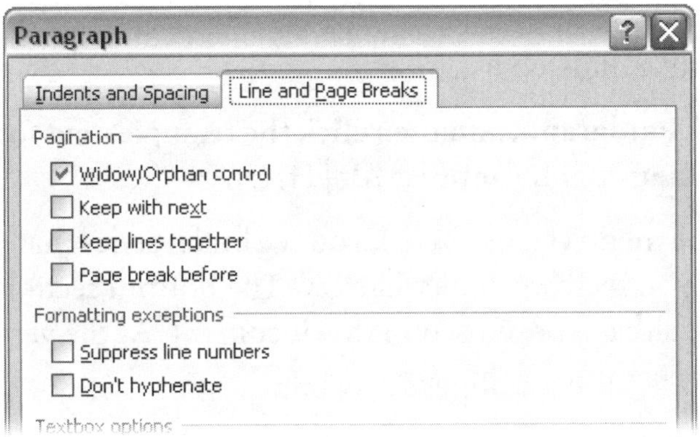

**Figure 3-10.** Use the Line and Page Break settings to control the appearance of your text and to avoid awkward transitions between pages.

# Creating Bulleted and Numbered Lists

Bullets and numbers add impact and help organize information. The bullets in the previous section call attention to the Line and Page Breaks commands and show that the commands are related to each other. Numbered paragraphs send a different signal, implying that the items listed are sequential or have a hierarchy. This book uses numbered paragraphs for step-by-step instructions. Meeting minutes are usually numbered, both as a point of reference and to indicate the order of the meeting's events.

Like the other paragraph formatting options, you don't have to select a paragraph to format it. It's enough just to have the insertion point in the paragraph. When using bullets or numbers, you usually want to format more than one paragraph. To do that, make a selection, and then click the bullet or number button.

### Bulleted paragraphs

It's easy to turn an ordinary paragraph into a bulleted paragraph—Word does all the heavy lifting for you. You may spend more time choosing a bullet style than applying it.

Here's how to create a bulleted list:

1.  **Go to Home → Paragraph, and then click the triangle next to the Bullet button to open the Bullets menu (or press Alt+H, U).**

    At the top of the menu (Figure 3-11), you see bullet styles that you used recently. In the middle, you see your Bullet Library. The bottom section shows bullet styles that have already been used in the document. At the very bottom are two commands for customizing bullets.

2.  **On the Bullets menu, click to choose a bullet style.**

    When you click a bullet to apply that style to the paragraph, a couple of things happen. Word adds the bullet and automatically formats the paragraph with a hanging indent (page 96), so that the first line of the paragraph extends farther to the left than the other lines. The bullet appears in this overhang, calling attention to the bullet and setting off the paragraph from the other body text.

3. **Type some text, and then press Enter to start a new paragraph.**

When you hit Enter to create a new paragraph, Word assumes that you're continuing with your bulleted list, so it adds the same bullet and indent automatically. You don't have to do anything; just keep on writing.

4. **When you're through with your bulleted list, press Enter, and then click the Home → Paragraph → Bullet button again to turn off bullet formatting.**

The paragraph with the insertion point changes from a bulleted paragraph to a normal paragraph.

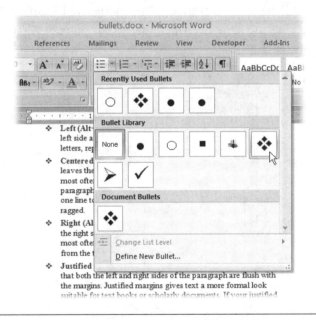

**Figure 3-11.** The Bullet menu provides choices from the traditional filled circle to more contemporary options. If you have your own ideas for bullet design, at the bottom of the menu click Define New Bullet.

If you have a few paragraphs that you've already written, and you want to change them to bulleted paragraphs, just select all the paragraphs, and then click the Bullet button.

## Customizing bullets

You don't have to settle for the bullets shown on the menu—Word has more choices tucked away. You can even use your own graphics for bullets, like a miniaturized version of your company logo. To explore the Bullet options available to you, open the Bullet menu (Alt+H, U), and then, at the bottom of the menu, click Define New Bullet. The Define New Bullet Box opens, showing you three buttons at the top: Symbol, Picture, and Font. Use the Symbol to browse through additional bullet options that are built into Word's type libraries. Use the Font button to apply character styles to your choice such as font size, shadow, or bold formatting.

The middle button is the most interesting—it opens the Picture Bullet box (Figure 3-12) where you see a whole slew of bullets based on picture files.

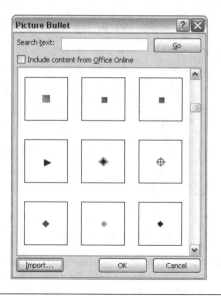

**Figure 3-12.** Open the Picture Bullet box to see bullets based on picture files like JPEG and GIF. If you have pictures or drawings on your computer that you want to use as bullets, then click the Import button in the lower-left corner.

These files are the same sort used for drawings and photographs, with filename extensions like .jpg, .gif, .pct, and .emf. In addition to these dozens of bullet options, you can use your own picture or graphic files as bullets. Just click the Import button at the bottom-left corner to open the Add Clips to Organizer box. Use this Windows file box to select any picture on your computer and add it to your bullet library.

## Numbered paragraphs

In most cases, numbered paragraphs work just like bulleted paragraphs. You can follow the step-by-step instructions in the previous section for making bulleted paragraphs to make numbered paragraphs. Just click the Numbering button, and then choose a number style (Figure 3-13).

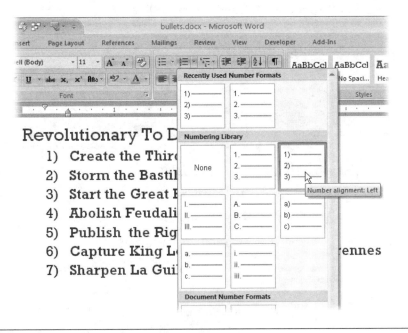

**Figure 3-13.** Word provides several styles for numbered paragraphs. In fact, a better term would be sequenced paragraphs, because not all of the styles use numbers. You find recently used styles at the top of the list. To customize your numbered lists, click Define New Number Format (not shown) at the bottom of the list.

The main distinction between the numbered paragraphs and the bulleted paragraphs is in the options. For numbered paragraphs, you can choose from Arabic numbers, Roman numerals, numbers set off by parentheses, and alphabetic sequences. You can even use words such as One, Two, Three, or First, Second, Third.

## Multilevel lists

Multilevel lists are a more advanced numbering format. They help you create project and document outlines, as well as legal documents divided into articles and sections. In a multilevel list, each new level is indented (nudged to the right), and usually each new level has a new number format (Figure 3-14). In addition to outline and legal numbering, multilevel lists can use bullets instead of numbers. So for example, you can create a bulleted list that uses squares for level one, triangles for level two, and circles for level three. If you choose a bulleted multilevel list, the lines within the levels aren't sequenced; they're just bulleted.

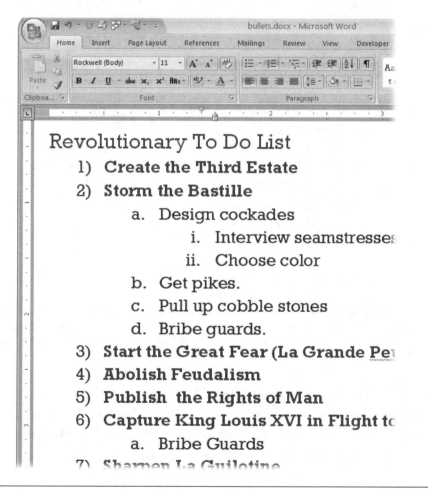

**Figure 3-14.** Multilevel lists add an extra twist to the numbered format. They're like outlines and provide a new sequence of characters for each new outline level.

# Setting Tabs

The lowly Tab key contains more power than you may think. Sure, you can use the Tab key to scoot the insertion point across the page in half-inch increments. But Word's tab tool is capable of much loftier feats: You can use it to design a dinner menu, create a playbill, or develop a series of consistently formatted reports.

Tab stops are all about precision alignment, giving you control over the way you present text and numbers to your readers. For example, on your dinner menu you can use *tab leaders* (dotted lines like the ones in this book's table of contents) so that your reader's eye tracks from Wild Salmon to the exceptionally reasonable price you're asking. Once you have settings you like, you can save and reuse them. (How's that for efficiency?)

Before you start working with tabs, you need to know a few basic terms:

▶ **Tabs.** Technically considered *tab characters*, tabs are hidden formatting characters, similar to space characters. Tabs are embedded in your document's text.

▶ **Tab stops.** These paragraph settings define the position and characteristics of tabs in your document. Think of tab stops as definitions, describing your tabs. To define them, you use Word tools, like the Ruler or the Tabs dialog box.

▶ **Tab key.** The key on your computer keyboard that inserts tabs into your text.

Press the Tab key, and Word inserts a tab in the text at that point. The tab character makes the insertion point jump left to right and stop at the first tab stop it reaches. If you haven't set any new tab stops, Word uses the built-in set of tab stops—one every half inch across the width—that every new, blank document starts out with.

## How Tab Stops Work

Tab stop settings apply to paragraphs. If a paragraph has several lines, the tab stops are the same for all the lines within that paragraph. If you haven't deliberately set tab stops, Word provides built-in tab stops at half-inch intervals. These stops are left tab stops, meaning the text aligns on the left side. You can see all tab stops on the horizontal ruler—they show as small vertical tick marks in the gray area below the number scale (Figure 3-15).

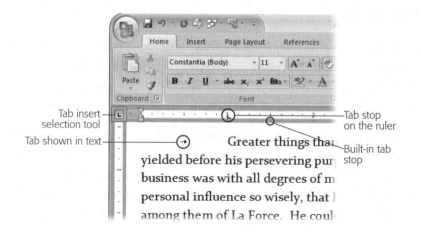

Figure 3-15. Tabs are just white space in your text, but for Word, they're these little arrow characters that position your text on the line. You can change your Word Options (Office button → Word Options → Display) to show tabs on your screen.

**TIP**

If you don't see tab stops in the ruler, click within a paragraph. Remember, tab stops are paragraph settings, so your insertion point must be in a paragraph to see them.

## Viewing Tab Marks in Your Text

Tabs are invisible on the printed page, like spaces or paragraph marks. Sometimes, when your document behaves unexpectedly, it helps to reveal the hidden characters so you can see if tabs are the culprit. After all, when they're hidden, all you see is white space on the page, however, spaces, tabs, and indents each behave quite differently.

To view tabs within your text:

1.  **Choose Office button → Word Options to open the Word Options dialog box (Figure 3-16).**

    The Word Options button is at the bottom of the Office menu.

2.  **On the left side of the Word Options box, choose the Display option.**

    The panel on the right is divided into three parts. The top section shows page display options, the middle section shows formatting marks, and the bottom section holds printing options.

3.  **In the middle group, turn on the "Tab characters" checkbox to make your tabs visible.**

    An icon next to this checkbox shows you the symbol for tab characters. This mark shows up on your computer screen but not in printed text.

4.  **Click OK to save the settings and close the dialog box.**

    The box closes and you see the tabs as small arrows in your text.

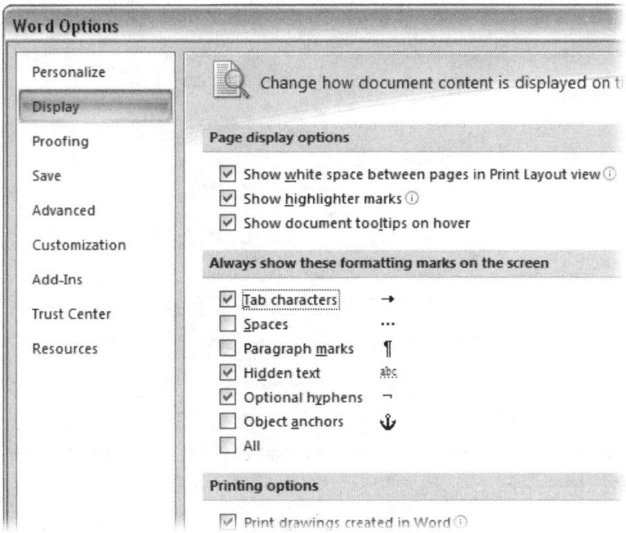

**Figure 3-16.** Use the Word Options box to reveal formatting characters like tabs, spaces, and paragraph marks. When you turn on the checkbox next to the mark, you see these nonprinting characters on your screen.

## Deleting and Editing Tabs

Because tabs are characters within your document, you can delete, copy, and paste them, just as you would any other character or text fragment. Maybe you want to delete a tab just click immediately after a tab character, and then press the Backspace key. You can also use the Tabs box (Figure 3-17) to control tabs.

With tabs, you can use almost any editing trick that you'd use on other characters. You can select and drag a tab to a different place in your text. You can use shortcut keys, such as Ctrl+X to cut a tab and Ctrl+V to paste it someplace else. (All of these activities are much, much easier when you've set your Word Options to view tab marks as described previously.)

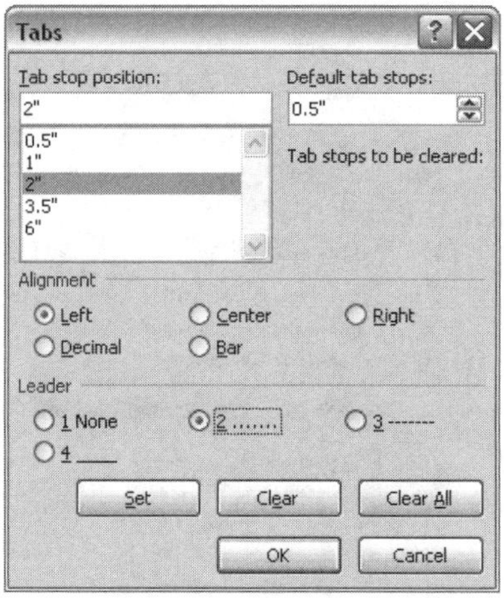

**Figure 3-17.** The Tabs box puts you in complete control of all things tabular. When you select a specific tab in the upper-left box, you can customize its alignment and leader characters.

## Types of Tabs

Five types of tabs are available in Word—one of which isn't a true tab but works well with the others:

▶ **Left tab.** The most common type of tab, it aligns text at the left side; text flows from the tab stop to the right. When you start a new, blank document, Word provides left tabs every half inch.

- **Center tab.** Keeps text centered at the tab stop. Text extends evenly left and right with the tab stop in the middle.

- **Right tab.** Aligns text to the right. Text flows backwards from the tab stop, from right to left.

- **Decimal tab.** Used to align numbers, whether or not they have decimals. Numbers align with the decimal point centered on the tab stop. Numbers without decimal points align similar to a right tab.

- **Bar tab.** The Bar tab is the oddball of the group and, no, it has nothing to do with your local watering hole. It also has nothing to do with aligning text. It inserts a vertical bar in your text as a divider. The bar appears in every line in the paragraph. This tab stop ignores tabs inserted in your text and behaves in the same manner whether or not tab characters are present.

___ **NOTE** _____

There may be a certain Microsoftian logic in grouping the bar tab with the tab feature, but Word provides other ways to place vertical lines on your pages that you may find more intuitive. You can use Insert → Insert Shapes → More and choose the line for free-form lines. Or you can use borders for paragraphs or tables.

## Tab Leaders

Tab leaders help readers connect the dots by providing a trail from one tabbed item to the next. They're ideal for creating professional-looking menus, playbills, and more. As visual aids, leaders are quite helpful, and they work equally well for text and numbers.

Here are some examples:

```
Hamlet, Prince of Denmark..........Sir Laurence Olivier
Ophelia, daughter to Polonius.......Roseanne Barr
```

Four Leader options can be used with each type of tab stop except the bar tab:

```
None                        No leader here
Dotted........................... You've seen this before
Dashed _ _ _ _ _ _ _ _ _ _ _ _    For a different, intermittent look
Underline_____  When only a solid line will do
```

# Using Word's Rulers

If you're visually oriented, you may prefer the ruler for futzing with tab stops, page margins, and indents. Two rulers are available—horizontal and vertical. The horizontal ruler appears at the top of the page, giving you quick access to your tab, indent, and margin settings. To make the rulers visible, press Alt+W, R, or click the View Ruler button at the top of the right-hand scroll bar (Figure 3-18).

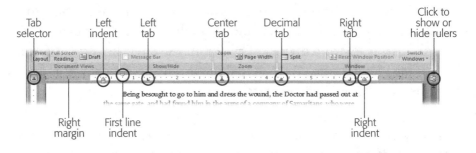

**Figure 3-18.** Word's ruler provides lots of information about the formatting of the current paragraph, that is, the paragraph that contains the insertion point. Use the button just above the scroll bar for a quick way to show and hide your ruler.

— **TIP** —

> The ruler marks off your page in the measuring units of your choice. The factory setting uses inches, but if you want to make changes, you can do that in Word Options. Go to Office button → Word Options → Advanced. Scroll down to the group under Display, and then change the drop-down menu labeled "Show measurements in units of" to your preferred units of measurement.

## Managing Tab Settings with the Ruler

In Figure 3-18, the ruler measures the page in inches. The grayed areas at both ends of the ruler indicate the page margins. The numbers on the ruler mark the distance from the left margin in both directions, left and right. Note the number 1, at the left edge of the page in Figure 3-18.

## Setting tab stops

Word's every-half-inch tab stops can work for many of your documents, but sooner or later, you may need to put a tab stop in a different place or change its style. No problem—it's easy enough to do with the ruler.

Setting a new tab stop is a two-step process:

1. **Using the selection box to the left of the ruler, choose the type of tab you want.**

   The icon in this box shows what kind of tab you're about to apply—Left, Center, Right, Decimal, or Bar. When you hold your cursor over the box for a second or two, a little screen tip appears describing the formatting option. Click the box to cycle through the tab stop and indent options.

2. **Once you've selected the tab type you want, click the ruler to position the tab.**

   Click the point on the ruler where you want to place the tab stop. An icon appears on the ruler showing the position and the type of tab stop.

---

__ TIP _____

If you find the tab icons a little confusing, here's some help: Think of the vertical line as the tab stop and the horizontal line at the bottom as the direction your text flows. For example, the Left tab icon is L shaped, indicating that text flows to the right, away from the tab stop. The Center tab icon has the vertical line in the middle.

---

You can add an almost limitless number of tab stops—one for every tick mark on the ruler. If you need greater precision, use the Tab dialog box described on page 105. Setting a tab stop removes all the built-in tab stops to its left, but the ones to the right remain.

## Adjusting and removing tab stops with the ruler

If a tab stop isn't exactly where you want it, you don't have to delete it—just drag it to a new position on the ruler. If you wish to remove a tab stop, drag it up or down off the ruler, and it disappears. When you make these changes, your document shows the consequences. Any tabs in your text shift over to the next readily available tab stop, which can be a built-in tab stop or one that you've set.

## Setting Margins with the Ruler

You can always use the Page Layout tools (Page Layout → Page Setup → Margins or Alt+P, M) to set your margins with a click of the mouse, but for visual control, nothing beats the ruler (Figure 3-19). The lighter part of the ruler shows the text area, and the darker part shows your margins. Making adjustments is simply a matter of clicking and dragging the margin to a new location. Keep in mind that changing your margin affects the entire document section; more often than not, that means it affects the entire document because many documents are a single section. (For more details on working with sections, see page 155.)

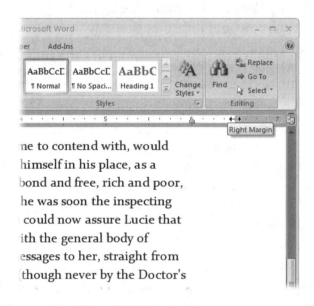

**Figure 3-19.** Hold your cursor over the margin boundary on the ruler, and it changes to a double arrow, as shown here. The screen tip shows what you're pointing to—the right margin, in this case. Drag the boundary to a new location to change your document margins.

**TIP**

To avoid confusion, remember that indents are used to change the width of a single paragraph, while margins are used to change the paragraph width for an entire section or document.

## Adjusting Paragraph Indents with the Ruler

Using the ruler to adjust indentation is similar to changing margins. It's just a matter of clicking and dragging. Indents are bit more complicated because you have a few more options, and that means more tools and widgets (Figure 3-20).

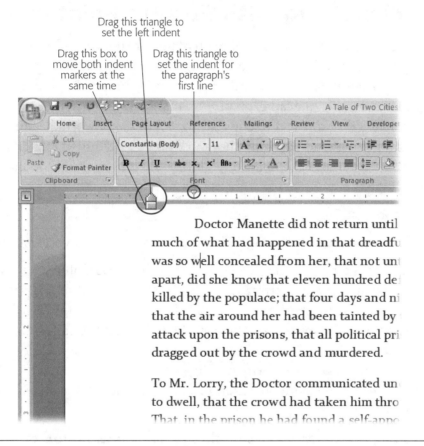

**Figure 3-20.** To adjust paragraph indents, slide the little triangles along the ruler. The changes you make affect the paragraph with the insertion point. If you want to make changes to more than one paragraph, make a multiple selection before you start.

It can take awhile to get used to adjusting paragraph indents with the ruler. For one thing, you need a steady hand and accurate clicking to zero in on those little triangle buttons. The top triangle sets the first line indent and moves independently. The bottom triangle creates a hanging indent, and you can move it independently too, as long as you grab only that triangle. That little box below the triangle is your left indent, and if you drag it, both it and the top (first line) indent marker move together.

# Fast Formatting with Format Painter

Whether it's a special heading or a paragraph of text, formatting a paragraph just the way you want it is a lot of work. Once you have the margins, indents, and tabs in place, and you've got the font style and size set, you've invested a chunk of time in the project. Fortunately, you can capitalize on that investment. The Format Painter works like magic. You can use it to copy the formatting of a word, heading, or paragraph onto something else. You don't have to worry about any of the formatting details. You don't even need to *know* how something is formatted, so long as you like the way it looks.

Here's how it works:

1. **Select the character or paragraph with the formatting that you want to copy.**

   You can copy and paint either the character or the paragraph formatting. If you want to copy just text formatting (font, size, text color, and so on), select a few letters or a word with that formatting, not the whole paragraph. Selecting an entire paragraph, complete with the paragraph mark at the end, copies both the character formatting and the paragraph formatting. If you don't select anything, the Format Painter uses the formatting from the current paragraph, so to copy paragraph formatting alone (for example, tabs and indents), just click anywhere in the paragraph.

2. **Go to Home → Clipboard and click the Format Painter button, or just press Alt+H, FP.**

   Your cursor acquires a tiny paintbrush icon. If you have only one quick change to make, just click the Format Painter once. However, if you want to copy the same formatting to several different locations, double-click the Format Painter. When you double-click, the button stays locked down, indicating that it will stay on and let you paint multiple times until you're ready to stop.

3. **Drag the Format Painter over the text or paragraph that you want to change.**

   Here's the fun part. Like magic, your selection takes on all the formatting that you copied. If you double-clicked for multiple format painting, you can keep on dragging over text or clicking paragraphs. When you're through, hit Esc. The Format Painter button pops back up, and your cursor changes back to its normal I-beam appearance.

# Formatting with Styles

Like the Format Painter, Word's styles are great time-savers because they let you apply a whole bunch of formatting commands in one fell swoop. Unlike Format Painter, Word's styles are permanent repositories of formatting information that you can always apply with one click. So, if you've discovered or created the perfect style (formatting) for a heading, you can apply that same style to headings today, tomorrow, or a week from tomorrow.

Microsoft provides sets of predesigned Quick Styles. These sets include a Normal style for body text and a number of Heading styles. You can also find a variety of styles for lists, quotes, references, and for paragraphs or text that deserve special emphasis. With a click of your mouse, you can apply any one of these styles and make dramatic changes to your document (Figure 3-21).

Some styles define character formatting, such as font, font size, font style, and special effects such as underlining or strikethrough. Other styles define both character formatting and paragraph formatting. Paragraph formatting includes things like paragraph alignment, line spacing, bullets, numbering, indents, and tab settings.

## Applying Quick Styles

It's easy to preview and apply a style to your text. The action takes place in the Styles group on the Home tab. Follow these steps:

1. **Select the text or paragraph that you want to format.**

   When you want to apply a style to an entire paragraph, just click to put the insertion point in that paragraph. When you want to apply a style to text, you need to select the text first.

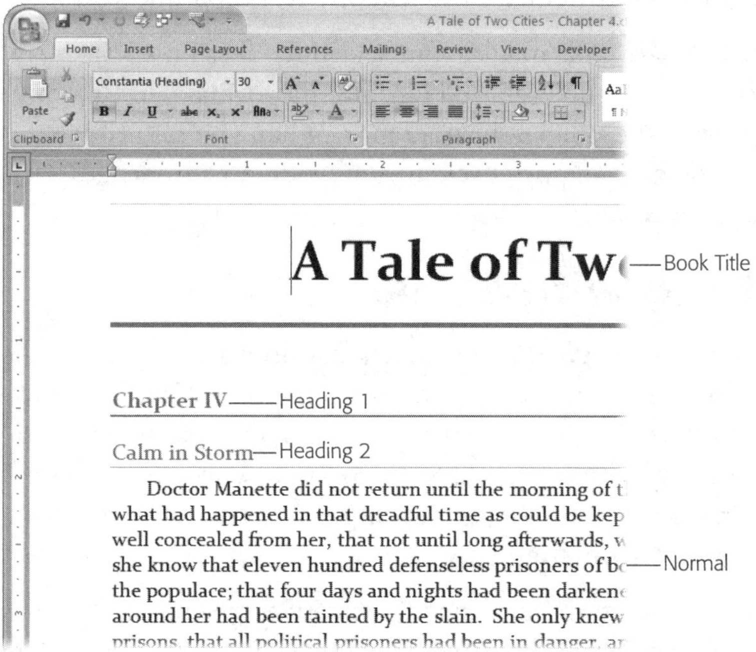

**Figure 3-21.** This attractive page uses four Quick Styles: Book Title style centers the text and sets the font to 30-point Constantia with colored borders above and below. Heading 1 for the chapter heading uses a different color and generous paragraph spacing. The Heading 2 spec uses a complementary color and closer paragraph spacing. Finally, the body text uses the Normal style, which provides, among other things, an indent for the first line of each paragraph.

2. **Go to Home → Styles and hold your cursor over a style to see a live preview in your document.**

   The Styles group shows a few styles right on the ribbon. To see more styles, use the arrows on the right to scroll through the list, or click the double down-arrow button at bottom to open the entire menu (Figure 3-22).

   When you hold the mouse cursor over a style, the text in your document changes, showing you the effect of applying that style.

3. **Click to apply the style.**

   When you click a style on the ribbon or in the menu, Word applies that style to your paragraph or text selection.

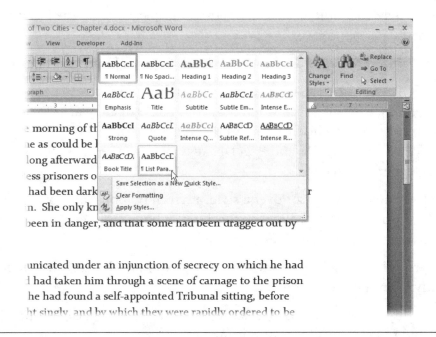

**Figure 3-22.** Each style is a collection of formatting commands that you can apply with a mouse click. To browse the available styles, go to Home → Styles. When you hold your mouse over a style, the text in your document changes, giving you a live preview of the style. Word offers dozens of pre-designed Quick Styles, or you can create your own.

# Modifying Styles

When you apply a style to a paragraph of text, you do more than just change its formatting. In essence, you've attached that style to the paragraph. If you make changes to that style later, the paragraph reflects those changes. Imagine that you have a style called Heading 1 that centers the headings on the page. You've used this style repeatedly throughout your 400-page novel about the French Revolution. Say, you decide your novel would look better with that heading aligned on the left margin rather than centered. Instead of making the change to each individual heading, you edit the Heading 1 style. When you change the style definition, all your headings that are based on the Heading 1 style change to match.

Here are the steps to modifying a style. In this example, you give the Heading 1 style left alignment:

1.  **Go to Home → Styles and click the Styles dialog box launcher (Figure 3-23).**

    In the Styles box, you can click to apply any one of the styles to your current selection or paragraph. Even when the Styles box is open, you can click within your text to move the insertion point to a different paragraph. And you can use the scroll bar, the PageUP and PageDN keys, or any other method to navigate through your document.

    When you hold your cursor over a style, a screen tip pops up showing you details. Turn on the Show Preview checkbox at bottom to see a more visual representation of each of the styles.

2.  **Right-click Heading 1 (or whatever style you want to change), and then choose Modify from the shortcut menu.**

    The Modify Style dialog box opens (Figure 3-24). Here you can get under the hood and tinker with all the formatting options.

    ---
    **TIP**

    When you right-click anywhere on the style name, or click the V button in the Styles dialog box, a context menu shows you several choices for changing and working with the selected style. At the top of the list is "Update Heading 1 to Match Selection." This option changes all the formatting in the selected style so that it's identical to the current paragraph or selection.

    ---

3.  **In the lower-left corner of the Modify Style box, click the Format button, and then choose Paragraph.**

    The Paragraph dialog box opens. Yep, it's exactly the same box you open when you click the Paragraph dialog box launcher on the ribbon or press Alt+H, PG (see Figure 3-8). In fact, the Format button leads you to many familiar dialog boxes, from Fonts to Borders to Tabs. The difference, of course, is that you're now changing a style format, not just a few paragraphs.

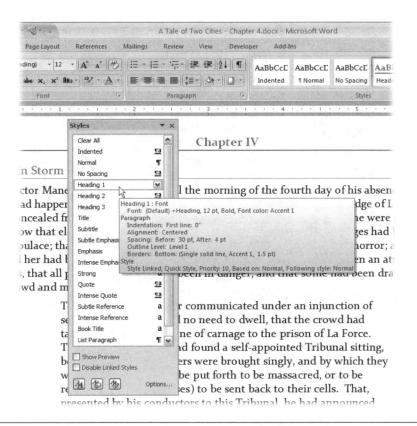

**Figure 3-23.** Open the Style dialog box to see a complete list of all available styles. On the right side, a paragraph mark shows that a style includes paragraph formatting. The lowercase "a" shows that the style includes character formatting. Click the down arrow button to open a menu where you can modify the style definition.

4. **At the top of the Paragraph box, in the General group, click the Alignment drop-down menu, and then choose Left.**

   In this example, you're just making a single change, but you can also make changes to any of the other formatting options in this box.

5. **Close the Paragraph box, the Modify Style box, and the Styles box.**

   Everything's done except the cleanup. Close each of the boxes you've opened to go back to your text and continue editing.

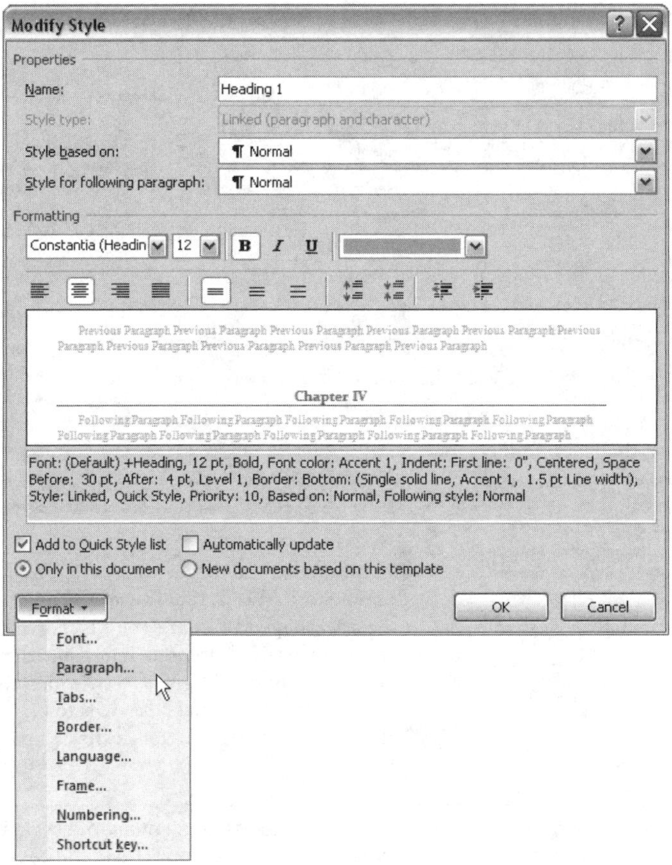

**Figure 3-24.** The Modify Style box is command central for tinkering with your style definitions. The properties at the top determine the behavior of the styles when you're working with text. The preview window in the center shows an example of the style in action. Use the format button in the lower-left corner to open dialog boxes to make changes in the character and paragraph formatting.

# Managing Style Sets

A *style set* is a collection of styles. Microsoft includes several predesigned style sets with Word, with names like Classic, Distinctive, Elegant, Formal, and Modern. Go to Home → Styles → Change Styles (or press Alt+H, FQ) to see them listed under the Change Styles button (Figure 3-25). Each of Word's predesigned style sets includes a Normal style, several heading styles (Heading 1, Heading 2, and so on), and other paragraph and character styles (like Title, Subtitle, Intense, Strong, and Reference). Even though a style has the same name in different sets—like Heading 1—the formatting is likely to be quite different. So when you change your document's style set, you can get a radically different look.

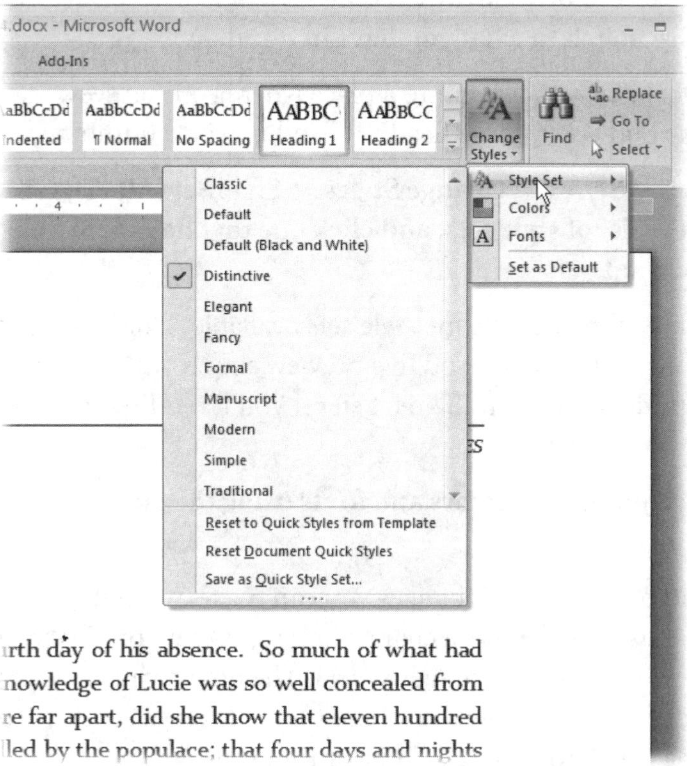

**Figure 3-25.** Click the Change Styles button, and then click Style Set to see the different style sets available. Using the Colors and Fonts options, you can make quick changes to the look of your document. Second thoughts? Click "Reset to Quick Styles from Template" to undo any changes made in haste. At the very bottom, you can use the "Save as Quick Style Set" command to immortalize your current styles as a brand-new style set.

The style set that's in use has a checkmark next to the name. If you move your cursor over the name of a different style set, Live Preview shows you your text formatted with that new style set. To make the change permanent, just click the name. The menu closes, and your text has a whole new look.

# Creating Your Own Style Set

The best way to create your own style set is to start with one of Microsoft's predesigned sets, and then modify it. Here's a basic procedure for customize an existing style set to meet your needs.

1. **Use live preview to browse the existing style sets and choose one that's a reasonably close match to what you have in mind.**

   For example, open a document to a place where you can see a few different types of styles, like body text, some headings, and maybe a numbered or bulleted list.

2. **Go to Home → Styles → Change Styles → Style Set (Alt+H, GY). Work your way down the list of style sets, and click one that has a look that's similar to the one you want.**

   The Style Sets submenu lists the style sets available. Hold your mouse cursor over the name of a style set, and live preview shows you how that style set changes your document. In the next steps, you'll modify the style set to be exactly what you want.

3. **If necessary, modify the colors and fonts using the options on the Change Styles menu.**

   The first and most obvious changes you can make are to the colors and fonts. The commands to make those changes are right there on the Change Styles menu (Home → Styles → Change Styles). The previewing procedure is the same: Just hold your mouse cursor over a Font or Color style, and you see your document change. Click to choose a color or font style.

   Start with the Normal paragraph style. Consider the font, font size, color, and any other character formatting that you may want to change. (But don't get crazy; after all, this is the *Normal* paragraph style.) After the Normal paragraph style, move on to the Heading styles. The font size and color you choose for your headings set the tone for your entire document.

4. **Examine the existing paragraph styles, and if necessary, make changes.**

   Consider the line spacing and indents for normal paragraph. Do you want more or less space around them on the page? Choose the paragraph spacing for each heading style. Think about borders—perhaps you'd like a nice line above or below a heading. Work your way through any of the existing paragraph or character styles that you know you'll use.

5. **Consider the paragraph styles you need, and add new ones if they're missing.**

   After you've modified the existing styles, think about styles that you'd like to have but aren't part of the set. Maybe you need a numbered list, or a special sidebar paragraph with a border running all the way around it. Create whatever styles you need, and then add them to your style set.

   Don't worry if you can't think of everything just now. You can always add new styles later when you're using the style set.

6. **When you're done customizing your style set, go to Home → Styles → More → Save Selection as Quick Style Set (or Atl+H, L), and then save it with a new name.**

   The Save command is at the very bottom of the submenu. As a last step, save your style with a name, and it becomes one of the available style sets (Figure 3-26). A standard Windows Save dialog box opens. Type a name for your style set in the "File name" text box, and then click Save. After you've saved it, your customized style shows on the Change Styles menu with all the rest.

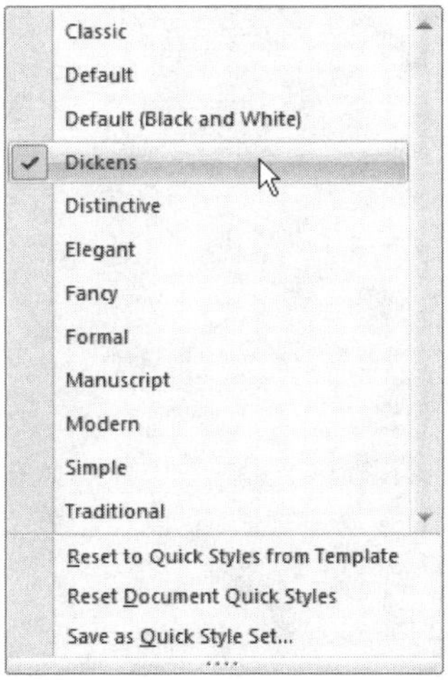

**Figure 3-26.** You can create a custom style set that's fine-tuned to your own specs. Once saved, your style set shows up on the Change Styles menu.

# SETTING UP THE DOCUMENT: MARGINS, PAGE BREAKS, AND MORE

- ▶ Choosing Paper Size and Layout
- ▶ Setting Document Margins
- ▶ Applying Page Borders
- ▶ Adding Headers and Footers
- ▶ Working with Multiple Columns
- ▶ Hyphenation
- ▶ Dividing Your Document into Sections

YOUR DOCUMENT MAKES A FIRST IMPRESSION before anyone reads a word. The paper size, color, and borders give the reader an overall sense of the document's theme and quality. Margins, the text layout, and perhaps a watermark send further visual clues. Making the right choices about your document setup helps you send the right message to your readers. Say you're working on an invitation; using a smaller, elegant paper size and adding a subtle border lets your recipients know right away that they're in for a sophisticated event.

In this chapter, you'll learn how to set and change all the page layout features that people notice first, starting with paper size, orientation, and margins. You'll also learn how to adjust margins and make changes to the headers and footers. Finally, you'll learn how to work with multiple columns and how to control Word's hyphenation inclinations.

# Choosing Paper Size and Layout

When you edit a document in Word, what you see on your computer screen looks almost exactly like the final printed page. To get that correct preview, Word needs to know some details about the paper you're using, like the page size and orientation. You have two different ways to change the page settings: using the Page Layout tab (Figure 4-1) or the Page Setup dialog box (Figure 4-2). When you click the Page Layout tab, the ribbon's buttons and icons change to show you options related to designing your page as a whole. Your options are organized in five groups: Themes, Page Setup, Page Background, Paragraph, and Arrange.

## Changing Paper Size

If you want to quickly change the page size to a standard paper size like letter, legal, or tabloid, the Page Layout → Page Setup → Size menu is the way to go (Figure 4-1). With one quick click, you change your document's size. If there's text in your document, Word reshapes it to fit the page. Say you change a ten-page document from letter size to the longer legal-size page. Word spreads out your text over the extra space, and you'll have fewer pages overall.

# Of Menus and Boxes

Word gives you two ways to set options: through ribbon menus and dialog boxes. In general, the ribbon's drop-down menus give you access to quick, predesigned solutions, while dialog boxes give you greater control over more details. Menu options usually focus on one or two settings, while dialog boxes are much more complex affairs, letting you change several settings at once.

The Page Layout → Page Setup → Size menu, shown in Figure 4-1, lets you choose a standard paper size with one click. But what if you're not using one of the standard paper sizes on the Size menu? In that case, click More Paper Sizes (at the bottom of the Size menu).

The Page Setup dialog box opens to the Paper tab (Figure 4-2). Here, you can customize the page size—by entering numbers in the Width and Height text boxes—and tweak other paper-related settings. These other settings, such as the Paper Source settings (which let you tell your printer which tray to take the paper from), are typical of the fine-tuning controls you find in dialog boxes.

On the Margins and Layout tabs, you can control your document's margins, orientation, headers, and footers. You'll learn more about all of these settings later in this chapter.

## Customizing paper size and source

If you can't find the paper size you need on the Size menu, then you need to customize your paper size, which you do in the Page Setup dialog box's Paper tab. Here are the steps:

1. **Choose Page Layout → Page Setup → Size. At the bottom of the Size menu, click More Paper Sizes.**

   The Page Setup dialog box appears, with the Paper tab showing (Figure 4-2). Why the Paper tab? Because you opened the box using the More Paper Sizes button.

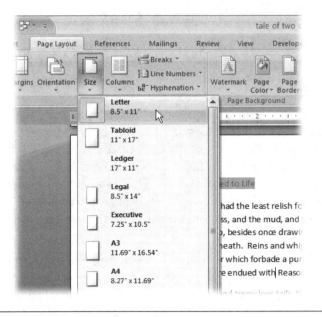

**Figure 4-1.** The Size menu, like many Word 2007 menus, uses icons as well as text to give you quick visual cues. Your choices include Letter (8.5" x 11"), Tabloid (11" x 17"), and more. If you're using standard-size paper (including standard international sizes like A3 and A4), you can click one of these choices, and you're done.

2. **In the Width and Height boxes, enter the size of your custom paper.**

   The quickest way to change the Width and Height settings is to select the numbers in the boxes and type your new page dimensions. Your new numbers replace the previous settings. You can also click the up and down arrows to the right of the text boxes, but it's slow going as the sizes change in tenths of an inch. Notice that as you change the dimensions, the Preview image at the bottom of the Page Setup box changes to match.

3. **Click OK at the bottom, to close the dialog box and make the changes.**

   The Page Setup box closes, and your custom-sized document shows in Word.

**Figure 4-2.** Using the Paper tab of the Page Setup box, you can choose from standard paper sizes or set your own custom paper size. Dialog boxes are great for making several changes at once. On this tab you can also choose a paper source (if you're lucky enough to have a printer with more than one paper tray). You can read more about printing in Chapter 7.

---

**NOTE**

At the bottom of the Page Setup dialog box is an "Apply to" option with two choices: "Whole document" and "This point forward." If you choose "Whole document," Word applies these paper size and other page layout settings to your entire document. If you choose "This point forward," Word creates a page break at the insertion point, and starts using the new settings only after the break.

## Setting Paper Orientation

Most business documents, school papers, and letters use a *portrait* page orientation, meaning the page is taller than it is wide. But sometimes you want a short, wide page—*landscape* page orientation—to accommodate a table, chart, or photo, or just for artistic effect. Whatever the reason, using the Orientation menu (Page Layout → Page Setup → Orientation) is the easiest way to make the change (Figure 4-3). Just click one of the two options: Portrait or Landscape.

If you've already got the Page Setup box open, you'll find the Orientation options on the Margins tab (Page Layout → Page Setup → Margins → Custom Margins).

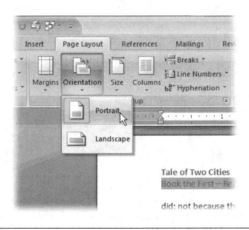

**Figure 4-3.** Click Portrait or Landscape to choose a page orientation for your document.

# Setting Document Margins

Page margins are more than just empty space. The right page margins make your document more readable. Generous page margins make text look inviting and give reviewers room for notes and comments. With narrower margins, you can squeeze more words on the page; however, having too many words per line makes your document difficult to read. With really long lines it's a challenge for readers to track from the end of one line back to the beginning of the next. Margins become even more important for complex documents, such as books or magazines with facing pages. With Word's margins and page setup tools, you can tackle a whole range of projects.

## Selecting Preset Margins

Word's Margins menu (Page Layout → Page Setup → Margins) gives you a way to quickly apply standard margins to your pages. The preset margins are a mixed bag of settings from a half inch to one and a quarter inches. For most documents, you can choose one of these preset margins and never look back (Figure 4-4).

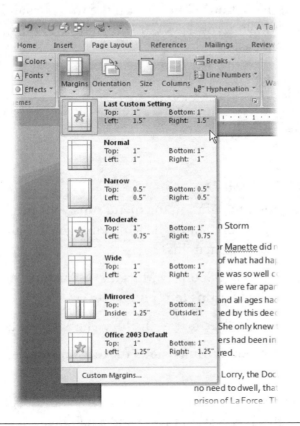

**Figure 4-4.** The Margins menu provides some standard settings such as the ever popular one inch all the way around. Word calls this favorite of businesses and schools the Normal margin. If you've customized your margins, your most recent settings appear at the top of the menu.

For each of the preset margin options you see dimensions and an icon that hints at the look of the page:

▶ **Normal** gives you one inch on all sides of the page.

▶ **Narrow** margins work well with multicolumn documents, giving you a little more room for each column.

- **Moderate** margins with three-quarter inches left and right let you squeeze a few more words in each line.

- The **Wide** preset gives you more room for marginal notes when you're proofing a manuscript.

To select one of the preset margins, go to Page Layout → Page Setup → Margins, and then click one of the options. You can also use the shortcut key Alt+P, M, and then use your up and down arrow keys to highlight one of the margins. Press Enter to use the highlighted margin.

---

**NOTE**

Word measures margins from the edge of the page to the edge of the body text. Any headers and footers that you add (page 139) appear *in* the margin areas.

---

## Setting Custom Margins

What if none of the preset margins on the menu suits your needs? Say your company's style guide insists on one-and-a-half-inch margins for all press releases. Here's how to customize your margins:

1. **Go to Page Layout → Page Setup → Margins → Custom Margins to open the Page Setup box to the Margins tab** (Figure 4-5).

   The Page Setup box has three tabs at the top. The Margins tab is on the left.

2. **At the top of the box, enter dimensions for top, bottom, left, and right margins.**

   The boxes in the Margins section already contain your document's current settings. To change the Top margin to one and a half inches, select the current setting, and then type *1.5*, or you can click the arrows on the right side of the box to change the margin number. Make the same change in the Bottom, Left, and Right margin text boxes.

— TIP —

While you're here in the Page Setup box, double-check the page Orientation setting. Margins and page orientation have a combined effect. In other words, if you want a quarter-inch top margin, make sure the orientation is set correctly depending on whether you want the "top" of the page to be on the long side or the short side of the paper.

**3. Click OK to apply the changes to your document.**

The Page Setup box closes and your document takes shape with the new margins. If the changes are substantially different from the previous settings, you may find that you have a different number of pages in your document.

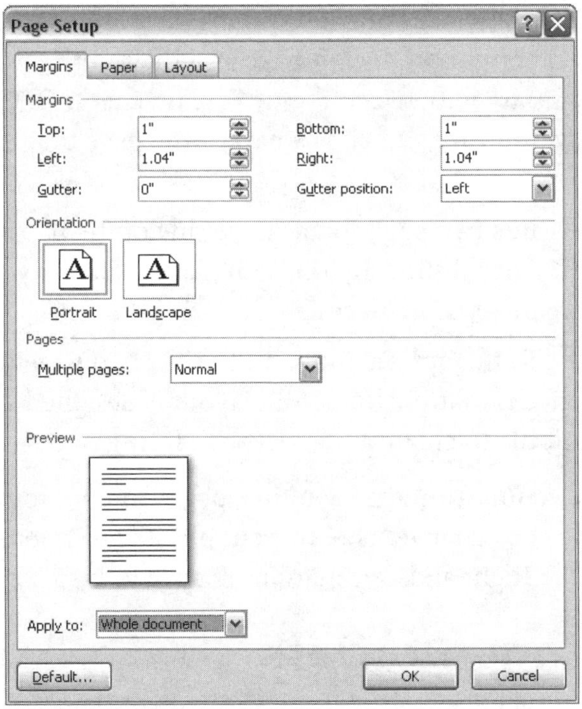

**Figure 4-5.** The Margins tab is divided into four groups of controls: Margins, Orientation, Pages, and Preview. Use the text boxes at the top to set your top, bottom, and side margins. Use the gutter settings to specify the part of the page that's hidden by a binding.

## Setting Margins for Booklets

The vast majority of the documents spewing forth from our collective printers are printed on a single side of the page. If they're bound at all, it's likely to be with a staple or a paper clip in the upper-left corner. Documents like this don't need fancy margins or page setups. But, if you're putting together a booklet, corporate report, or newsletter, you need more sophisticated tools.

Open the Page Setup box to the Margins tab (Page Layout → Page Setup → Margins → Custom Margins or Alt+P, MA). In the Pages group, click the "Multiple pages" drop-down menu to see the options.

- ▶ **Normal** is the setting you use for most single-sided documents.

- ▶ **Mirror margins** are great for documents with facing pages, like bound reports or newsletters. This setting makes outside and inside margins identical. Outside margins are the left margin on the left page and the right margin on the right page. Inside margins are in between the two facing pages. Documents with facing pages may also have a gutter, which is a part of the page that is hidden when the document is bound.

- ▶ **2 pages per sheet** prints two pages on a single side of the paper. If you've defined headers and footers, they'll show up on both pages. Usually you cut these pages after printing to create separate pages.

- ▶ **Book fold** is similar to the option above and prints two pages on one side of the paper. The difference is that the book fold layout is designed so you can fold the paper down the middle to create a booklet with facing pages.

When you make a selection from the "Multiple pages" menu, some of the other options in the Margins box change too. For example, if you choose "Mirror margins," the labels above for the Right and Left margins change to Inside and Outside.

# Applying Page Borders

A tasteful, properly applied border can add a certain flare to your document. However, an inappropriate border can make your document look cheesy (Figure 4-6). Enough said?

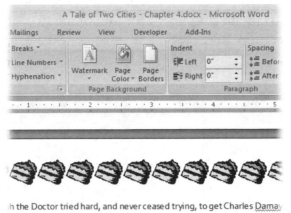

**Figure 4-6.** The Page Layout → Page Background → Page Borders menu lets you add a simple line border around a paragraph, picture, or page. You can also add an art border, but don't get carried away. This cake border is a bad choice for Marie Antoinette and most other adults.

Okay, now that you've been warned, here's how to add page borders:

1. **Choose Page Layout → Page Background → Page Borders to open the Borders and Shading box.**

   The Borders and Shading box has three tabs. Make sure you're using the Page Border tab. (The first Borders tab puts borders around paragraphs, pictures, and other objects on the page.)

2. **On the left, choose a setting to define the border.**

   Start with the five settings on the left, to define the border in broad strokes ranging from no border to drop shadows. You can select only one of these settings.

3. **Choose a line style, color, and width, or choose an art border.**

   If you're going with a line border, choose a line type from the Style drop-down menu. You can choose from more than two dozen lines, including solid, dotted, double, and wavy. Then use the drop-down menus to choose a Color and Width (Figure 4-7).

If you want an art border-trees, hearts, pieces of cake, and so on-select your design from the Art menu (just below the Width menu). Note that some of the art styles use different patterns for different sides of the page and for the corner design.

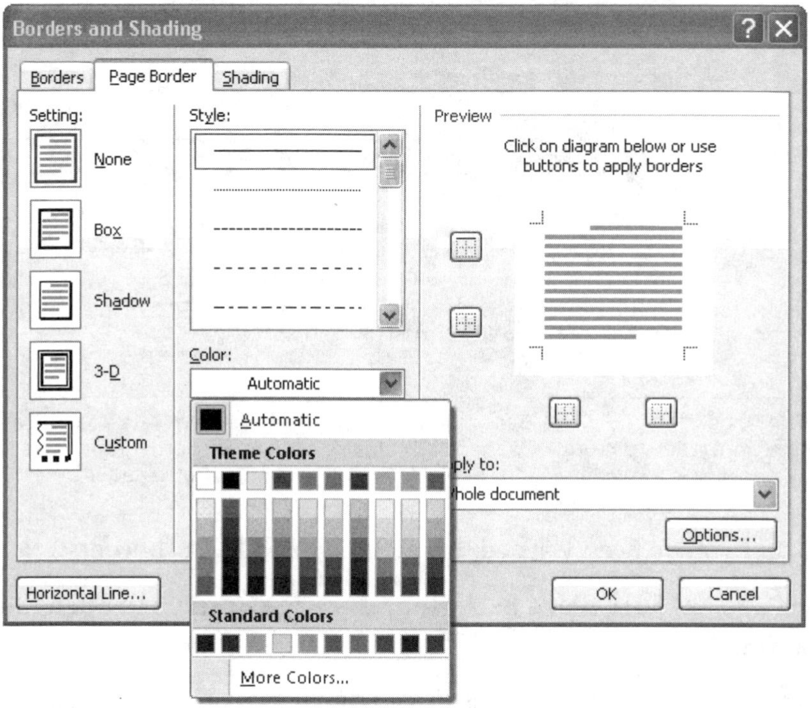

**Figure 4-7.** If you choose a line border, you can choose a color as well as a style.Selecting from the Theme Colors palette ensures that your color coordinates with the document's current theme. The Standard Colors palette gives you access to several basic, bright colors. Preview the border, and then select the sides of the page that will have borders.

___ **NOTE** _____

Whether you choose lines or art for your border, you can adjust the width. You can increase line widths to a thick 6 points and art widths to 31 points.

_____

# A Colorful Background

The Page Color option lets you fill in the entire background of a page. Avoid the temptation to use this feature to create a pretty background. Nothing screams "Amateur designer!" more than loud background colors and patterns that fight with the text on the page.

Printing a colored background also drinks up gallons of expensive printer ink, so if you just want a colored background, print your document on colored paper instead. In truth, Microsoft intended the Page Color feature more for those rare birds who use Word to create Web pages, rather than for printed documents.

However, you may occasionally use a background color (with heavy stock) to create postcards, colored covers, business cards, and so on.

If you use a dark text color, make sure you use a light page color and vice versa. Avoid extremely busy background patterns, textures, and images that make it hard to read your text.

Choose Page Layout → Page Background → Page Color, and you'll see a drop-down menu of options as shown previously in Figure 4-7. If you move your mouse over a color (without clicking), then you see the page change color, immediately giving you a preview. In fact, if you're previewing a very dark page color, Word's smart enough to change the text from black to white. That doesn't mean it's impossible to come up with some garish page color options. When you settle on a color, click to choose it.

The Preview on the right side of the Borders and Shading box shows what sides of your page will have borders. Click the borders to toggle them on or off. Using this technique, you can choose to show a border on a single side of the page or on any combination of sides.

4. **In the lower-right corner of the box, use the "Apply to" control to set the pages that will have borders.**

Maybe you want your first page to have a different border from the rest of the document. If the first page of your document uses letterhead, you may want a first page with no border at all, so select "This section - all except first page." Or, to put a border around the cover page but no other pages, choose the "This section - first page only" setting. As with paper size and other page layout settings, Word lets you apply borders differently in different sections of your document. See the tip on page 136.

5. **Click OK to accept the settings and to close the Borders and Shading box.**

# Adding Headers and Footers

Headers and footers are where Word puts the bits of information that appear at the top or bottom of every page of most multipage documents (Figure 4-8). They remind you of the page number, chapter title, and so on, as you read along. For business memos and reports, headers are a great place to repeat the document's subject and publication date. (If you're the author of the report and want your boss to know, consider adding your name under the title.)

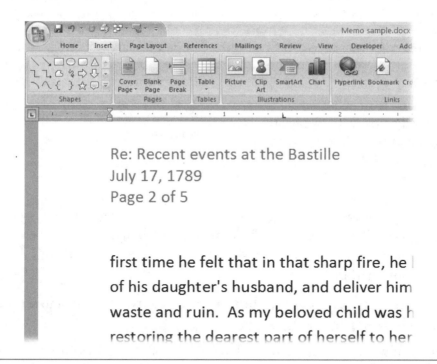

**Figure 4-8.** Document headers give the reader additional information that's not found in the text. For example, the header for a business memo can include the subject, date, and page number. Word lets you enter this information manually or with the help of fields that automatically update the information.

── NOTE ────────────────────────────────────────────────

Word's *fields* are bits of text automated with the help of some behind-the-scenes computer code. You can insert fields into your document to show information that's likely to change, like today's date or a page number. Because it's a field, this text updates itself automatically, as discussed on page 142.

## Introducing the Header and Footer Tools

Unlike some of the other features in this chapter, the header and footer tools are on the Insert tab (not the Page Layout tab). As you can see in Figure 4-9, three menus appear in the Header & Footer group—Header, Footer, and Page Number. Each of the menus provides predesigned page elements, known in Word-speak as Building Blocks. So, for example, if you select a header Building Block, it may add text and several graphic elements to the top of your page.

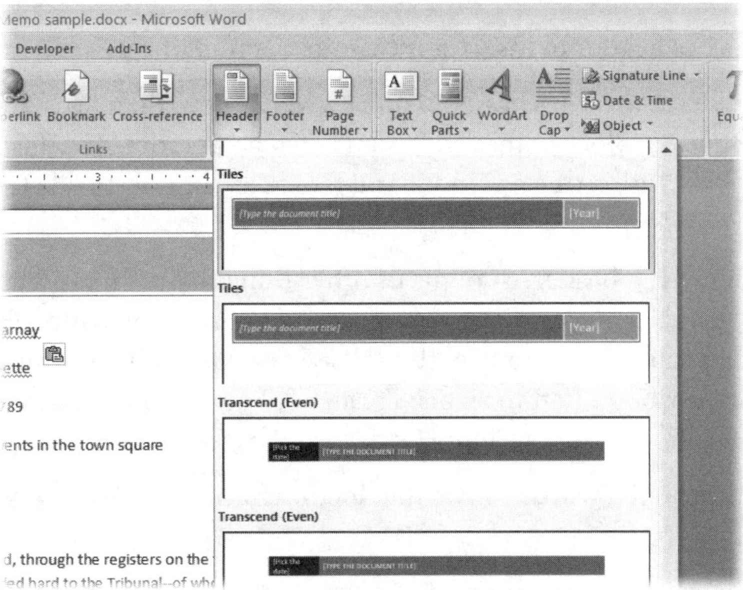

**Figure 4-9.** The Header, Footer, and Page Number menus help you insert predesigned page elements, known as Building Blocks, into your document. You can see what each one looks like right on the menu. At the bottom of the menu, you find options to create (or remove) custom headers, footers, and page numbers.

## Inserting and Modifying a Header Building Block

Go to Insert → Header & Footer → Header, and you see more than a dozen predesigned header options. You can keep these canned headers as they are, or use them as a starting point for your own imagination. The following steps show you how to use a Building Block to add a header to your document and then tweak it a bit by inserting an additional field.

1. **Go to Insert → Header & Footer → Header to open the Header menu.**

   If you've used earlier versions of the program, you'll notice that the drop-down menus in Word 2007 are larger and much more visual. The Header menu is a good example, as it gives you a clear representation of the available predesigned headers.

2. **Use the scroll bar on the right to find the Tiles header.**

   You can drag the box in the scroll bar to move quickly through the menu, or use the arrow buttons to browse through the examples.

3. **Click the Tiles header to insert it into your document.**

   When you select the Tiles header, you're adding more than text to your document: A Building Block comes with all its own accessories. The Tiles header includes a box with a rule around it and two tiles of color. Inside the tiles are bracketed words.

   When you insert a header, a couple of other things happen too. The Header menu closes and a new Design tab appears on your ribbon, with a Header & Footer Tools tab above. Along with that, a whole slew of new buttons and tools appear on the ribbon (left to right): Header & Footer, Insert, Navigation, Options, Position, and the Close Header and Footer button.

4. **Click the bracketed words "Type the document title," and then type a title of your choice.**

   The bracketed words are a prompt that you're supposed to enter new text in that spot. A single click anywhere on the words selects the entire group. Type your title, say, *A Tale of Two Cities*. When you type, the other words and the brackets disappear. When you add a title to the header, Word uses this text to update the title shown in the Document Properties (Office button → Prepare → Properties). For details, see the box on page 142.

5. **Click the bracketed word "Year," and then use the calendar control to update the header's Year field.**

   This standard Word tool lets you enter a date by selecting it. At the top, you see the month and year. Click the buttons on either side to move backward or forward through the months. Click a date on the calendar below to select a specific date. Word uses the year from the date you selected to update the Year text in the header. Or you can enter a year simply by typing it.

   You can modify Building Blocks after you add them to your document by typing your own text, which you'll do next.

6. **Click the header to the right of your title. If the title is highlighted, use the right arrow key to deselect the title, and then type a hyphen (-) followed by a space.**

   You can also add automatically updating text by inserting a field, which is how Word creates those ever-changing dates and page numbers. Word has fields for lots of other stuff too. You can't create (or edit) a field by typing directly in your document, though. You must use the Field dialog box.

7. **Choose Insert → Quick Parts → Field.**

   The Field dialog box opens showing an alphabetical list of field names on the left side, as shown in Figure 4-10. Fields store information about your document and keep track of other information that you can use in your documents.

8. **Double-click the Author field name to insert it into the header.**

   The author's name appears next to the title in the header. (If you're working on your own computer, it's probably your name.) This text is grayed out to show that it's a field and that you can't edit it directly.

9. **Double-click anywhere on the document's body text to close the Header & Footer Tools contextual tab.**

   You have two options for closing the header and going back to editing your document. You can double-click anywhere outside the header, or, on the right side of the ribbon, you can click the Close Header and Footer button. Either way, the header fades out and the text of your document sharpens up. Your insertion point appears back in the body text, and you're ready to work.

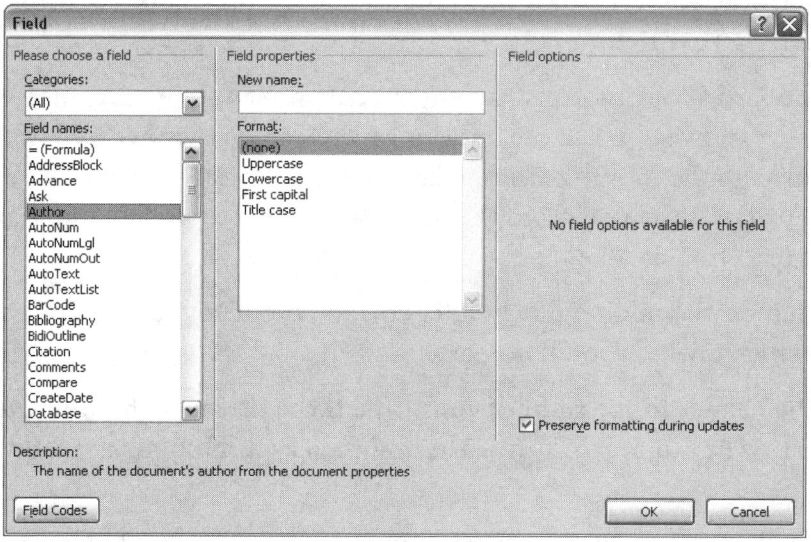

**Figure 4-10.** Using fields, you can add automatically updating page numbers, dates, and names. The Field dialog box shows a whole list of fields (left) and provides ways to format them (right) so that they work just right.

# Inspecting Your Document's Properties and Fields

When you type to replace placeholder text in a Quick Part (like the header title in step 3 on page 140), something else happens behind the scenes. Every Word document has *properties*—defining information like author, title, and subject. You can check them out in the Document Information Panel: Choose Office button → Prepare → Properties. (When you're done, click the X button at the upper-right to close the box.) When you give the header a new title, Word takes those words and inserts them in the Title field of the Document Information Panel.

Word keeps track of the title and other document properties and uses them to fill in the fields you insert into your documents. You can insert a field in a header, a footer, or indeed anywhere in your document by choosing Insert → Quick Parts → Field. For example, the number of pages in a document is stored in the NumPages field. So if you'd like to put "Page X of XX pages" in your header or footer, just replace X with the Page field and XX with the NumPages field.

## Adding a Matching Footer Building Block

Most of the header Building Blocks have complementary footers. For example, the Tiles header used in the step-by-step example provides title and date information, while the Tiles footer provides company and page information (Figure 4-11). The steps for inserting the Tiles footer are nearly identical to the header steps. Just start with the Footer menu: Choose Insert → Header & Footer → Footer or press Alt+N, 0.

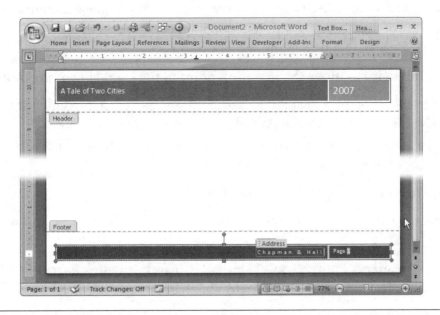

**Figure 4-11.** Most of the header and footer Building Blocks come in pairs. By using a header and footer with the same name, you can be sure of having a consistent design. You can modify Building Blocks—like this predesigned header and footer—after you insert them in your text. Just edit as you would any text. It's best to leave the page numbers as they are, though. This page number is grayed out to indicate that it's a field that automatically changes for each page.

## Creating Custom Headers and Footers

Microsoft provides a lot of competently designed headers and footers with Word, but you're free to create your own. After all, Microsoft's Building Blocks may not be to your taste, or maybe you have to follow company guidelines for your documents.

It's not difficult to create your own headers in Word. Here's how to create a custom footer with a company name on the left and page numbers on the right:

1. **Go to Insert → Header & Footer → Footer → Edit Footer.**

   The insertion point moves from the body of your document to the footer space at the bottom.

2. **Type your company name, press Enter, and then type your city and country.**

   Pressing Enter puts the city and country on a new line below the company name. Text that you type directly into the footer appears on every page unless you make changes to the header and footer options.

3. **Press Tab twice to move the insertion point to the right side of the footer.**

   The first time you press Tab, the insertion point moves to the center of the page. If you enter text at that point, Word centers the text in the footer. The second time you press Tab, the insertion point moves to the right margin. Text that you enter there is aligned on the right margin.

4. **Type *Page*, and then press the Space bar.**

   As you type, the insertion point remains on the right margin and your text flows to the left.

5. **Choose Header & Footer Tools | Design → Insert → Quick Parts → Field (or press Alt+JH, Q, F) to open the Field dialog box.**

   The Quick Parts menu shows several different options: Document Property, Field, and Building Blocks Organizer.

6. **In the list of Field Names, double-click Page to insert the Page field in the footer.**

   Remember, if you simply type a number into the footer, you'll end up with the same number on every page. Instead, you place the Page field in your footer to tell Word to insert the correct number on each page. The page number appears in the footer next to the word "Page." The number is grayed out, indicating that it's a field and you can't edit the number.

7. **Type *of* and then a space. Press Alt+JH, Q, F to open the Field box again, and then double-click the NumPages field to insert it in your footer after the space.**

The NumPages field keeps track of the number of pages in your document. When you're done, your footer looks like the one in Figure 4-12.

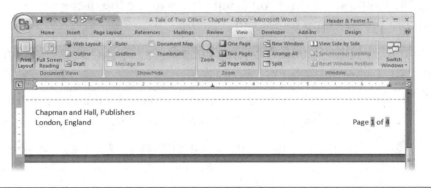

**Figure 4-12.** This custom footer may not be as flashy as Microsoft's Building Blocks, but what Chapman and Hall wants, Chapman and Hall gets. The company name and city are plain typed-in text, while the page number and number of pages are fields that update automatically.

## Removing Headers, Footers, and Page Numbers

It's easy to remove any headers, footers, or page numbers that you've added to your document. You'll find a command at the bottom of each of the respective menus to do just that. If you want to remove a header, follow these steps:

1. **Go to Insert → Header & Footer → Header to open the Header menu.**

   You see the same menu that you used to insert the header Building Block into your document. At the bottom of the menu, below all the Header examples, you see the Remove Header command.

2. **Click Remove Header.**

   The Header menu closes, and the entire header disappears from your document—text, graphics, and all.

The steps for removing a footer or a page number Building Block are nearly identical. Just start with the Footer menu (Insert → Header & Footer → Footer) or the Page Number menu (Insert → Header & Footer → Page Number).

# Working with Multiple Columns

Word makes it easy to work with multiple newspaper-style columns. Instead of your having to use tabs or spaces to separate the column one line at a time, Word lets you set up the column guidelines and then type away. When you type text in a multicolumn layout, your words appear in the left column first. After you reach the end or bottom of the column, the insertion point jumps to the top of the next column and you begin to fill it, from top to bottom.

To use multiple columns, go to Page Layout → Page Setup → Columns, and then click one of the following options:

▶ **One.** Whether you know it or not, every page in Word has a column layout. The standard layout is one big column stretching from margin to margin.

▶ **Two.** With two columns, your document begins to look like a pamphlet or a school textbook.

▶ **Three.** Three columns are about as much as a standard 8.5 × 11-inch page can handle, unless you switch to Landscape orientation. In fact, you may want to reduce the body text size to about 9 or 10 points and turn on hyphenation. Otherwise, you can't fit very many words on a line.

▶ **Left.** This layout has two columns, with the narrower column on the left. The narrow column is a great place to introduce the text with a long heading and subheading or a quote pulled from the larger body text.

▶ **Right.** The mirror image of the Left layout, this option uses two columns with a narrow column at right.

▶ **More Columns.** Use the More Columns option to open the Columns dialog box (Figure 4-13) where you can create a customized column layout.

---

**TIP**

If you want to use keyboard shortcuts to select column options, press Alt+P, J and then use the up and down arrow keys to highlight one of the options. With your choice highlighted, hit Enter.

---

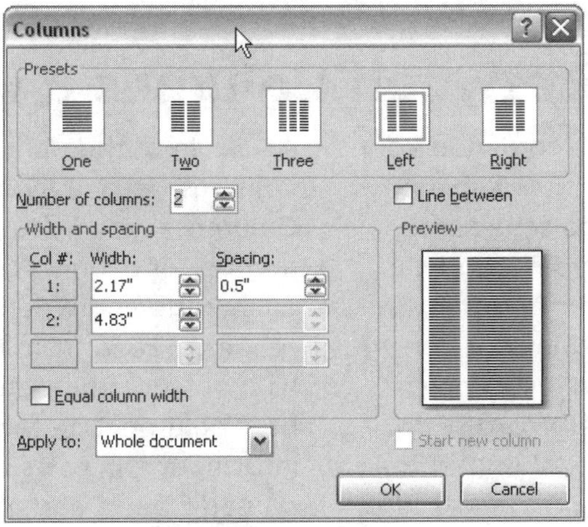

**Figure 4-13.** At the top of the Columns dialog box, you see the same presets as on the Columns menu. Below them, controls let you create your own multicolumn layouts. The preview icon on the right changes as you adjust the settings.

When you get to the bottom of a column, Word automatically flows your text to the top of the next one, but you can also force Word to end the column and jump to the next one. There are two ways to create a *column break*. The quickest way while you're typing is to use the keyboard shortcut Ctrl+Shift+Enter (or Alt+P, BC). Or, if you forget the shortcut, you can use the ribbon: Page Layout → Page Setup → Breaks → Column.

## Customizing Columns

Go to Page Layout → Page Setup → Columns → More Columns to open the Columns box (Figure 4-13) where you can create custom page layouts with multiple columns. By entering a number in the "Number of columns" text box, you can create more than three columns per page.

If you turn on the "Equal column width" checkbox, Word automatically sets all the columns to the same width, so you don't have to do the math (Figure 4-14). Turn off this checkbox, and you can get creative by entering a different width and spacing for each column. Use the scroll bar on the right if you can't see all of the columns.

## Choosing Between Columns and Tables

Word gives you two tools to divide your text into strips—Columns and Tables. Even though they may look the same on paper, they work and act differently. If you're writing a newsletter or a pamphlet, you probably want newspaper-style columns, so you can just type (or paste in) your text and let Word distribute it smoothly from one column to the next. But if you're listing the names of volunteers who joined the PTA each semester, you're better off using a table to create the columns, so you can keep each name on its own line.

As a rule of thumb, use newspaper-style columns (Page Layout → Page Setup → Columns) when you need a consistent number of evenly spaced columns on each page and when you expect the reader to read from the top to the bottom of a column before moving to the next column. Use tables to organize information in rows and columns, like a spreadsheet. Readers are just as likely to read tables left to right as they are from top to bottom. There's more information on tables on page 254.

Turn on the "Line between" box to place a line (also known as a *rule*) between your columns for a crisp professional look.

Near the bottom of the Columns box is a drop-down menu labeled "Apply to." If you want to use your column settings for your entire document, leave this set to "Whole document." If you want to create a new section with the column settings, select "This point forward" from the menu.

## Hyphenation

Without hyphenation, if a word is too long to fit on the line, Word moves it down to the beginning of the next line. If a word is particularly long, it can leave some pretty big gaps at the end of the line. Justified text is aligned on both the left and right margins, like most of the text in this book. If you have justified text and no hyphenation, you often get large, distracting gaps between words, where Word is trying to spread out the text along the line. When used properly, hyphenation helps make text more attractive on the page and easier to read. In most cases, you can relax and let Word handle the hyphenating.

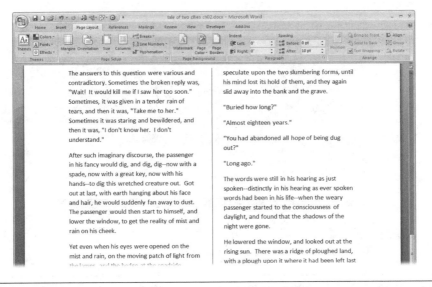

**Figure 4-14.** You can fine-tune your columns options to create just the right effect. This example uses the "Equal column width" and the "Line between" options.

You just have to choose one of three basic hyphenation styles from the Page Layout → Page Setup → Hyphenation menu (Alt+P, H), as shown in Figure 4-15:

▶ **None.** No hyphenation at all. For informal letters, first drafts, and many reports, you may choose not to use hyphenation. It's a good-looking choice for documents that have fairly long lines (60 to 80 characters) and left-aligned text.

▶ **Automatic.** Word makes hyphenation decisions based on some simple rules that you provide. Consider using automatic hyphenation for documents that have line lengths of about 50 characters or less, including documents that use newspaper-style columns.

▶ **Manual.** In this scheme, Word asks you about each word it wants to hyphenate, giving you the final decision. Use manual hyphenation when you need to be particularly scrupulous about your grammar and when you need to be certain that you don't hyphenate a company name, a person's name, or some other equally important word.

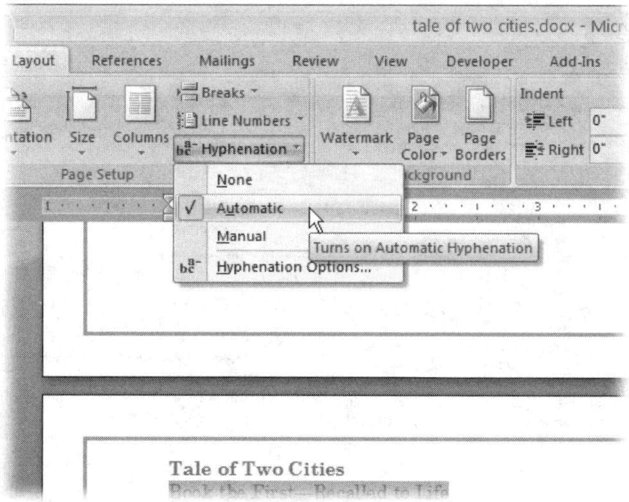

**Figure 4-15.** Choose Automatic from the hyphenation menu, and Word takes care of all hyphenation decisions. Word's hyphenation feature works quite well and usually needs no help from you.

## Automatic Hyphenation

It's easy to turn on automatic hyphenation. Just choose Page Layout → Page Setup → Hyphenation (or press Alt+P, H). Still, you may want to assert some control over how and when Word uses hyphenation. To do that, open the Hyphenation box (Figure 4-16) by choosing Page Layout → Page Setup → Hyphenation → Hyphenation Options (Alt+P, HH). This box has two important options that let you control hyphenation:

▶ **Hyphenation zone.** This zone is the maximum space that Word allows between the end of a word and the right margin. If the space is larger than this, Word hyphenates a word to close the gap. For most documents, .25" (a quarter of an inch) is a reasonable choice. A larger distance may give you fewer hyphens but a more ragged look to your right margin.

▶ **Limit consecutive hyphens to.** A "ladder" of three or more hyphens makes text difficult to read. Enter *2* in this box, and Word won't hyphenate more than two lines in a row.

# Hyphenation Rules of Thumb

Hyphenation rules are notoriously complicated, and, to make matters worse, they change by language and country. For example, Americans and British hyphenate differently. Still, you should follow these basic rules of thumb:

* **Use hyphenation with documents that have shorter lines.** A document that uses two or three columns on the page needs hyphenation to avoid large gaps in the text.

* **Use hyphenation with justified text.** Justified text, which is aligned on both the left and right margins, makes documents look formal and tidy—but not if big gaps appear between letters and words. Avoid those gaps by letting Word hyphenate your justified text.

* **Avoid hyphenating company names and proper names.** Most people don't like to have their name messed with, and your boss feels the same way about the company name. Use manual hyphenation to prevent Word from dividing certain words.

* **Avoid hyphenating more than two lines in a row.** According to many standard style guides, it's wrong to use hyphenation on more than two consecutive lines. Use manual hyphenation to remove a hyphen if you see too many in a row.

* **Avoid overusing hyphens.** Excessive hyphenation, even if not on consecutive lines, distracts the eye and makes a document more difficult to read.

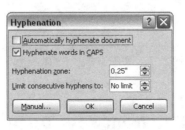

**Figure 4-16.** Use the Hyphenation box to set the ground rules for hyphenation. Turn on the "Automatically hyphenate document" checkbox at top to have Word automatically hyphenate words according to the rules you set.

# Manual Hyphenation

The term manual hyphenation sounds like more work than it actually is. Computer-assisted hyphenation would be a better term. When you turn on manual hyphenation (Alt+P, HM), Word automatically finds and shows you words that fall within the hyphenation zone, using the hyphenation rules you set in the Hyphenation box (Figure 4-17, below).

Word then shows you the word in a box and suggests where to place the hyphen. If you agree, click Yes. If you'd rather hyphenate the word in a different spot, click to put the insertion point where you want the hyphen, and then click Yes.

You many not always agree with Word when it comes to hyphen placement. For example, as shown here, Word wants to put the hyphen in the wrong spot in the word "mischance." To manually set the hyphen, click to put the insertion point between the "s" and the "c," and then click Yes.

It's best to run the Manual Hyphenation command (Page Layout → Page Setup → Hyphenation → Manual or Alt+P, HM) immediately before you print or save the final draft of your document. If last-minute edits change the line lengths and line breaks, you need to run manual hyphenation again.

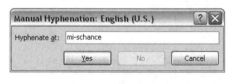

**Figure 4-17.** You may not always agree with Word when it comes to hyphen placement. In this case, the hypen is in the wrong spot in the word "mischance." To manually set the hyphen, click to put the insertion point between the "s" and the "c," and then click Yes.

## Removing Hyphenation from Your Document

It's easier to remove hyphenation from your document if you've used automatic rather than manual hyphenation. In the case of automatic hyphenation, you simply turn it off: Choose Page Layout → Page Setup → Hyphenation → None, or use the keyboard shortcut Alt+P, HN. All the automatic hyphens in your document disappear and the words rearrange themselves accordingly.

But when you use manual hyphenation, Word inserts optional hyphens in your document that don't go away even if you turn hyphenation off. If you set Hyphenation to None (Alt+P, HN), then Word continues to split words at the end of lines using the optional hyphens. The only way to find and delete the optional hyphens is with Word's Find and Replace dialog box.

Here are the steps to remove optional hyphens from your document:

1. **Choose Home → Replace (or press Ctrl+H) to open the Find and Replace dialog box to the Replace tab.**

   If you don't see a Special button at the bottom, click the More button on the left to expand the box. (If the box is expanded, the More button is labeled "Less" and clicking it shrinks the box.)

2. **Click in the "Find what" box to put the insertion point in the box.**

   Normally, you'd just type in the text that you're searching for, but the optional hyphen is a special character that you won't find on your keyboard. Searching for optional hyphens requires a couple of extra steps.

3. **Click the Special button to reveal the list of special characters.**

   The Find and Replace tool can search for a number of special characters. Some of them, like the optional hyphen and the paragraph mark, are nonprinting characters. Others, like the em dash need more than a single keystroke to produce.

4. **From the menu of special characters, choose Optional Hyphen.**

   The Special menu closes when you make a choice from the list. In the "Find what" box, you see ^-, the code Word uses to indicate an optional hyphen. Leave the "Replace with" box empty, because you want to replace the optional hyphens with nothing, which effectively removes them.

5. **Click Replace All to remove all optional hyphens from your text.**

   Word quickly removes the optional hyphens and displays a message telling you how many changes were made. Click Close to dismiss the alert box, and then, in the Find and Replace box (Figure 4-18), click Close. Mission accomplished.

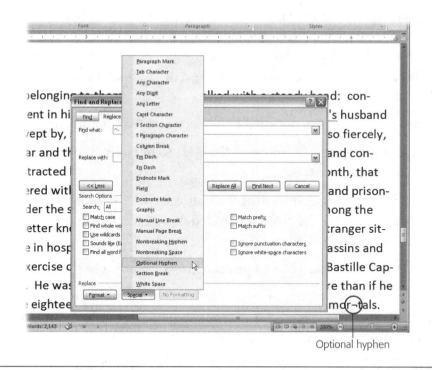

**Figure 4-18.** Click the Special button on the Replace tab (Ctrl+H) to enter nonprinting characters like optional hyphens in the "Find what" or "Replace with" field. You can change your display settings to always show optional hyphens. When they aren't at the end of a line, optional hyphens look like the character between the "r" and "t" in the word "mortals" (circled).

Optional hyphen

# Dividing Your Document into Sections

The longer and more complex your document is, the more likely it is to contain different *sections*. Word's sections don't have anything to do with how you've divided your document with headings and subheadings. They're electronic divisions you create by adding *section breaks* to your document. Section breaks are a close cousin to page breaks, except that a section can contain any number of pages. More important, each section in a Word document can have its own page formatting.

Many people work with Word for years without ever really understanding Word's sections. But breaking your document into different sections gives you a lot more flexibility within the same document. For example:

- **To change the page orientation.** If you want to have some pages in portrait orientation and others in landscape orientation (charts or graphs, for example), you need to insert a section break where the format changes (Figure 4-19).

- **To use different sizes of paper in a single document.** If you want to insert some tabloid-size pages in the middle of a document that's the standard 8.5 × 11 inches, you need to use page breaks where the format changes.

- **To change the number of columns on the page.** Perhaps you want to change from a single column format to a double column format; you need to insert a section break where the format changes. You can even put the break right smack in the middle of a page.

- **To change page margins in a single document.** When you want to change page margins, not just adjust a paragraph's indentation, you need to create a section break where the margins change.

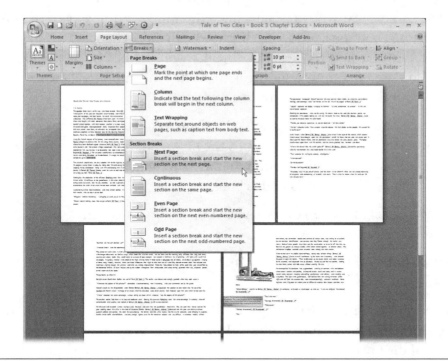

**Figure 4-19.** Use section breaks to make major changes to your page format. For example, after you insert a Next Page break, you can change the page orientation or the paper size.

## Inserting Section Breaks

As you can see from the previous list, sections are all about page formatting, so it's not surprising that the section break commands are found under the Page Layout tab (Page Layout → Page Setup → Breaks or Alt+P, B). When you click the Breaks button in the Page Setup group, the menu is divided into two parts: Page Breaks and Section Breaks.

___ **NOTE** _____

When you use the Breaks menu (Figure 4-19), remember that the breaks shown at the top aren't section breaks. They're just text formatting breaks like page breaks and column breaks. The commands on the bottom are section breaks, as advertised.

_____

Section breaks have two major distinctions. There are Next Page breaks, which create a new page for the new section, and there are Continuous breaks, which place a divider mark in the text with no visible interruption. Everything below that mark is in a new section. You use a Next Page break when you're changing the paper size or orientation. Or you can use a Next Page break if you want each chapter to start on a new page. You use the Continuous break to change the number of columns or the margins in your document in the middle of a page.

The other two options—Even Page and Odd Page—are just variations on Next Page. They create section breaks and start the new section on the next even or odd page. For example, you use this option to make sure that all your chapters begin on a right-hand page (like the ones in this book).

Here's how to insert a section break and change the paper orientation for the new section from Portrait to Landscape.

1. **Click within your text to place the insertion point where you want the section break.**

   You're going to insert a Next Page break, so click after the end of a sentence or paragraph. Also, make sure you're in Print Layout view, so you can see the results of the break.

2. **Choose Page Layout → Page Setup → Breaks, and then select Next Page from the drop-down menu.**

   If you're at the end of your document, Word creates a new empty page, and your insertion point is on the new page, ready to go. If you're in the middle of a document, Word creates a page break and moves your insertion point and all the remaining text to the new section.

3. **With the insertion point in the new section, click the Orientation button (Page Layout → Page Setup → Orientation), and then choose Landscape.**

   When you make Page Setup changes in your new section, they affect only the new section. So when you change the page orientation to landscape, you see pages before the break in portrait orientation and pages after the break in landscape orientation.

In Print Layout view, you see how your document looks with section breaks inserted. In Draft view, section breaks appear in your document as dotted lines. The line doesn't print, but it's visible on your computer screen (Figure 4-20).

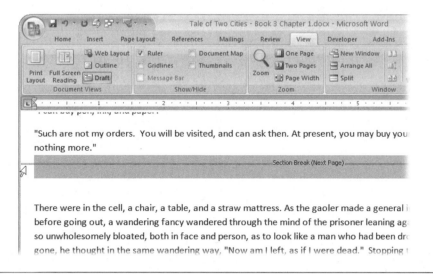

**Figure 4-20.** To delete a section break, change to Draft view. Section breaks show as dotted, double lines. Select the break by clicking the line, and then press Delete.

# THEMES AND TEMPLATES

5

- ▶ Choosing a Theme
- ▶ Choosing a Template

FORMATTING YOUR TEXT, headings, lists, and other page elements individually—as described in the previous couple of chapters—takes time that you may not have. And with so many choices in fonts, colors, and graphic ornaments, putting together a good-looking document can be overwhelming. No wonder so many people stick with Times New Roman body text and Arial headings! Fortunately, graphic designers at Microsoft have created *themes*, a new Word 2007 feature that lets you apply a complete, coordinated package of fonts, colors, heading styles, and more with a single click.

While themes are all about style and appearance, *templates* are about content. Part of Word for more than a decade, templates provide boilerplate text and blank spaces for you to fill with your own information. Templates also set you up with snappy graphics and consistent margins, indents, and paragraph formatting. A good template even provides cues to tell you what information you need to fill in the blanks.

Word's themes and templates help you make your documents look like they came from a Fortune 500 company's publications division. Even if you don't know a font from a fondue, you can crank out professional looking business proposals, resumés, and more.

## Choosing a Theme

When you're on deadline putting together, say, a business proposal, you don't want to waste precious minutes worrying about fonts, heading colors, and the design of tables, charts, and graphs. Instead, simply choose a theme with a click of your mouse (Figure 5-1), and you've got a professional looking document.

Themes are made up of three parts:

▶ **Colors.** Each theme contains twelve colors, each of which is assigned to a specific document part. One color (usually black) is used for body text. Another color (dark blue, say) is used for Heading 1 paragraphs. Lesser headings—like Heading 2 and Heading 3—may use a lighter shade of the same color. Other complementary colors are used for accent and hyperlinks (links to the Internet).

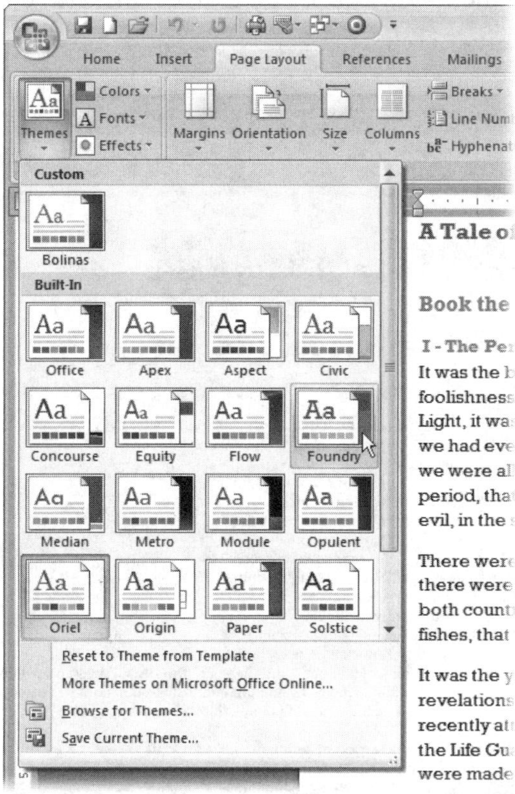

**Figure 5-1.** Word 2007's themes are prepackaged collections of colors, fonts, and effects that work together to create attractive pages. Hold your mouse cursor over a theme to preview its effect on your document. Applying a theme is as simple as clicking the design you like best.

▶ **Fonts.** Each theme specifies one or two fonts—one for the body text and one for headings. Also known as typefaces, fonts define the actual shape of the letters on the screen and on the page. They have a subtle but significant effect on the appearance and feeling of a document. Some typefaces don't always play well with others, but fortunately, you don't have to worry about that when you choose themes, since their typeface combinations are always compatible.

▶ **Effects.** Each theme uses one of Word's 20 built-in graphic effects. These effects include design touches like shadows, line styles, 3-D, and so on. Most of these effects have more of an impact in PowerPoint presentations than in Word documents, but they come with the theme's package.

When you choose a theme, you're applying color, font, and effect formatting to the elements in your document (Figure 5-2).

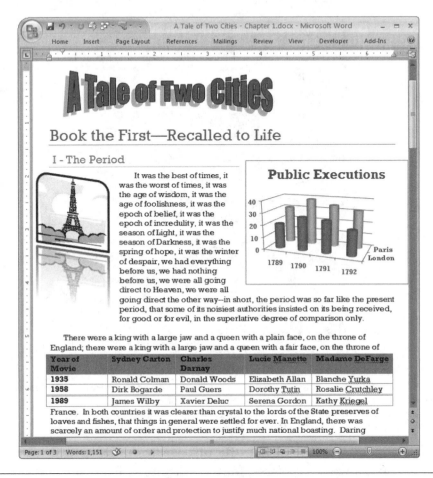

**Figure 5-2.** This document shows the Foundry theme in all its glory. The theme defines the fonts and the colors used for headings, chart objects, picture borders, and tables. As you can see, even with professionally designed themes, amateurish excess can still produce an ugly page.

If you use Excel or PowerPoint as well as Word, you'll be glad to know that all Microsoft Office programs use the same themes. That makes it very easy to keep a consistent, professional look across all documents you create for a specific job or project. Figure 5-3 shows you an example. And if you need help getting up to speed in these programs, check out *Excel 2007 for Starters: The Missing Manual* and *Powerpoint: The Missing Manual*, both from O'Reilly.

Here are examples of the parts of your document that take their formatting cues from the selected theme:

▶ **Body text.** Font, size, style, and color.

▶ **Headings.** Font, size, style, and color.

▶ **Tables.** Font specs (same as above), border and line styles, and colors.

▶ **Charts.** Font specs, borders, lines, chart graphic styles, and colors.

▶ **Picture.** Border colors.

▶ **Smart-Art.** Font specs, graphic colors.

▶ **Clip art.** Major outline and border colors.

▶ **Drop caps.** Font specs and color.

▶ **WordArt.** Font colors change, but the actual typestyle remains the same.

Here's how to choose a theme for your document:

1. **Go to Page Layout → Themes (or press Alt+P, TH).**

   The Themes menu is on the far left of the Page Layout tab (Figure 5-1). It's like an artist's palette where you see sample colors and typefaces. Themes are divided into two categories with Custom themes at the top and Built-In themes below.

You see Custom Themes only if you've created your own custom document themes. For tips on how to roll your own themes, see page 166.

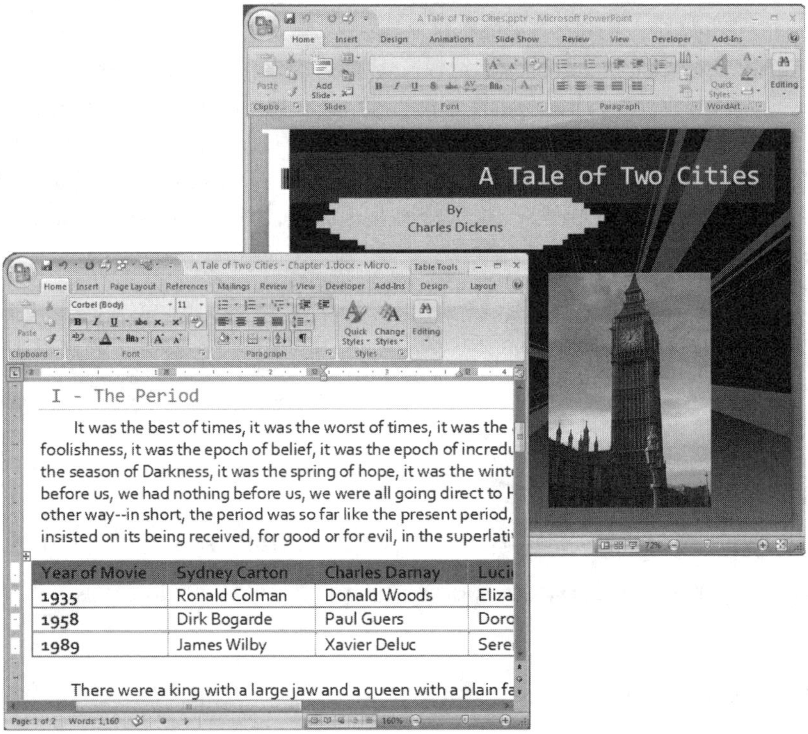

**Figure 5-3.** Word, PowerPoint, and Excel share the same themes. This Word document (front) and PowerPoint presentation (rear) both use the Metro theme, giving them consistent typestyles and graphic specifications.

2. **If the themes aren't all visible, drag the scroll bar on the right to get a better view.**

   In the lower-right corner, the three dots indicate that you can click that spot to drag the corner and resize the menu. If you'd rather have the menu stretch across the top of your window so you can see your document beneath, then just drag the corner.

3. **With your mouse, point to a theme (but don't click) to see a Live Preview.**

The Themes menu uses Microsoft's new Live Preview feature—all you have to do is point to a theme, and your document changes to show you how it will look using that theme. You can quickly view and compare the available choices. (See, computer games aren't the only programs that use all of your computer's graphics power.)

4. **Once you decide on a theme, click to select it.**

One click chooses a theme and applies formatting changes throughout your document. Headings, borders, and lines change color. Body text, headings, and title fonts also change (Figure 5-4).

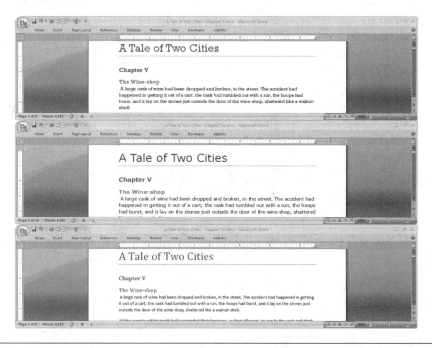

**Figure 5-4.** Here's the same document with three different themes. On top is the Foundry theme with a font that looks a little like something that would come out of a typewriter. In the middle is the Aspect theme featuring Verdana—a modern looking sans-serif type. On the bottom is the Office theme, ensconced in hues of Microsoft.

## Finding More Themes

Word comes with 20 built-in themes, but you may still find yourself looking for more. Perhaps you work in an office on a computer that was set up by your employer, and someone has created official company themes that you need to use. If that's the case, then you need to know where to look for those themes on your computer, especially if you (or someone you love) have inadvertently moved them. You can also look beyond your computer: Creative types are constantly coming up with new, exciting themes and sharing them on the Web.

### Browsing for themes on your computer

Open the Themes menu (Page Layout → Themes → Themes or Alt+P, TH), and you find custom themes at the top of the list (Figure 5-5). Custom themes are ones that you or someone else created, and they're stored in the Document Themes folder inside your Template folder (*C:\Documents and Settings\[Your Name]\Templates\Document Themes*).

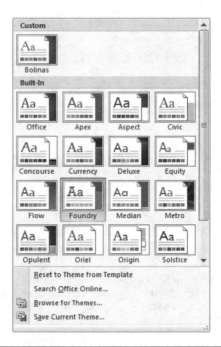

**Figure 5-5.** The Themes menu shows two types of themes—Built-In and Custom. Built-In themes are predesigned themes that come with Word. Themes that you or someone else created appear at the top of the list.

If themes are stored (or moved) somewhere else on your computer, then they won't show up on the Themes menu, but Word can help you look for them. To search for themes, click the Browse for Themes button near the bottom of the Themes menu. The Choose Theme or Themed Document box opens. As shown in Figure 5-6, this standard Windows file box is set up to show you *.thmx, *.docx, *xlsx, and other file types that contain Office themes. The "Files of type" menu is set to Office Themes and Themed Documents, which acts as a filter, so the main window shows you only files that match these types (and folders that contain them).

**Figure 5-6.** If you click Browse for Themes, then you get a standard Windows file box. You can use this box to navigate through your system to seek out files that end in ".thmx." And if you can't find themes this way, see the box on page 169 for another way to search.

# Moving Themes to Your Themes Folder

If you frequently browse to use a custom theme, then you'll save time copying the theme to your Document Themes folder. That way, the theme always shows up in the Custom group on the Themes menu, and you'll never have to search for it again. Here's how to move a theme from your My Documents folder to your Document Themes folder:

1. Choose Page Layout → Themes → Themes → Browse for Themes to open the Choose Theme or Themed Document box (Figure 5-6).

2. Use the buttons on the left and the drop-down menu at the top to hunt down a folder with Office themes. (Theme files end in .thmx.)

3. When you find the file you want to copy, right-click it, and then choose Copy from the File shortcut menu.

4. Navigate to your Document Themes folder. If you sign on to your computer with the name *Christopher*, then start in your My Computer window, and go to *C:\Documents and Settings\Christopher\Templates\ Document Themes* (Figure 5-7).

5. Right-click an empty spot in the Document Themes folder, and then choose Paste.

You see your Themes document added to the Document Themes folder. Open your Themes menu, and it's there at the top of the list.

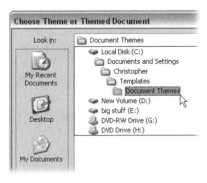

**Figure 5-7.** Word stores themes in a folder inside your Templates folder. Microsoft likes to hide this folder so you won't find it with your other files in your My Documents folder. Instead, you must look in the Documents and Settings folder on your hard drive. On most computers that's Local Disk (C:).

# Searching for Themes on Your Computer

If you think themes may be hiding on your computer that aren't in your My Documents folder, then you can search them out using Windows Explorer.

1. Go to Start → My Documents.

   Windows Explorer opens and you see the contents of a folder in the large box on the right. The panel on the left changes as you click buttons and menu commands.

2. Near the top of the window, click Search (or press Ctrl+F) to open the Search task pane.

   At the pane's left, click the "All files and folders" button (since you want to search your entire computer).

3. In the "All or part of the file name" box, type *.thmx*. (The asterisk (*) character is a wild card that matches any file name with any number of characters.

So when you enter *.thmx* you're telling your computer to look for all files that end with ".*thmx.*")

4. In the "Look in" drop-down menu at the bottom, choose My Computer to tell Windows Explorer to search *all* the files and folders on your computer. (Those theme files can't hide from you!)

5. Click Search. Before long, you see files ending in .thmx start to pop up in the window on the right.

Ignore themes that show up in expected places, like \*Program Files\Microsoft Office\Document Themes 12* and \*Templates\Document Themes*, because all these themes already show up in Word's Theme menu. You're looking for themes in other locations. When you find likely candidates, copy and paste them into your *C:\Documents and Settings\Christopher\Templates\Document Themes* folder.

## Searching for themes online

You can look for themes on the Internet, too. A good place to start is Microsoft Office Online (*www.microsoft.com/office*), shown in Figure 5-8. As time goes on, it's likely that more themes, fonts, and colors will be available. And don't forget to do a Google search. Type *Office 2007 themes* in Google's search box, and you'll see at least a half million entries.

**Figure 5-8.** Microsoft's Office Web site is a good source for information and add-ons. Currently you'll find help files, predesigned templates, and an active Office community. More themes, colors, and font sets should be available soon.

# Choosing a Template

When you use a template, you're taking advantage of the work and wisdom of those who have gone before you. As the saying goes, "Why reinvent the wheel?" Microsoft must adhere to this philosophy because, in Word 2007, they've made templates an even more integral part of the program. Just look at the New Document dialog box (Alt+F, N). Your computer screen fills up with templates (Figure 5-9). You'll find templates for resumés, newsletters, calendars, and greeting cards. The business category alone contains hundreds of templates. When you're working on deadline or you need a professionally designed document, finding the right template to do the job will save time in the long run.

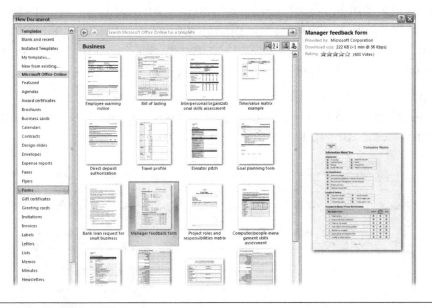

**Figure 5-9.** Open the New Document box and suddenly you see more than a dozen template options. The list on the left shows installed templates at the top. In the lower part of the list are hordes of templates that you can access from the Microsoft Office Online site.

Here's a partial sampling of the types of templates you'll find. In the New Document dialog box, they appear alphabetically in the left panel:

▶ **Planning.** Agendas, calendars, lists, planners, schedules.

▶ **Stationery and mailing.** Business cards, greeting cards, envelopes, faxes, invitations, labels, letters, postcards.

▶ **General business.** Contracts, forms, invoices, memos, minutes, purchase orders, receipts, reports, resumés, statements, time sheets.

▶ **Marketing.** Award certificates, brochures, gift certificates, flyers, newsletters.

If that's not enough, in typical Microsoftian overkill there's even a category called More Categories, where, believe it or not, you find 50 more categories, which run the gamut from Address Books, Games, and Paper Folding projects to Quizzes and Scorecards.

When you use a template, you're not opening a template file, you're opening a copy of it, sort of like pulling the top sheet off a pad of forms. The original template file remains untouched. Here are some of the goodies you'll find in a new document you've opened from a template:

▶ **Graphics.** Templates for brochures, business cards, greeting cards, and newsletters almost always include drawing, clip art, lines, and borders. Frequently you'll find templates that include photos (Figure 5-10).

**Figure 5-10.** When you use a template, you get a professionally designed, preformatted document. Many templates include impressive graphics and high quality photos. All you need to do is fill in your message.

- ▶ **Formatting.** Setting up the page formats, indents, and line spacing, and positioning every single bit of text on the page can be a big job. For projects like forms, purchase orders, and invoices, you may end up tearing your hair out. Fortunately, using a template is a lot easier on your scalp.

- ▶ **Boilerplate text.** Often in templates the text is just there for position. You replace the text with your own words. However, some templates include boilerplate text that you want to leave in place. Contracts, fax cover pages, forms, and even resumés may include body text or headings that you want to keep.

- ▶ **AutoText entries.** Sophisticated templates sometimes add automated features like AutoText entries (page 180). A template designed to handle a common complaint may include a lengthy AutoText entry that begins, "We are so very sorry that the widget didn't live up to your expectations." To insert the diatribe, all you have to do is type *sorry*, and then press the F3 key.

- ▶ **Content controls.** Some templates include widgets, like text boxes and drop-down menus, that let you create electronic forms in Word, just like the forms you fill out on Web sites.

- ▶ **Macros.** Templates that include a lot of automatic features probably use macros—mini-programs that run inside Word documents—to create their magic. Macros let you run several commands with the click of a button or a keyboard shortcut.

## Starting a Document from a Template

The New Document dialog box lets you access the hundreds of Office templates that are available online—many more than Word installs on your computer. If you have a computer with a cable or DSL Internet connection, then using an online template is almost as fast as using an installed one.

Here's how to download a business card template and use it to create your own cards:

1. **Go to Office button → New (or press Alt+F, N).**

   The New Document box opens, offering several ways to create a new document (Figure 5-9). To find a business card template, look to the Templates categories list on the left.

# Templates Behind the Scenes

Every Word document has at least one template attached to it, whether you know it or not. Even when you start a blank document, the Normal template is what provides a basic page layout and serves up your preferred font and Auto-Text entries. The tools and formats in the Normal template are always available to all your documents, so it's called a *global template*.

Document templates are different from global ones. They often provide extensive formatting, boilerplate text, and in some cases macros and other tools to help you get the job done. The settings and tools in document templates are available only to documents that are based on that template. So you won't find AutoText from your invoice template in a document you created using a greeting card template.

2. **In the left panel, under the Microsoft Office Online heading, click "Business cards."**

   Each category contains dozens of templates. When you select "Business cards," you see cards for just about every industry on earth—except English Novelist (Figure 5-11).

3. **Scroll down the middle panel, and then click the "Financial services business cards" template to preview it in the rightmost panel.**

   The preview shows how your document will look. It creates 10 cards per page when you print on a full-sized sheet. You'll find some additional details about the card below the preview panel. Note the file size is 225 KB. Even a 56 Kpbs (slow dial-up Internet access) takes less than a minute to download this template.

   At bottom is a rating showing that this particular design has received four out of five stars, according to votes from 196 people like you. The rating system is a way for you to learn if a certain template has been helpful to others. You can vote on this template, too, as described in Figure 5-12.

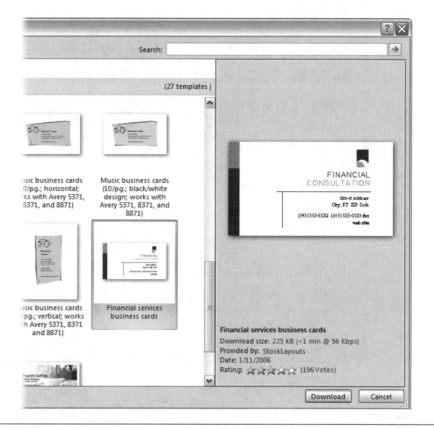

**Figure 5-11.** Use the New Document box to see previews of templates before you download them for use. If you click one of the categories at left, then you see thumbnails and descriptions. Click a thumbnail to see a larger version in the preview window at right. Like what you see? Click the Download button.

4. **In the middle panel, double-click the template to start the download.**

   If all goes well, then you see an alert box telling you that the download is taking place (Figure 5-13). When the download is complete, Word opens a new document based on the template.

   ___ **NOTE** _____

   The Microsoft Genuine Advantage box may rear its head during the download process. When you see this message box, Microsoft is checking whether you have legal and licensed versions of their programs. If you don't, then you won't be able to download the template.

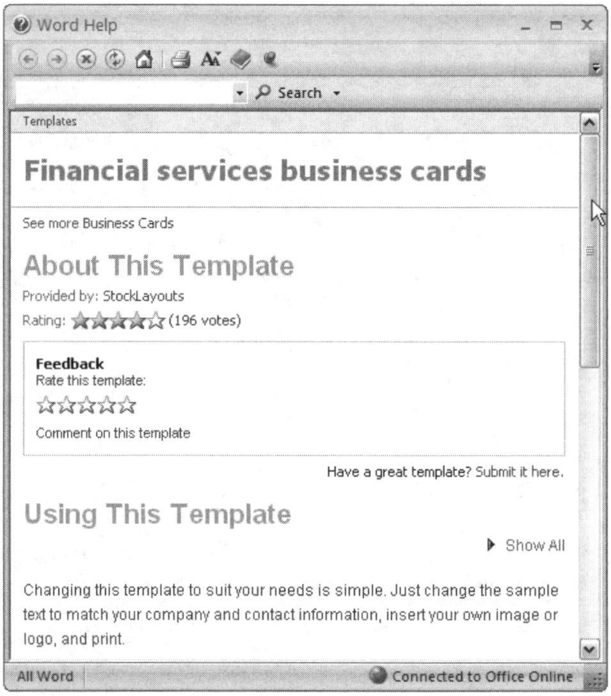

**Figure 5-12.** In the New Document box, select a template, and then click Help to view details about that template in a window like this one. Add your vote to the rating by clicking one of the stars under the Feedback heading.

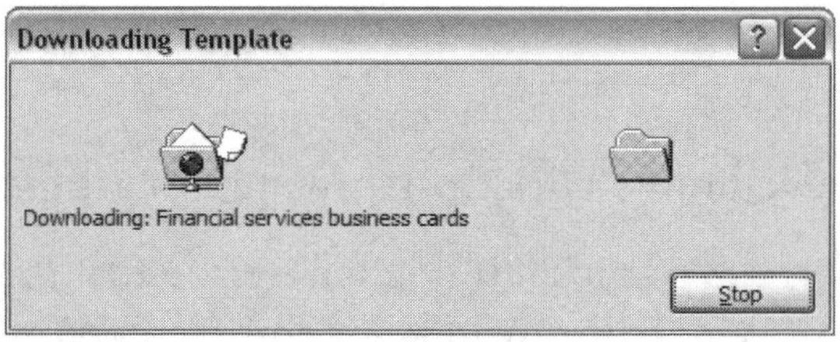

**Figure 5-13.** The download alert box appears when the download begins. If you change your mind, click Stop. Otherwise, the box automatically goes away when the download is complete.

5. **Replace the boilerplate text with your own text.**

As with any template, you need to replace the boilerplate text with your own information. Figure 5-14 compares the newly inserted text next to the original template. In the case of the business cards, you need to copy (Ctrl+C) and paste (Ctrl+V) your text in each of the cards on the page.

6. **Save the file with a new name.**

When you're happy with the changes, save your document in a folder where you can find it later.

7. **Print the document.**

When you're ready, run the presses. You probably don't want to print business cards on regular flimsy paper. Instead, you can find sturdier card stock at an office supply store. Avery, one company that makes labels and other forms, has several products for business cards including some with micro-perforated edges that give you a clean, professional result.

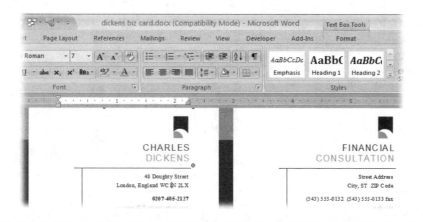

**Figure 5-14.** The card on the right shows the boilerplate text for the Financial Services business card. The card on the left shows the text changed to accommodate a more creative and noble profession.

## Using Installed Templates

Using a template that's already on your computer isn't much different than using one of the templates from Microsoft Office Online (Figure 5-15). After you open the New Document box (Alt+F, N), click Installed Templates at the top of the left panel. The middle panel shows you thumbnails of all templates on your computer. (You won't find as much variety here as you get online.)

You can preview the installed templates just like you did the online counterparts. Click a template thumbnail to preview it in the right panel. Using an installed template works exactly the same as using one from Microsoft Office Online, as described in the previous section, except that you skip the download process. Just double-click the template to open a new document from it, and then get to work as described starting in step 5 on page 177.

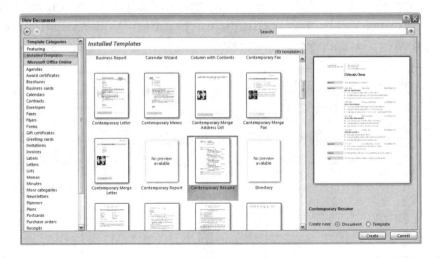

**Figure 5-15.** If you're lucky enough to have a fast Internet connection, then you'll hardly notice whether your templates are online or installed on your computer. The process of selecting, previewing, and using a template is almost exactly the same.

After you've used a template, the next time you start a new document, you'll see the template's name in the Recently Used Templates list (Figure 5-16). The templates that you use most frequently end up as permanent members of this list—how's that for handy?

Search: [_____] →

Recently Used Templates

New from existing...

Oriel Resume
Equity Fax
Business Fax
A Tale of Two Cities - Chapter 1
Meeting Minutes.dotx
tale of two cities
_CRA Agenda.dot

Business card for small business

**Figure 5-16.** Templates that you used recently appear on the right side of the New Document dialog box. To create a new document using a template, just double-click the name, or select it, and then click Create in the lower-right corner (not shown).

# SPELLING, GRAMMAR, AND REFERENCE TOOLS

▶ **Turning on Spelling and Grammar Checking**

▶ **Checking Spelling**

▶ **Checking Grammar and Style**

▶ **Controlling AutoCorrect**

▶ **Exploring Word's Research Tools**

▶ **Accessing Word's Thesaurus**

▶ **Translating Text**

▶ **Checking Your Word Count**

WHEN YOU'VE WORKED FOR HOURS on a resumé or a report, the last thing you want to do is send it out with goofs. Word's spelling and grammar tools help you avoid that kind of embarrassment. In this chapter, you'll learn how to use these tools. You'll also get a clear understanding of when and how Word makes automatic changes to your text. Even more important, you'll learn how to set up these tools to work the way you like to work.

If you really want to sound smart, Word can help you with some extra research, giving you access to a comprehensive Web-based reference library, including dictionary, encyclopedia, thesaurus, Web search, and language translation tools (Figure 6-1).

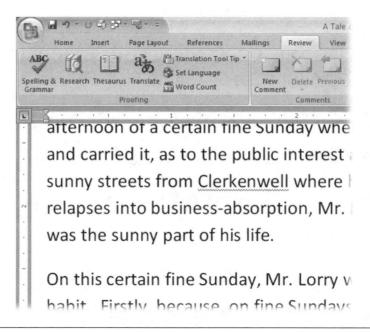

**Figure 6-1.** Access to Word's Spelling and Grammar checker is on the Review → Proofing group, along with the thesaurus, the translation tool, and a slew of Web-based research tools.

# Turning on Spelling and Grammar Checking

Spelling errors make any document look unprofessional, so ignoring Word's spell checker is just plain silly. And while grammar and style are largely subjective, the grammar-checking tool can help you spot glaring errors (like mixing up "it's" and "its"). When Microsoft first added these tools to Word, some people resented the intrusion, as discussed in the box on page 187. The fact is, you're in control. You can choose whether you want Word to check your work as you type, flagging misspelled words and questionable grammar (Figure 6-2), or whether you prefer to get the words on the page first, and then review the spelling and grammar at the end.

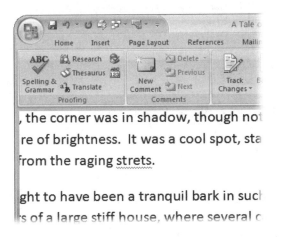

**Figure 6-2.** When you use the "Check spelling as you type" option, Word places wavy red lines under possibly misspelled words. Some people consider this a distraction from their writing and choose to do a manual spell check when they've finished writing.

Follow these steps to set up Word's spelling and grammar-checking tools to work the way you like to work:

1.  **Click the Office button (Alt+F) and in the lower-right corner of the menu, click Word Options.**

    The list on the left gives you several buttons that divide the Options into different groups. The options for the spelling and grammar tools are in Proofing.

2. **Click the Proofing category (Figure 6-3).**

The panel on the right changes to show checkboxes and buttons grouped into four categories: "AutoCorrect options," "When correcting spelling in Office programs," "When correcting spelling in Word," "When correcting grammar in Word," and "Exceptions for."

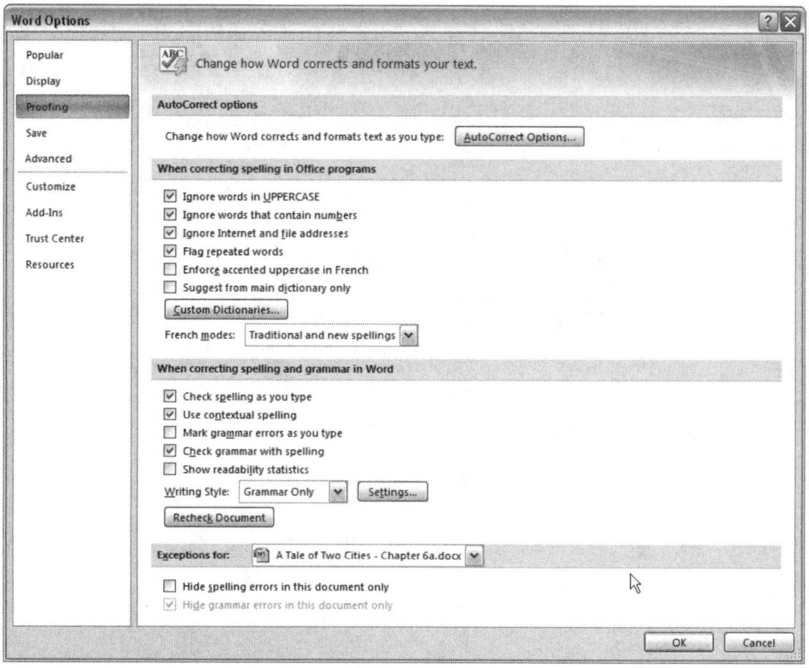

**Figure 6-3.** Not only can you choose whether Word checks your spelling and grammar as you type, but Word also gives you a bunch of ways to fine-tune the program's level of persnicketyness. (By the way, this chapter was originally written in Word, and that last word was flagged with a red underline.)

3. **Turn on the options in "When correcting spelling for Office programs" for the types of errors you want Word *not* to worry about.**

For example, Internet addresses and filenames often set off the spell checker, resulting in a distracting sea of red waves. You can also tell Word to ignore words in uppercase and words that include numbers, which are often company names or special terms that Word doesn't know how to spell. Use the checkboxes to have the spell checker ignore these types of words.

_ TIP _____

> You can "teach" Word how to spell these unfamiliar words and include
> them in spell checks by adding them to Word's spelling dictionary
> (page 188).

4. **Word starts out with background spell checking turned on; if it annoys you, turn off the "Check spelling as you type" checkbox.**

   This unassuming checkbox is the most important option. Turning it on turns on the wavy red lines under misspelled words.

   Sometimes the word you type is spelled correctly, but it's the wrong word in the context. For example, "I'll see you in too weeks" is a contextual error. Word checks for this type of mistake if you turn on the "Use contextual spelling" checkbox.

5. **If you're interested in some grammar help from Word, turn on the "Check grammar with spelling" checkbox.**

   This setting makes Word flag questionable construction as you work, with a wavy *green* underline. Or you can leave it turned off and check grammar when you're through writing, as described on page 194.

   If you don't want Word checking your grammar at all, turn off the "Check grammar with spelling" checkbox.

_ TIP _____

> To fine-tune your grammar options, click the Settings button to open
> the Grammar Settings box (Figure 6-4). In this box, you can control
> whether the grammar checker flags capitalization, run on sentences,
> and so on.

6. **Click OK to close the Word Options box.**

   Your new spelling and grammar settings go into effect.

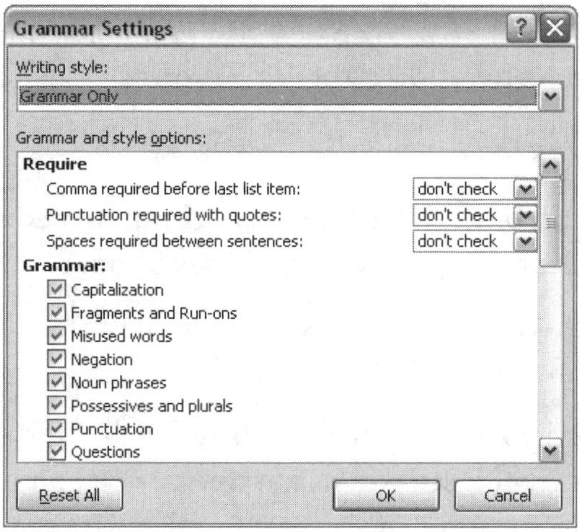

**Figure 6-4.** You encounter even more debate and personal opinion when it comes to setting rules about grammar and style. Word gives you more options for controlling the program's tendency to flag your immortal prose.

# Checking Spelling

Word's spell checker reads every word in your document and looks it up in its behind-the-scenes dictionary file. If the word isn't in the dictionary, the spell checker flags it as a possibly misspelled word. Spell checker handles misspelled words in three ways:

▶ **AutoCorrect.** The spell checker looks to see if the word is in its list of words to correct automatically. Words like "hte" for "the" or "shwo" for "show," for example, are in the AutoCorrect list. (You can add and remove words from the Auto-Correct list, and if you prefer, you can turn off AutoCorrect entirely. To see how, flip ahead to the next page.)

▶ **Check spelling as you type.** If you've set up Word to check spelling errors as you type, the spell checker puts a wavy red line under the word in question (Figure 6-2).

▶ **Check spelling manually.** Check spelling in one pass. The spell checker asks you about each questionable word when you run a manual spell check.

# The Wavy Line Debate

When Microsoft first introduced background spell checking and the wavy red line, it was roundly pooh-poohed by a large portion of the Word-using population. Some people didn't like the distraction of the red snakes popping up all over. These lines interfered with their concentration on their work. Other people noticed that background spell checking slowed down already slow computers. And, of course there were the folks who considered it unnecessary. "I always check my spelling when I'm *finished* writing." Microsoft continued to ship Word with background spell checking turned on. After all, people who didn't like it had the option to turn it off.

Over the years, the wavy lines have won some converts. Folks who once found background spell checking distracting began to leave it on as they upgraded Word.

Those people who were new to Word probably didn't know they could turn it off. Computers continued to increase in horsepower, so speed was no longer a big issue. If your computer can edit video, it probably won't be stressed by handling spell checking in the background, even for a very long document. The Automatic spell checking isn't going away and the solution is the same as always. Pick your path to pristine prose and set up Word accordingly.

By the way, if you *don't* want Word to check spelling in the background, you can make it stop. Open Word Options (Alt+F, I), and then click the Proofing option on the left. The third group of options is named "When correcting spelling and grammar in Word." Turn off the "Check spelling as you type" checkbox, and you've turned off background spell checking.

## Checking Spelling as You Type

Unless you've turned this option off, as described in the previous steps, Word checks the spelling of each word you type, comparing it to its spelling dictionary. When a word is not in the dictionary, the spell checker brings it to your attention—not with a whack across the knuckles with a ruler, but with a wavy red underline (Figure 6-2).

To correct a word flagged with a wavy red line, right-click it. A shortcut menu shows suggested spellings for the word you flubbed (Figure 6-5). To choose a word from the list, just click it, and the correctly spelled word replaces the misspelled word.

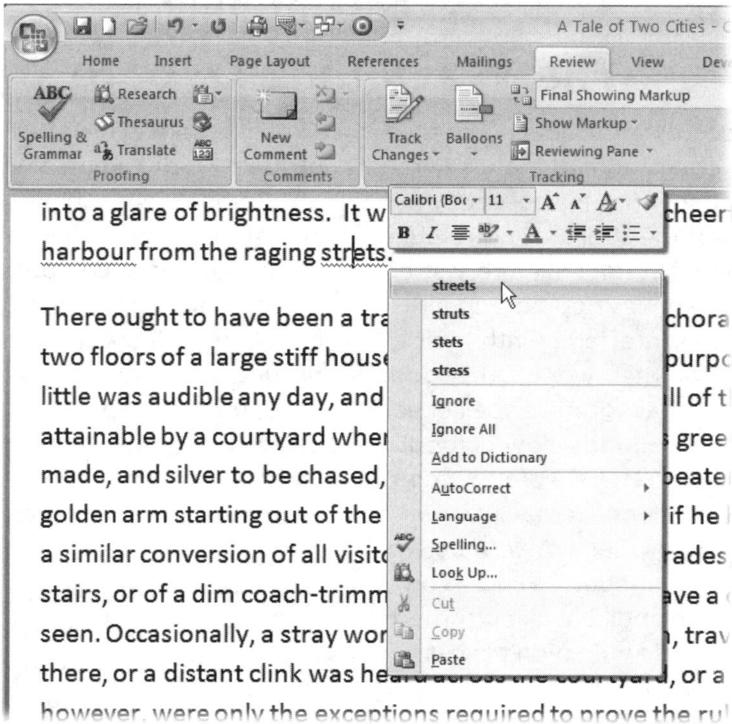

**Figure 6-5.** Right-click words flagged with the wavy red line, and you see a pop-up menu suggesting a few correctly spelled possibilities. You have some other options, including adding the word to your spelling dictionary so it won't be flagged again.

Sometimes the spell checker flags a word, but you want to keep it in your document just the way it is (and make Word stop underlining it, for heaven's sake). For these words, the shortcut menu gives you three courses of action (Figure 6-6):

▶ **Ignore.** Click Ignore, and the spell checker ignores this instance of the word (in this document only) and removes the underline.

▶ **Ignore All.** When you choose this option, the spell checker doesn't flag any occurrence of the word in this document. No more wavy red lines for that baby.

▶ **Add to Dictionary.** When you add a word to the dictionary, you'll never see a wavy line under the word again, in this document or any other. Word adds the word to a file named CUSTOM.DIC. Over time, your custom dictionary collects all the special words that you don't want flagged in a spell check.

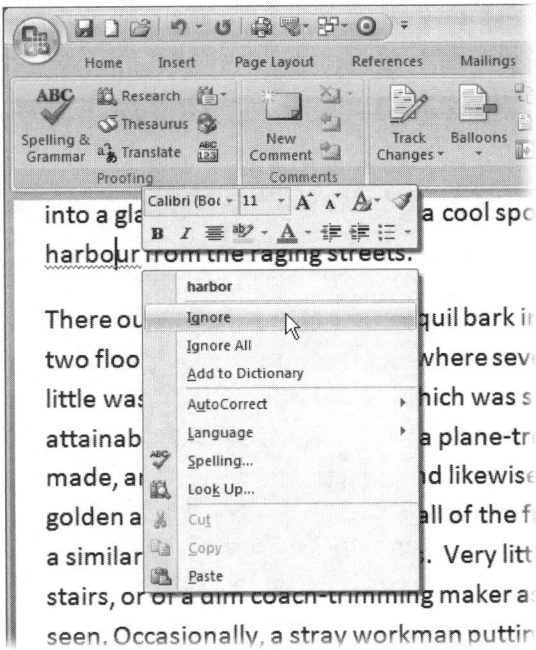

**Figure 6-6.** In addition to a spelling suggestion, Word gives you three other options. You can ignore the word just this once, you can ignore all occurrences of the word in the document, or you can add the word to your dictionary, so that Word won't flag it as misspelled in any document.

## Checking Spelling Manually

When you opt for manual spelling and grammar checking, you can do these tasks in one pass, at your leisure, like after you've finished writing. To start a spelling and grammar check, choose Review → Proofing → Spelling and Grammar or press Alt+R, S. (F7, that old favorite spelling key, still works too.) You see a dialog box like the one in Figure 6-7.

Often, you're checking the spelling and the grammar at the same time, so in the upper-left corner, the Spelling and Grammar box tells you about the problem. In the case of a misspelled word, you see "Not in Dictionary" over a text box that shows the entire sentence with the word highlighted. The box below offers suggestions. On the right side of the dialog box, you see several buttons. Use one of the top three buttons—Ignore Once, Ignore All, and Add to Dictionary—when you want to keep the word spelled as it is. These options do the same thing as the shortcut menu options described earlier.

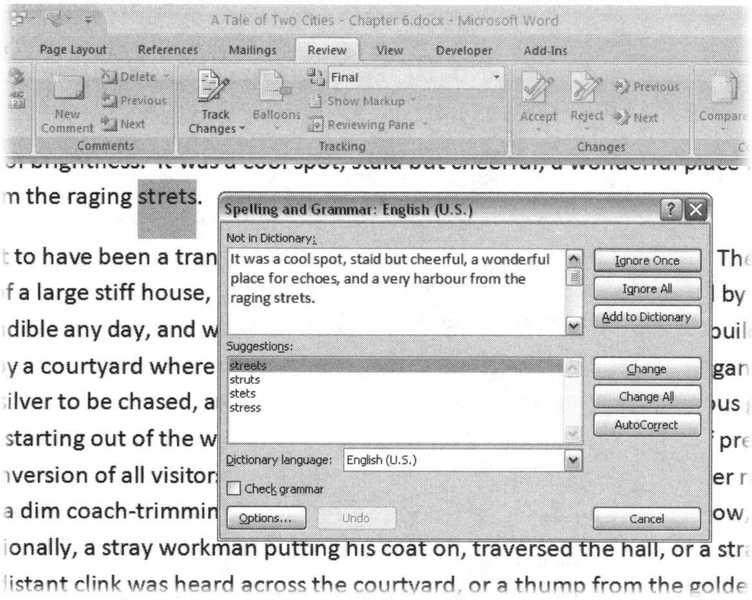

**Figure 6-7.** When you use the manual spell checker, you work in this dialog box. The top text box shows you your word in context. The bottom text box offers suggested spellings.

The bottom three buttons let you make changes to the misspelled words. When you select a word from the Suggestions list, and then click Change, Word replaces the highlighted word with the suggestion. When you click Change All, Word looks through your whole document, and corrects any other occurrences of the misspelled words at the same time. Clicking the AutoCorrect button tells Word to make the correction automatically, as you type, every time you misspell the word.

## Managing Custom Dictionaries

Word has a standard spelling dictionary, which is just one huge list of common words in their correct spellings. When you tell Word to add a word to the dictionary, it doesn't actually add the word to its standard dictionary. It adds it to a new file that's all yours. This file, CUSTOM.DIC, contains your personal preferred spellings. Over time, your CUSTOM.DIC file collects the oddly spelled names of your friends and family, slang terms you frequently use, and a host of other words.

__ TIP _____

You can transfer your custom dictionary to another computer by
simply copying your CUSTOM.DIC file to the new machine. (Your
CUSTOM.DIC file lives in a folder named *C:\Documents and
Settings\**User Name**\Microsoft\Application Data\Proof.*)

### Removing a word from your custom dictionary

Oops! You've added a misspelled word to your custom dictionary. Now Word won't
ever flag "dosn't" again. All is not lost. You can edit your custom dictionary right
within Word. Here are the steps:

1. **Go to Office button → Word Options (Alt+F, I). In the list on the left, click
   Proofing.**

   Access to the custom dictionary is with the Spelling and Grammar tools.

2. **Roughly in the middle of the window, among the Spelling settings, click the
   Custom Dictionaries button.**

   The Custom Dictionaries box opens (Figure 6-8).

3. **In the list on the left, choose CUSTOM.DIC.**

   When you add words to your dictionary while checking spelling, Word stores
   them in the CUSTOM.DIC file. If you've created any additional custom dictionaries, you'll see them in this list too.

4. **Click Edit Word List to open the dictionary.**

   Yet another dialog box opens with CUSTOM.DIC in the title bar (Figure 6-9).
   Your custom words are in the list labeled Dictionary.

5. **Select the misspelled word, and then click Delete.**

   The list is alphabetized, so you can use the scroll bars on the right to find your
   misspelled word. As a shortcut, you can click the first word in the list, and then
   type the first letter of the word you want. Say you're looking for "dosn't"; press
   D, and the list jumps to words starting with D.

   Once you find the word, click it, and then click Delete at bottom.

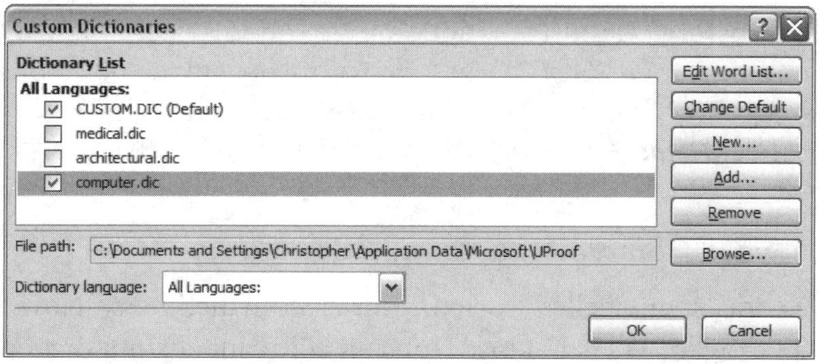

**Figure 6-8.** Use the Custom Dictionaries box to manage your personal dictionary and add professional dictionaries to Word. Here's where you choose the dictionaries in use, add new dictionaries, and open your custom dictionaries for editing.

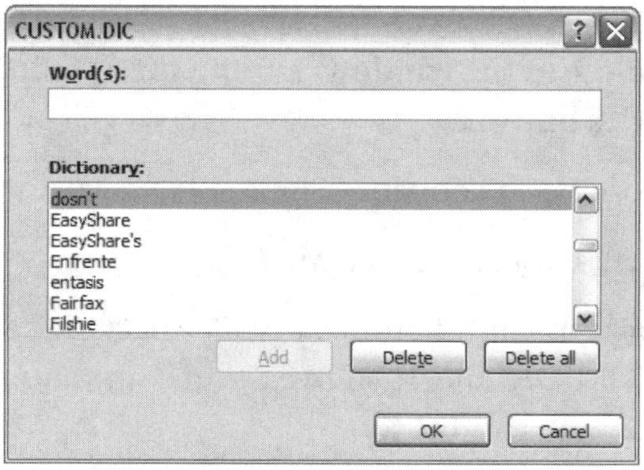

**Figure 6-9.** You can add and delete words from your custom dictionary CUSTOM.DIC. To add a word, type it in the box at the top, and then click Add. Remove words from the list by selecting the word in the Dictionary button, and then clicking Delete. Be careful with that Delete All button—it really does delete all the words in your custom dictionary.

6. **Close the windows by clicking OK.**

You've opened three dialog boxes to get to edit your dictionary. Clean things up by clicking OK in each. Now the non-word "dosn't" officially earns a wavy line.

## Adding professional dictionaries to Word

It seems that every profession, business, and industry has its own language, and often that means it has its own custom dictionary for Word too. You can find all sorts of custom dictionaries, either free or for a price. Search the Web, and you'll find dictionaries for everything from architecture to zoology. And if it's not out there, you can always create your own. Google is a good place to start the search. Just type "Microsoft Word" .dic dictionaries in the search box and see what pops up. If you want to zero in on a specific business like construction or computers, then add that word to your search.

Once you find a dictionary and download or copy it to your computer, you can add it to Word's dictionary list. Here are the steps:

1.  **Open the Custom Dictionaries box (Figure 6-8), as described in steps 1–2 on page 191.**

2.  **Click the Add button on the right to open one of Windows' standard file boxes.**

    A box labeled Add Custom Dictionary appears. You see the standard tools for navigating through your computer folders and hunting down files. Use the tools on the left and the drop-down menu on top to navigate to the folder containing your new dictionary.

3.  **Double-click your dictionary file, or select it, and then, at the bottom of the window, click Open.**

    The Add Custom Dictionary box closes, and you're back at the Custom Dictionaries box. Your new dictionary is listed along with CUSTOM.DIC and all the rest.

4.  **If you plan on using the dictionary right away, make sure there's a checkmark in the box next to its name.**

    Using the checkboxes, you can choose which dictionaries Word uses for its spell check. To minimize misspellings, use only the dictionaries relevant to your current document. A slip of the typing fingers could end up matching a medical term. Also, for each dictionary you add, it can take Word a little longer to check spelling, though you probably won't notice the difference.

# Checking Grammar and Style

Word's grammar and style tools work almost exactly like the spelling tools. You have the same choice between background checking and manual checking. If you check grammar and style in the background while you type, word puts a wavy green line under suspect sentences and phrases. If you check grammar manually, you view problem sentences in the Spelling and Grammar dialog box (Figure 6-10).

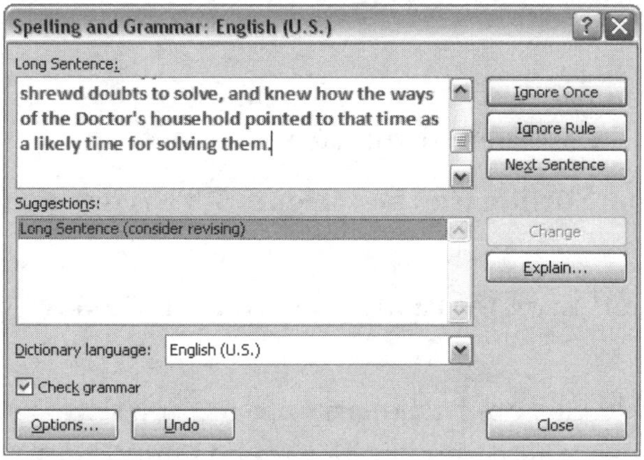

**Figure 6-10.** In the Spelling and Grammar dialog box, text in the upper-left corner describes the error, and suggestions appear at bottom. For a more detailed description of the problem, click Explain.

You may feel that Word's grammar police are a little too strict for your personal style of writing. If that's the case, you can tinker with the settings (Office button → Word Options → Proofing). Here are some of the options you toggle on or off in the Grammar Settings box (Figure 6-4):

▶ **Capitalization.** Finds words that should be capitalized, (like *madame* DeFarge).

▶ **Fragments and run-ons.** Checks for complete sentences and flags overly long meandering sentences that seem to just go on and on and you can't wait for them to stop but they never do.

▶ **Misused words.** Looks for the incorrect use of adjectives and adverbs.

▶ **Negation.** Flags double negatives.

- **Noun phrases.** Checks for proper usage of "a" and "an" and finds phrases where the number doesn't agree with the noun. For example, it wouldn't like "A Tale of Two City."

- **Possessives and plurals.** Leave this option checked if you have a problem forgetting apostrophes in phrases like "the ships hold."

- **Punctuation.** Checks your usage of quotation marks, commas, colons, and all those other little marks.

- **Questions.** Checks for question marks, and flags questions with non-standard structure.

- **Relative clauses.** Finds errors in relative clauses, such as the use of "which" instead of "who" in a clause referring to people.

- **Subject-verb agreement.** Flags sentences where the verbs don't match the nouns, as in "All of the nobles has gone to the guillotine."

- **Verb phrases.** Finds errors in verb usages such as incorrect tense.

Style checking is even more subjective than grammar checking. If you feel there ain't no reason Microsoft should meddle when you say you're real mad at the congressman, you can turn this feature off.

You can tweak the Style checking settings in the Word Options dialog box (Office button → Word Options → Proofing). For example, the "When correcting spelling and grammar in Word" section has a Writing Style drop-down menu with two options: Grammar & Style or Grammar Only. If you choose Grammar & Style, Word hunts down problems such as clichés, passive sentences, and run-on sentences. It's always your choice though; turn on the suggestions that you find helpful and that match your own personal style.

# Controlling AutoCorrect

The AutoCorrect feature packs more punch than you may expect, and it works across several of the Office programs, including Word, Publisher, and Outlook. With AutoCorrect, if you accidentally type *hte,* Word changes it to "the." The program doesn't ask you for permission (it comes with AutoCorrect turned on). You may not even notice when Word makes the change. Obviously, AutoCorrect is not a feature for control freaks. On the other hand, there's some surprising power in the concept. Have you ever tried to figure out how to type the © symbol? If you have AutoCorrect on, and you type (c), it magically turns into the copyright symbol. That's just the beginning. AutoCorrect lets you enter a lot of other symbols right from the keyboard, from math symbols to arrows to smiley faces. And just imagine, if you work for the *American Gastroenterological Association*, wouldn't it be great to type in *aga* and let AutoCorrect type in all those words, especially that middle one?

## How AutoCorrect Works

AutoCorrect changes words immediately after you type them, so you see the change when it happens right behind your insertion point. If you don't like what AutoCorrect did, press Ctrl+Z to undo it. The text goes back to the characters you typed, and AutoCorrect won't mess with it again.

## Fine-tuning AutoCorrect Options

Given that AutoCorrect's reason for being is to change the words that you write, it's important to know how to bring it under control. To adjust AutoCorrect settings, open the AutoCorrect dialog box (Office button → Word Options → Proofing → AutoCorrect Options). You can also jump to the AutoCorrect dialog box from any word in your text with a wavy red spelling line. Right-click the word, and then choose AutoCorrect → AutoCorrect Options from the shortcut menu. The Auto-Correct dialog box gives you access to a lot of settings, so it may take a few moments to sort out how all the options work. At the very top, the "Show AutoCorrect Options buttons" checkbox controls whether or not the little lightning-bolt menu buttons (Figure 6-11) show up in your text.

The checkboxes at the top of the AutoCorrect dialog box all deal with common typos and finger flubs (Figure 6-12).

___ TIP _____

> As shown in this example, you can use the AutoCorrect feature as if it were AutoText. The difference is AutoCorrect automatically turns *aga* into American Gastroenterological Association. When you use Auto-Text, you need to press the F3 key after you type *aga*. So, it's your choice: AutoCorrect for fewer keystrokes, or AutoText for manual control.

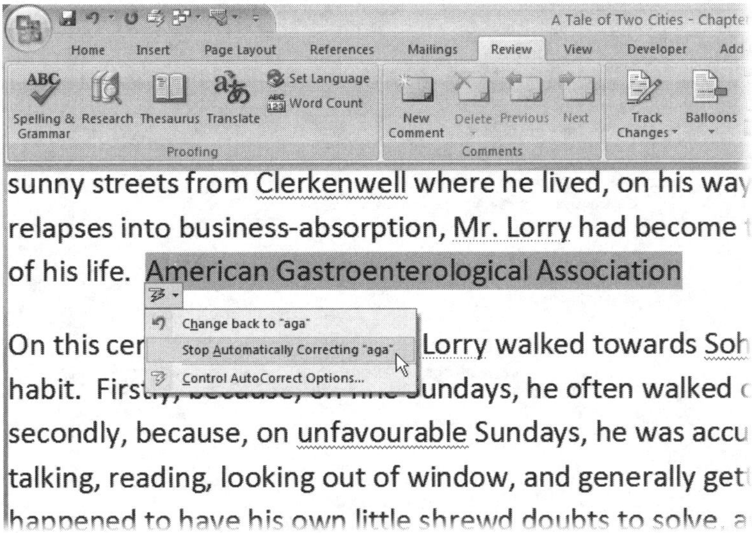

**Figure 6-11.** If you see a hollow blue line under a character or you see a lightning bolt, AutoCorrect is at work. When you move your mouse cursor to the spot, you see a shortcut menu like this providing AutoCorrect options. Using this shortcut menu is the fastest way to make AutoCorrect stop autocorrecting something you don't want it to!

The most important checkbox is smack in the middle of the box: "Replace text as you type." When this box is turned on, AutoCorrect corrects spelling errors and makes other replacements as you type. The list box below shows the text that Auto-Correct looks for (on the left) and the text that it uses as a replacement (on the right). Use the scroll bar to browse through the whole list. If you turn on the checkbox at the bottom, AutoCorrect also automatically corrects misspelled words using the same dictionary as for spell checks. No wavy underline. Just fixed spelling.

In addition to controlling how AutoCorrect works, you even get to decide what errors it corrects—by editing the Replace and With lists in this dialog box. Here's how to add your own entry to the list of replacements AutoCorrect makes:

1. **Choose Office button → Word Options → Proofing. At the top of the Proofing panel, click the AutoCorrect Options button.**

   The AutoCorrect dialog box opens.

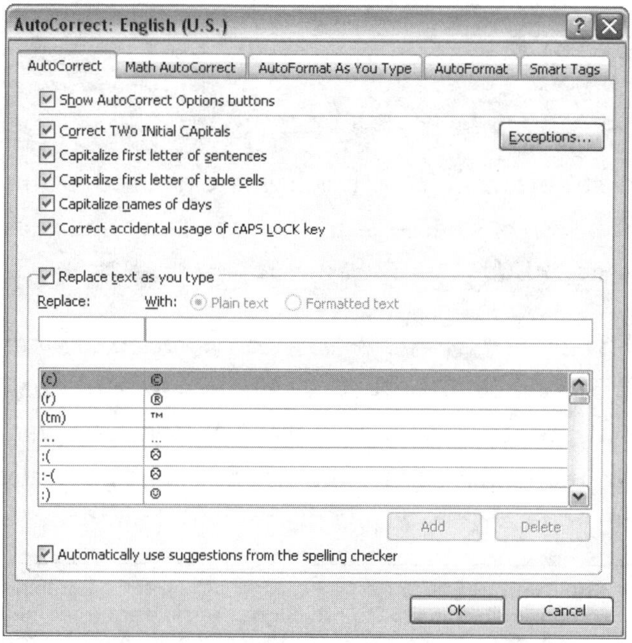

**Figure 6-12.** AutoCorrect likes to mess with your words as you type them. Fortunately, you can rein it in using this box. Use the checkboxes at the top to turn on (or off) AutoCorrect's fixes for some common typos. The box at bottom lists the changes AutoCorrect makes. By adding your own replacement pairs to this list, you can even use AutoCorrect as if it were AutoText.

2. **Make sure the "Replace text as you type" checkbox is turned on.**

   This checkbox is AutoCorrect's master on/off switch.

3. **In the Replace text box, type *aga*, and then press Tab. In the With box, type *American Gastroenterological Association*, and then click Add.**

   You've just told Word to be on the lookout for the sequence of letters "aga," and to replace it with "American Gastroenterological Association."

4. **Click OK to close the AutoCorrect box, and then click OK to close Word Options.**

If AutoCorrect is making replacements you don't like, you can fix this by deleting pairs from this list. Suppose every time you type *are*, Auto-Correct tries to replace it with "Association of Restaurant Entrepreneurs." To remove this annoyance, select the pair "are" and "Association of Restaurant Entrepreneurs," and then click Delete. If you choose "Stop Automatically Correcting" from the AutoCorrect Options button menu (Figure 6-11), Word deletes that entry from the list.

## Autocorrecting Math, Formatting, and Smart Tags

AutoCorrect is more than a spelling correction tool. A better term may be *AutoReplace*, since it can apply automatic formatting fixes to mathematical symbols and special text characters like quotation marks and dashes. The AutoCorrect feature also governs Smart Tags—those little "i" buttons that pop up and save you time by performing actions that you'd normally have to open other programs to do. (See the box on page 200 for more detail on Smart Tags.)

As on the AutoCorrect tab, the Math AutoCorrect, AutoFormat, and Smart Tag tabs let you turn certain kinds of fixes on or off. The Math tab also has Replace and With lists that let you type fancy math symbols by hitting a few letters on the keyboard.

▶ **Math.** Go to Office button → Word Options → Proofing → AutoCorrect Options and click the Math AutoCorrect tab to see how AutoCorrect gives you quick access to math symbols. Sure, you could hunt down some of these symbols with Word's symbol tool (Insert → Symbols → Symbol), but if you use the same math symbols frequently, AutoCorrect provides quicker, easier access. You can customize Math AutoCorrect by typing characters in the Replace and With boxes. It works just like the AutoCorrect tool for words.

▶ **Formatting.** Go to Office button → Word Options → Proofing → AutoCorrect Options, AutoFormat As You Type tab or AutoFormat tab. Have you ever wondered how Word's smart quotes feature works? You enter straight quotes (?), actually the symbol for inches, on both sides of a quote, yet Word automatically provides curly quotes, curled in the proper direction on both ends of the quote. That's AutoCorrect working behind the scenes. AutoCorrect can jump into action when you start making a numbered list or a bulleted list. It can provide a respectable em dash (—), every time you type two hyphens. The AutoFormat options are presented as checkboxes. Just turn on the ones you want to use.

▶ **Smart Tags.** Go to Office button → Word Options → Proofing → AutoCorrect Options, Smart Tags tab. Word's Smart Tags work behind the scenes as you type, looking for connections between your words and other resources. Type a name, and Smart Tags checks to see if that person is in your Outlook address book. If the person is, a dotted purple line appears under the name. Move your mouse over the word, and you see the Smart Tag "i" for information button. Click this button, and you can shoot an email off to your pal. Smart Tags perform a number of other tasks, like converting measurements and adding dates to your calendar. You can adjust the settings in the Smart Tags tab of the AutoCorrect box: Click the "Label text with smart tags" box to turn Smart Tags on, and then use the other checkboxes to choose the type of words you want tagged.

---

**POWER USERS' CLINIC**

## Smart Tags

As you're typing in Word, any number of little helpers pop up from time to time. There's the mini-toolbar, the AutoCorrect Options button, those wavy red lines that the spell checker lays down. And then there are Smart Tags (Figure 6-13). Microsoft's underlying idea is a perfectly good one—to let you share information and features among Office programs with fewer mouse clicks. For example, when you type the name of an Outlook Contact in a Word document, the Smart Tag appears in your document, with a dotted purple line and a little "i" for information button that reveals a shortcut menu when you click it.

You can choose from the menu and send an email, schedule a meeting, or insert an address without the extra steps of launching Outlook and tracking down the contact's name all over again. When you're typing somebody's name, Word figures that you may be thinking of that person and puts a few typical options at your fingertips.

If you're one of those "shut up and let me type" types, you can turn off Smart Tags in the AutoCorrect dialog box. Just click the Smart Tags tab, and then turn off the "Show Smart Tag Actions buttons" checkbox.

---

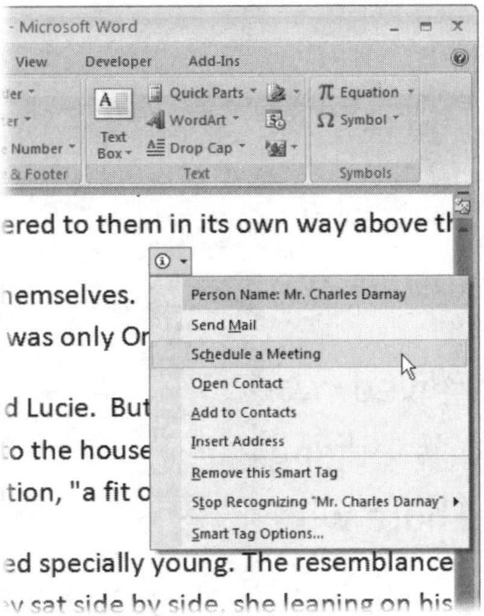

**Figure 6-13.** If you let them, Smart Tags appear in your document as little shortcut menus that link to information in other Microsoft programs. Choose from the menu to perform tasks like sending email or scheduling meetings.

# Exploring Word's Research Tools

Word's Research panel provides links to a library shelf of Internet research tools that you can use from within Word. To open the panel, go to Review → Proofing → Research. The Research task pane opens at the screen's left (Figure 6-14).

Here's a list of the tools tucked away in the Research panel:

▶ **Encarta Dictionary.** Like any dictionary, Microsoft's version provides definitions, parts of speech, and pronunciation.

▶ **Thesaurus.** Provides synonyms and alternate word choices.

▶ **Encarta Encyclopedia.** Finds links to articles in the MSN Encarta Encyclopedia.

> **NOTE**
> Encarta started life as a CD-ROM product before everyone was connected to the Internet. Originally, Microsoft purchased the rights to contents of the Funk and Wagnall's encyclopedia and merged that content with other sources.

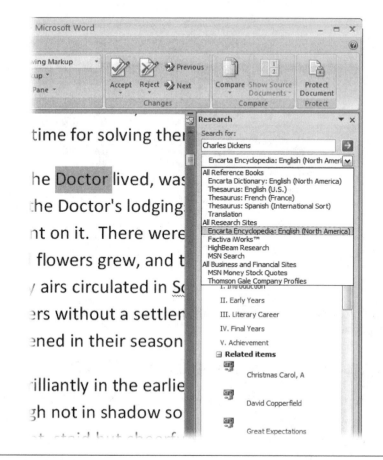

**Figure 6-14.** Use the drop-down menu at the top of the Research task pane to choose references when you're searching for information. Word provides dictionaries, encyclopedias, Internet search tools, and business reference resources.

▶ **Factiva iWorks.** A service of Dow Jones & Reuters, Factiva provides business and news information.

▶ **HighBeam Research.** Finds references in newspapers, magazines, journals, books, photos, maps, encyclopedia articles, dictionaries, thesauruses, and almanacs.

▶ **MSN Search.** Microsoft's Internet search tool.

▶ **MSN Money Stock Quotes.** Microsoft's financial information service.

▶ **Thomson Gale Company Profiles.** Provides business and financial details of companies.

If you're not connected to the Internet, obviously you can't use these online tools. Furthermore, their responsiveness depends on the speed of your connection. Some of the Proofing tools, such as the spell checker, thesaurus, and some of the translation tools, still work even if you're not connected. Encarta, Factiva, and the business research sites don't.

## Finding Information with the Research Task Pane

For the most part, anyone with an Internet connection and a browser can use all of Word's research tools. You use the same panel and the same quick and easy search process whether you're looking for company information in Thomson Gale, researching a topic for a school paper in HighBeam Research, or looking up the pronunciation of a word in the Encarta Dictionary. You don't have to go hunting all over the Web, and then learn how to use the tools on different sites.

Here's how to research a topic:

1. **Go to Review → Proofing → Research (Alt+R, R).**

   The Research task pane opens to the right of your document. If you want, you can click the top bar and drag the Research task pane out of the Word window so that it floats independently like a palette.

2. **At the top of the Research task pane, type your search terms in the "Search for" text box.**

   If your search words appear in your document, there's a shortcut: Select the words in your document, and then choose Review → Proofing → Research. The search words appear automatically in the "Search for" box, and Word immediately begins to search for references using your last selected reference source.

3. **Use the All Reference Books drop-down menu to select your reference source.**

   Say you're looking for information on Bulldog Brewing Company but don't need the dictionary definition of an English canine. Choose Thomson Gale Company Profiles. The search begins as soon as you make a selection.

Or, if you leave the menu set to All Reference Books, click the green Start Search button with the arrow. In this case, Word searches in all the reference books and lists the results in the Research pane.

Be patient. This is, after all, an Internet search. Sooner or later you'll see the results in a large text box (Figure 6-15).

4. **If necessary, use a link to follow up in your Web browser.**

Often the results include links to Web sites. If you want to continue your research, click the links, and your browser opens to the Web site, such as MSN Money or HighBeam Research.

# Accessing Word's Thesaurus

A well-thumbed thesaurus sits on many writers' bookshelves, somewhere between Strunk and White's *The Elements of Style* and Bartlett's *Familiar Quotations*. By providing synonyms and antonyms to common words, a thesaurus helps writers find what Flaubert called *le mot juste*—"the perfect word." Word's thesaurus (Figure 6-16) makes it so easy to look up a synonym that your hard-copy thesaurus may start gathering dust.

To use Word's thesaurus, just right-click any word in your document, and then point to Synonyms in the pop-up menu. A submenu appears with appropriate synonyms. If that's not enough for you, at the bottom of the menu, click the Thesaurus option to open the Research task pane, with your word entered in the "Search for" box (Figure 6-16). Click the green arrow to look up the reference.

# Translating Text

Word's research tools include language translation. When you select a word in your text and click the Translate button on the ribbon (Review → Proofing → Translate or Alt+R, L), Word begins to look up the word using the last language selection for the translation (Figure 6-17). (Word speaks Arabic, Chinese, Dutch, English, French, German, Greek, Italian, Japanese, Portuguese, Russian, Spanish, and Swedish.)

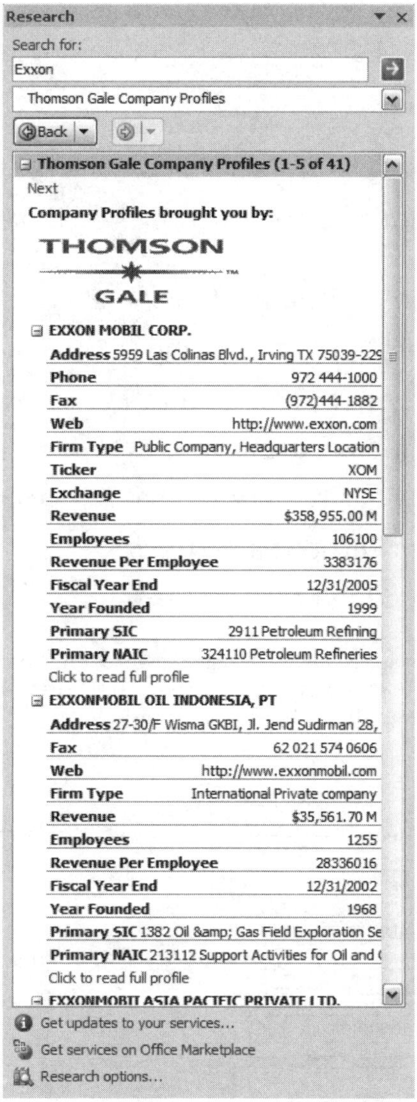

**Figure 6-15.** Use Word's Research task pane to get access to Word's thesaurus, Encarta dictionary, encyclopedia, and translation tools. Clicking the arrow next to the Back button opens a menu where you can return to the results of your last few searches.

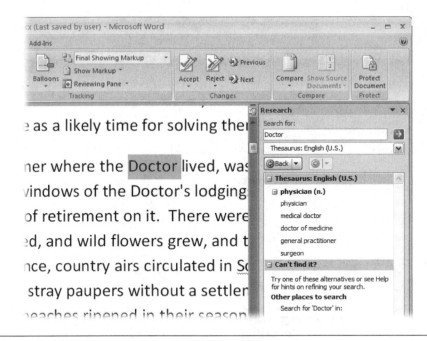

**Figure 6-16.** To use Word's thesaurus, just right-click a word, and then choose synonyms from the shortcut menu. Choose a word from the list, or, if you need more research, at the bottom of the menu, choose Thesaurus to open a thesaurus in the Research task pane.

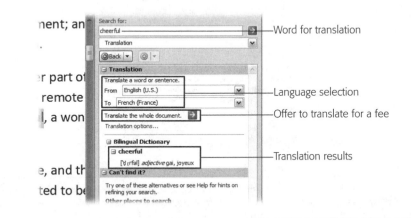

**Figure 6-17.** Translating words and phrases takes place in the Research task pane and, in fact, the process is very similar to the other research tasks.

Accurate translation is more of an art than a science. As a result, computer automation goes only part of the journey. Along with the translation of words and phrases, you get an offer to professionally translate your entire document for a fee (Figure 6-18). (Or, you can ask a friend who speaks the language for help.)

**Figure 6-18.** When you ask Word to translate for you, you get a computer translation and a commercial offer to have a pro do the job. In this case, Lingo offered to translate a 4,500-word chapter of *A Tale of Two Cities* for just over $1,000.

## Translation ScreenTips

Translation screen tips are another pop-up helper you can turn on. Go to Review → Proofing → Translation ScreenTip, and choose a language from the drop-down menu. Screen tips are available in English, French, Spanish, and other languages. Once you choose your language, all you have to do to see a translation and definitions for the word is to pause your mouse cursor over the word for a couple of seconds (Figure 6-19). The multilanguage details are surprisingly complete.

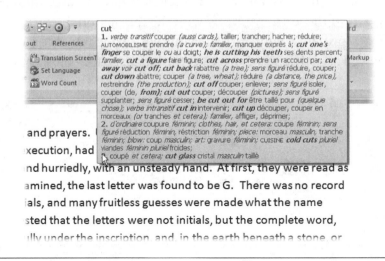

and prayers. [...]
[...]xecution, had [...]
[...]nd hurriedly, with an unsteady hand. At first, they were read as [...]
[...]amined, the last letter was found to be G. There was no record [...]
[...]ials, and many fruitless guesses were made what the name [...]
[...]sted that the letters were not initials, but the complete word, [...]
[...]lly under the inscription, and, in the earth beneath a stone, or [...]

**Figure 6-19.** Word's translation screen tips are great if you're in the process of learning a language or you're working in a language that isn't your first. Pause your cursor over a word, and you see a complete dictionary entry in two languages. Entries include parts of speech and idiomatic phrases.

# Checking Your Word Count

It's often necessary to count your document's words, lines, paragraphs, and pages. Word keeps a running tab of pages and words in the status bar at the document window's lower-right corner (Figure 6-20). To see more details, double-click the status bar to bring up the Word Count box. Addressing gripes from earlier versions of Word, Microsoft has added checkboxes that let you include or exclude text boxes, footnotes, and endnotes from the count.

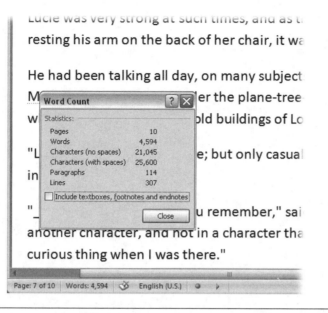

Lucie was very strong at such times, and as resting his arm on the back of her chair, it wa

He had been talking all day, on many subject

M̶ er the plane-tree
w̶ ld buildings of Lo

**Word Count**  [?][X]

Statistics:

| | |
|---|---|
| Pages | 10 |
| Words | 4,594 |
| Characters (no spaces) | 21,045 |
| Characters (with spaces) | 25,600 |
| Paragraphs | 114 |
| Lines | 307 |

[ ] Include textboxes, footnotes and endnotes

[ Close ]

"L̶ e; but only casua

in̶

"̶ u remember," sai

another character, and not in a character tha

curious thing when I was there."

Page: 7 of 10 | Words: 4,594 | English (U.S.)

**Figure 6-20.** Word keeps track of stats such as pages and word count in the lower-left corner of the window. Double-click this area, or go to Review → Proofing → Word Count to open the Word Count dialog box where you see stats on characters, lines, and paragraphs.

# PRINTING WORD DOCUMENTS

7

- ▶ Quick and Easy Printing
- ▶ Print Preview
- ▶ Choosing a Printer
- ▶ Printing to an Adobe PDF File
- ▶ Faxing with Word
- ▶ Changing Print Settings
- ▶ Printing Envelopes
- ▶ Printing Labels
- ▶ Setting Print Options

AT SOME POINT IN THEIR LIVES, most Word documents are headed for the printer. Even when you email a document or create an Adobe Acrobat (PDF) file, your recipient may want to print it. In fact, some people like to proofread a hard copy before sending off any document, believing they're more likely to catch mistakes that way.

Word puts a lot of printing power at your fingertips. This chapter shows you how to do things that would make Gutenberg drop his type, starting with the quickest and easiest ways to print your entire document. You'll learn how to choose and use the best printer for the job (say, your color inkjet for photos), a laser or fax for documents, and a PDF file for good measure. And if you're sending that document via snail mail, then you'll need to print an envelope or a label. Word's got you covered there too.

# Quick and Easy Printing

When you first install Word, the shortest route to the printer is the Quick Print button. With a document open in Word, go to Office button → Print → Quick Print. With a couple clicks your complete document begins to spew forth from your printer.

___ TIP _____

> To print with even fewer clicks, add the Quick Print button to the Quick Access toolbar, as described in Figure 7-1.

_____

The Quick Print process does have its limitations; it prints one copy of the entire document, single sided, every time. If you want to print just a few pages, print multiple or collated copies, or print on both sides of the paper, you must take a couple extra steps. Perhaps the biggest limitation of one-click printing is that your printer must be set up properly. It needs to be turned on, it needs to have paper, and it needs to be connected to your computer and set to run. Otherwise, the Quick Print button does nothing except give you an error message once it's given up.

You can use another quick and easy printing shortcut—printing a document directly from Windows Explorer. Select a file in Explorer, and then choose File → Print from Explorer's menu (Figure 7-2). Yet another Explorer option is to right-

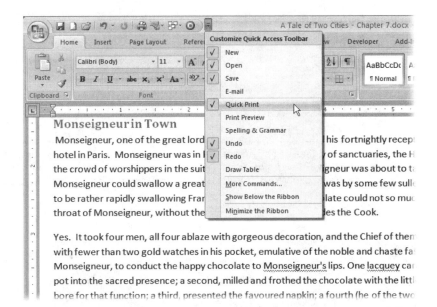

**Figure 7-1.** You can customize the Quick Access toolbar to hold any command button. For the convenience of one-click printing, add the Quick Print button. On the right side of the toolbar, click the Customize Quick Access toolbar button, and then turn on the Quick Print option.

click the file, and then choose Print from the shortcut menu. Windows opens the file in Word (launching Word first, if necessary), and Word then prints the document. (If Word wasn't already running when you gave the Print command, then it closes down when printing's done. If Word was already running, just the document closes.) Like the one-click print button, you can't specify any particulars when you print from Windows in this way, but it's a quick and easy way to spit out one copy of your document.

# Print Preview

Old movies have that great image of the writer ripping paper out of the typewriter, wadding it up in a ball, and throwing it on the floor. If you're not interested in that much drama (or wasted paper) when you work, then get to know Print Preview. You find Print Preview with a couple of other print commands on the Office menu. To see them, go to Office button → Print (Figure 7-3).

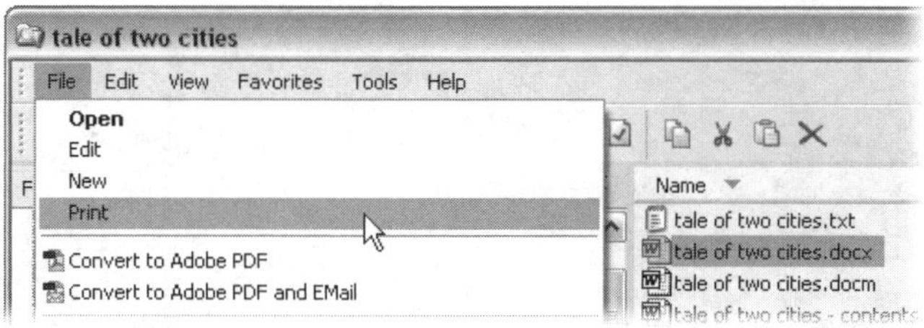

**Figure 7-2.** You can print Word files directly from Windows Explorer by selecting your document in Explorer, and then choosing File → Print. Windows' Print command works for just about any printable document, including those created in Word. Windows finds and runs the program needed to print the file.

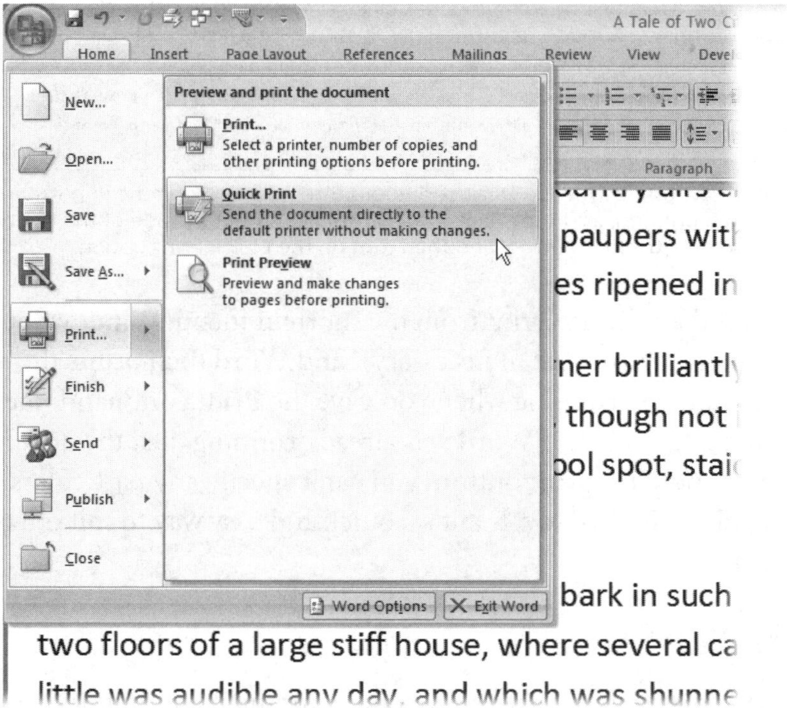

**Figure 7-3.** Go to Office button → Print, and you see three print options: Print, Quick Print, and Print Preview. The Print option opens the Print dialog box (just like pressing Ctrl+P). The Quick Print option does the same thing as clicking the Print button on the Quick Access toolbar: It prints one copy—no muss, no fuss, no options. The Print Preview button shows you how your document will look on the printed page.

When you click Print Preview, your Word window changes quite a bit. You can't edit text in this view; it's just for reviewing your work before you print. Up at the top, a single tab appears on the ribbon: Print Preview. On the left, you find two buttons with printer icons—Print and Options. Some familiar-looking tools occupy the Page Setup group. The launcher in the lower-right corner of that group indicates that, with a click, you can bring up the Page Setup dialog box. The tools in the Zoom and Preview groups help you view the page before you go to press. Click the big magnifying glass, and you bring up the Zoom box. The buttons give you a single-page view and a two-page view, so you can get a feeling for facing page layouts. In the Preview group, you can toggle the page rulers on and off. The Magnifier checkbox appears. It works like a toggle and turns your mouse cursor into a Zoom tool. One click and you zoom in; click again and you zoom out.

In Print Preview, you can use the Next Page and Previous Page buttons to look through your document, but it's just as easy to use the scroll bar on the right side of the window. The most curious and confusing button in the group is the Shrink One Page button. You may think this button performs some kind of Alice in Wonderland trick on one of your pages, but no, it makes an attempt to reduce the overall number of pages in the document. This button performs this magic by slightly reducing the type size and reducing the letter spacing. For example, if you preview your document and find it's 11 pages long, but page 11 has just a few lines at the top, then you can click Shrink One Page, and Word squeezes the material into a nice even 10 pages.

The whole purpose of Print Preview is to show you your document exactly the way it will look on the printed page. Word's Print Layout does a pretty good job of that when you're writing and editing, but Print Preview is more accurate. Headers and footers are positioned precisely, and they're not grayed out. Non-printing characters like tabs and paragraph marks don't show up in Print Preview. And if you're using facing pages, Print Preview gives you a good feel for the end result (Figure 7-4). Print Preview's a great place to check to see if your margins are wide enough and to catch widows and orphans (Chapter 3) and abandoned headers at the bottom of the page (Chapter 4).

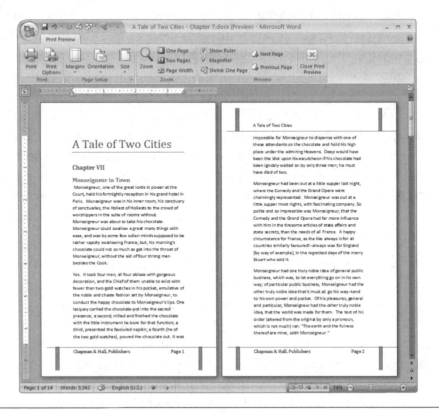

**Figure 7-4.** The Print Preview window shows you how your document will look on paper. Using the Zoom tools, Preview controls, and checkboxes on the Print Preview panel, you can get a good look at your document.

What's more, if you find something wrong, Print Preview puts all the tools you need for a quick fix right there on the ribbon (Figure 7-5). You can resolve a lot of last-minute problems with the Page Setup tools on the ribbon. You can also use the regular Page Setup dialog box; press Alt+P, PS to open it. You can adjust margins, change the page layout, and choose the paper source in your printer.

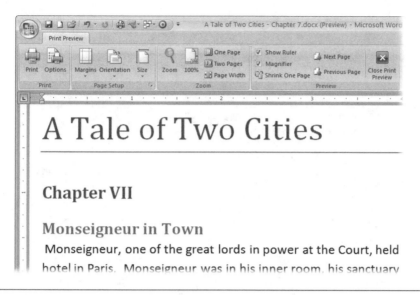

**Figure 7-5.** If you find a problem when you're viewing your document in Print Preview, then you've got the Page Setup tools close at hand.

# Choosing a Printer

These days, it's not unusual to have a couple of printers and printer-type options. For example, you may have a black and white laser printer for quickly and cheaply printing basic text documents. You may also have a color ink-jet printer for printing photos and the occasional color chart or graph. On top of that, perhaps you have a fax modem connected to your computer. (Windows thinks of fax machines as printers. When you think about it, they are sort of long-distance printers.) If you have the full-blown Adobe Acrobat program on your computer, Adobe PDF shows up everywhere you see your computer's printers listed. (Word considers creating PDFs, too, to be a type of printing.)

Having several printer options doesn't confuse Word one bit. You just need to let Word know which printer you want to use. To do that, open the Print dialog box, which in typical Microsoft fashion you can do at least three different ways. The quickest and easiest to remember is to press Ctrl+P. If you like to mouse up to the ribbon, then choose Office button → Print. For good measure, you can also use the new keyboard shortcut Alt+F, P. However you arrive at the Print dialog box, it looks like Figure 7-6.

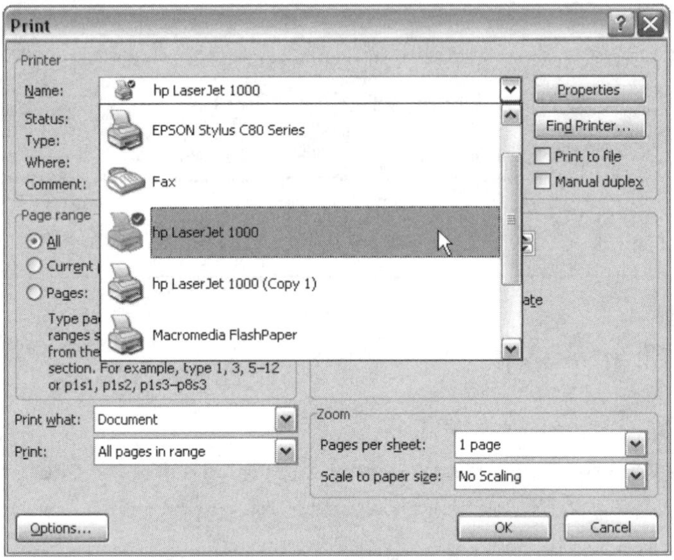

**Figure 7-6.** The Print dialog box has a bunch of buttons and menus that you can use to make your printer do exactly what you want. In the upper-left corner, use the drop-down menu to choose your printer. Details about your printer appear below the menu.

At the top of the Print box you find a group of controls labeled Printer. Use the drop-down menu at the top to choose the printer you want to use for this print job. Under this menu you see some details about your printer—its type and how it's connected to your computer. On the right, you see two buttons. The top Properties button opens a dialog with details specific to your printer. If you're on a network and share printers, the Find Printer button can help you locate a printer.

## Setting Your Default Printer

If you don't specifically choose a printer, Windows always uses one particular printer—known as the *default* printer. You'll see a checkmark next to its printer icon in the list (Figure 7-6).

You can promote any of your printers to this exalted position, but you can't do it within Word. You need to use the Windows system for this job. Here are the steps:

1. **In your screen's lower-left corner, go to Start → Printers and Faxes.**

   Printers and Faxes is in the Start menu's lower-right corner. When you click it, the Start menu goes away, and the Printer and Faxes box opens in a window that looks remarkably like Windows Explorer—because that's exactly what it is (Figure 7-7). You're in a special location in Explorer that's devoted to printers.

2. **In the Printers and Faxes box, right-click the printer you want to use most of the time, and from the shortcut menu, choose Set as Default Printer.**

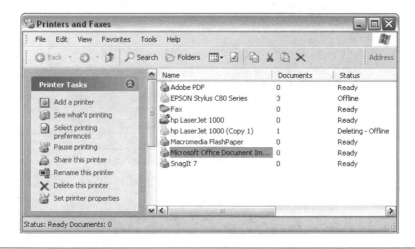

**Figure 7-7.** Your Printers and Faxes dialog box probably looks different from this one, because it lists the printers and devices connected to your own computer. The Task Pane on the left gives you the tools you need to add and remove a printer from your computer.

## Exploring Printer-Specific Properties

Different printers have different talents. Choose from color printers and black-and-white printers, printers that can print on both sides of the paper, printers that can use huge pieces of paper, and even computer thingys that behave like printers but aren't really printers. Adobe Acrobat and fax machines fall into this category. You need some way to get at the controls for these printers and, obviously, the controls are different for each one. You use the Printer Properties boxes to fine-tune the behavior of your printers and printing devices. For example, Figure 7-8 shows the properties for a black and white laser printer. Figure 7-9 shows the Properties box for a color inkjet printer. Figure 7-10 is the Properties box for the professional version of Adobe Acrobat. It's not really a printer at all; it just thinks it is.

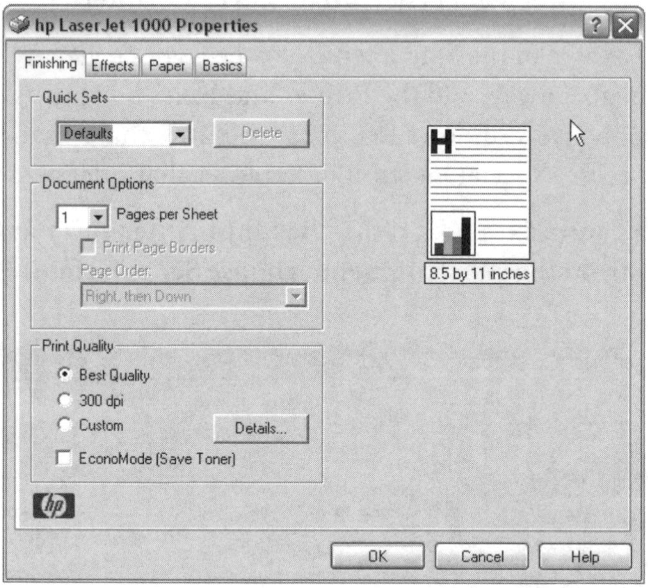

**Figure 7-8.** This Properties box for a Hewlett-Packard LaserJet is simple and utilitarian. It gives you a little bit of control over the quality of the print, and under the Effects tab, you can scale your document to print at a larger or smaller size.

# Printing to an Adobe PDF File

Say you want to create an attachment that you can email or put up on a Web site that anyone, on any computer, can open and print. First, read the box on page 222 and install the Adobe PDF add-in. Once you've installed the add-in, creating a PDF file is as easy as saving a file.

Go to Office button → Save As → PDF or XPS. The Publish as PDF or XPS dialog box opens. It looks just like a Save As dialog box. It has all the standard navigation tools, so you can choose a folder to hold the file. In the "Save as type" drop-down menu near the bottom, choose PDF, and then click the Publish button in the lower-right corner (where you'd normally see a Save button). When you're done, you've created a PDF file that you or anyone else can read and print with Adobe Reader.

**Figure 7-9.** The Properties for this Epson color printer give you lots of options that are helpful for printing photos. For example, you can adjust the printer for different types of photo paper, to make sure you get the best possible prints. Because it's an inkjet printer, the Utility tab provides tools to clean the print head and nozzles.

# Faxing with Word

Think of faxing a document as a form of long-distance printing. You tell Word to print a document, and it sends the pages over the phone lines and prints it out on your friend's fax machine. You need to have a fax modem in your computer, and the person on the other end needs a fax machine (see the box on page 228). Other than that, it's a lot like printing. Here are the steps:

1. **With your document open in Word, press Ctrl+P or choose Office button →
   Print.**

   The Print box, as shown in Figure 7-6, opens.

# Adobe Acrobatics

The dawn of the personal computer revolution generated talk about the paperless office. Of course, that never happened. If anything, personal computers and printers brought about a quantum leap in paper consumption. Still, if any computer tool came close to realizing an alternative to paper, it's Adobe Acrobat or PDF (Portable Document Format). The idea was to create a computer file format that can perfectly capture what's printed on the page—text, graphics, the whole kit and caboodle. The files need to be compact so they can be sent over the Internet. And anyone should be able to read and print these files without paying for additional software.

Adobe created Acrobat to meet all these needs, and before too long, everyone was using this new Portable Document Format to distribute reports and booklets over the Internet. Folks started calling them PDF files, because the filenames end in .pdf (Figure 7-11). Now you'll find PDFs online for just about everything. You can probably download the manual for your TV, your cell phone, and your refrigerator from the manufacturers' Web sites as PDF files. The Census Bureau and many other government agencies provide the information they collect as PDFs.

Businesses are using PDFs more and more as a way to distribute reports, spreadsheets, and other documents. Unlike an Excel spreadsheet, you don't need Excel to open a PDF, since the Adobe Reader program comes on all computers (and if not, it's only a free download away). Furthermore, with a PDF, no one can inadvertently erase or change your information once your document is open.

Adobe's format was so successful that it spawned some imitators. It doesn't make much sense to imitate a standard by creating an incompatible format, but that's what happened. Microsoft launched it's own format called XPS, which stands for XML Paper Specification. And an open source format has similar properties and aspirations—the Open Document format. After some wrangling, Microsoft decided to provide support for *all three* of these formats in Word 2007. The XPS format is included with Word. To add either Adobe PDF or Open Document support, you need to download an add-in program to make it part of Word. To find the add-in that installs both PDF and XPS capabilities to your computer, go to *http://www.microsoft.com/office* and enter *pdf xps* in the search box at the top of the page.

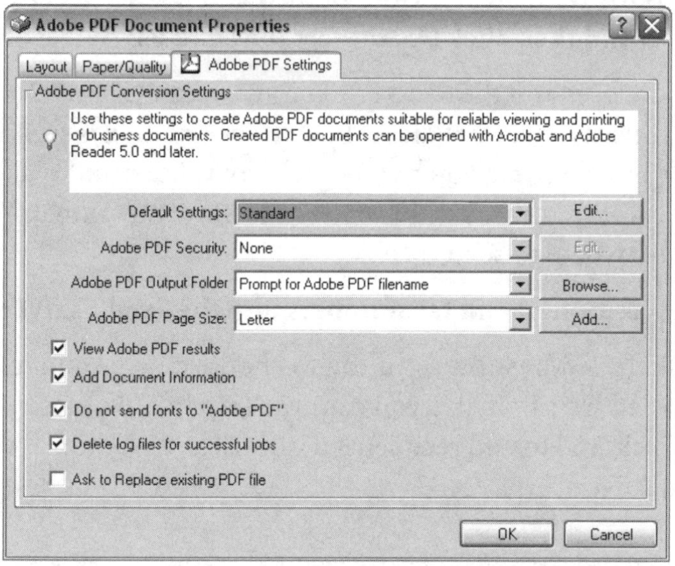

**Figure 7-10.** Adobe Acrobat isn't really a printer, but when you install Acrobat Pro (the commercial program used to create Adobe PDF files), it creates a "printer" for PDF files. When you "print" your document, you're actually writing a PDF file. The Properties box lets you choose options for file security and paper size.

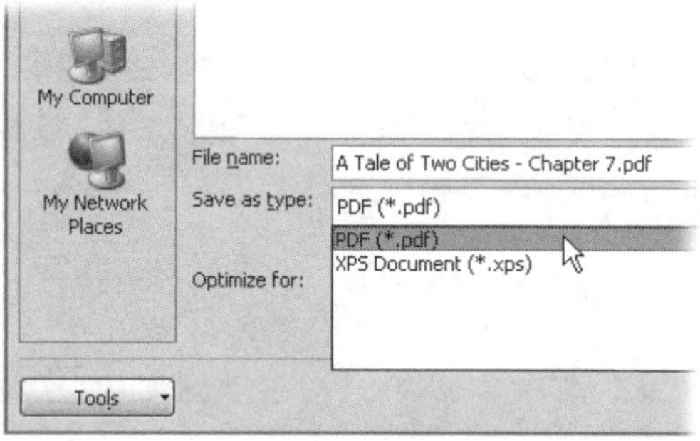

**Figure 7-11.** Use PDF files (also known as Acrobat) to distribute copies of your documents via email or over the Web. People who receive your files can view and print them using Adobe's free Adobe Reader available at *www.adobe.com/products/acrobat/readstep2.html*.

2. **Use the drop-down menu at the top of the Print box to select your fax modem as the printer, and then click OK to start the Send Fax Wizard.**

The Print box closes and the Send Fax Wizard opens (Figure 7-12). The Send Fax Wizard consists of several dialog boxes. The first box is stunningly useless. It does nothing but welcome you to the Send Fax Wizard and make you click the Next button an extra time. The next screen is more functional. You use it to tell your computer where to send the fax.

3. **Enter names (optional) and fax numbers into the Send Fax Wizard.**

You can click the Address Book button to choose a name and fax number from your Outlook address book, or you can type into the "To" and "Fax number" text boxes. Click Add to add recipients to the list at the bottom. When your list is complete, click Next.

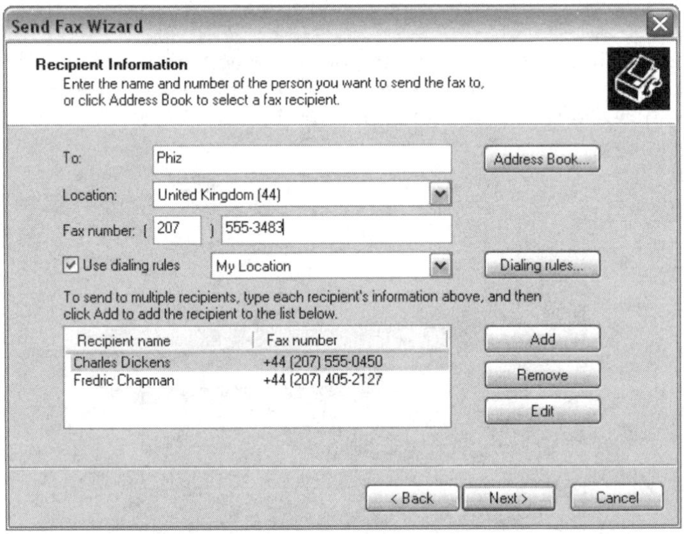

**Figure 7-12.** The Send Fax Wizard walks you through the process of addressing and sending your fax. You start by entering names and fax numbers or choosing recipients from your Windows address book.

4. **Choose whether to include a cover page.**

   If you turn on the cover page checkbox, the wizard prompts you for a subject and a note. The wizard automatically fills in details that Word collected when you installed the program, such as your name and contact info. If you need to, you can review and change those details by clicking the Sender Information button at right. When you're done with the details about the cover page, click Next.

5. **Use the next wizard screen to schedule your fax.**

   You have three options for scheduling. You can send it now, or you can choose to send it when discount rates apply. Last but not least, you can enter a specific hour and minute. When you've scheduled your fax delivery, click Next.

6. **Check the details and preview the fax, and then click the Finish button to send it.**

   The last box of the Send Fax Wizard gives you one last chance to review your fax recipients and to preview the fax by clicking the Preview Fax button (Figure 7-13). A viewer pops up where you can inspect your fax page by page before you send it. When you're certain that everything is okay, click Finish to send your fax on its way.

# Changing Print Settings

Sometimes clicking Quick Print doesn't do the trick. Perhaps you want to make several copies of your document, or maybe you want to print only certain pages. To tackle those chores and others, you need to give Word and your printer more specific instructions. To do that, open the Print box (Figure 7-14) by choosing Office button → Print → Print (or pressing Ctrl+P).

## Printing Part of Your Document

Word is pretty flexible when it comes to printing bits and pieces of your document. You can choose to print specific pages, or you can select a part of your document, and then tell Word to print only what you've selected. You make your choices using radio buttons in the Print dialog box's "Page range" section, described next.

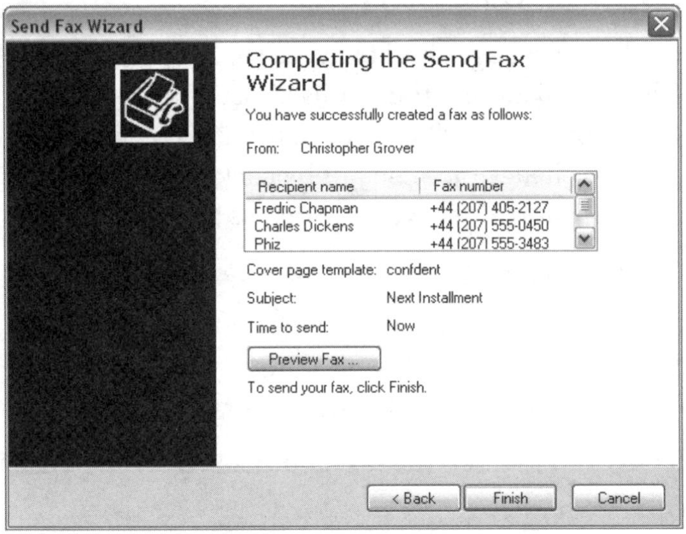

**Figure 7-13.** The last step in the Send Fax Wizard gives you a chance to preview your fax and double-check the names and numbers of the recipients.

- **All.** This option prints your entire document using the Print dialog box's current settings. You can choose to print and collate multiple copies of your entire document, if you want.

- **Current page.** This option is ideal for printing a test page. Word prints the page that's currently showing in the window (not the page with the insertion point).

- **Pages.** You can select consecutive pages, random pages, or a combination of the two. For example, if you type *7, 9, 12-15* in the Pages text box, then Word prints exactly those pages (Figure 7-15).

- **Selection.** Select the text you want to print before opening the Print box (Ctrl+P), and then click the Selection button. Word prints only the text that you've selected. This method helps you proofread a specific chunk of your text or print an individual element like a chart or a picture.

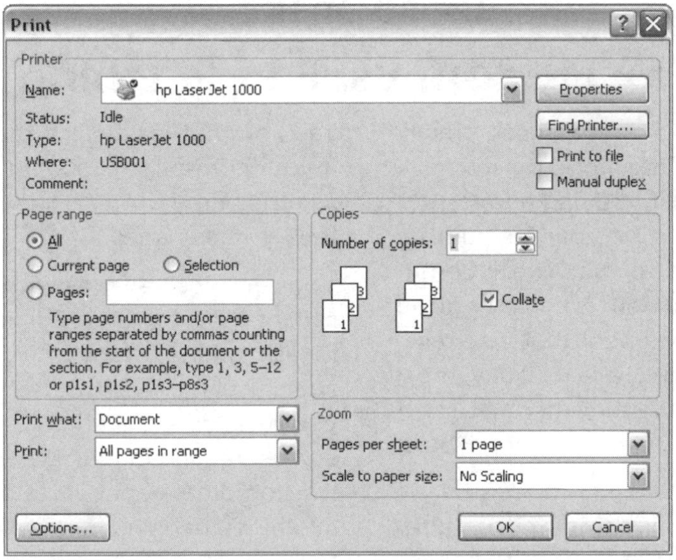

**Figure 7-14.** When your print job gets more complicated, you need to use the Print box. In addition to letting you choose a specific printer, the Print box lets you print multiple copies or print just a portion of your opus. You can also get at specific settings for your printer via the Properties box.

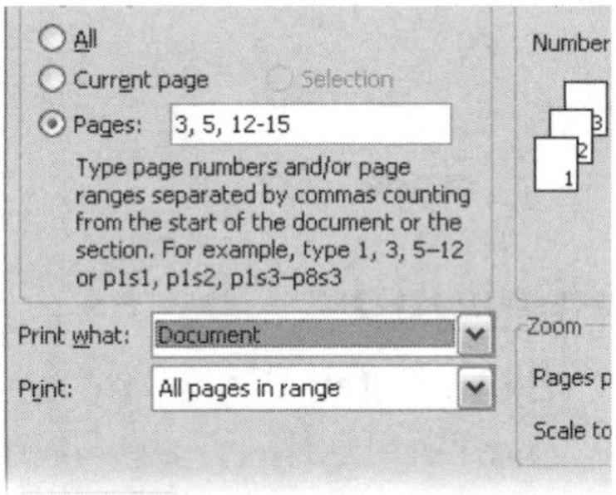

**Figure 7-15.** In the "Page range" section of the Print box, you can choose to print your entire document or just a part of it. Using the Print drop-down menu, you can print either your document alone, or the document with its properties, paragraph styles, and other technical details.

# Fax Modem vs. Fax Machine

In the days before everyone used email, fax machines took the world by storm. At first, people asked if you had a fax, and then they just asked for your fax number. If you don't have a fax machine, a computer with a fax modem is a pretty good substitute. Any document that you can print, you can send as a fax. Today, most modems also include the smarts to send a fax, and you can get one for only $50 or so.

To see whether your computer has a fax modem, go to Start → Control Panel → Printers and Faxes. When the control panel opens, you'll see Fax listed, but that doesn't necessarily mean you have a fax modem installed.  In the list, right-click the word Fax, and then choose Properties from the shortcut menu to open the Fax Properties box.

Last, but not least, click the Devices tab. If your computer can send a fax, you'll see the name of the fax modem listed in the Devices panel.

You can receive faxes with a fax modem too, but if you plan on receiving a lot of faxes, you may want to get a phone line specifically for fax traffic—otherwise your friends are likely to be greeted with a fax screech when they call. If you want the complete capabilities of a fax machine, then you need to add a scanner to your setup. Then you can scan newspaper articles, comic strips, and other important documents and fax them to colleagues.

## Printing and Collating Multiple Copies

Open the Print dialog box (Ctrl+P) to tell Word you want to print multiple copies and provide details about how you'd like them served up (Figure 7-16). The Copies section of the Print box is on the right side. Type a number in the "Number of copies" box, and then turn on the Collate checkbox if you'd like each copy ordered in sequence. If you don't turn on Collate, your printer will spit out all the page 1s, then all the page 2s, and so forth.

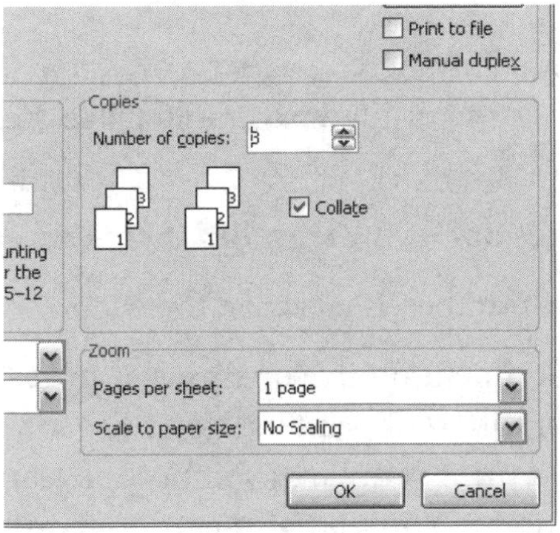

**Figure 7-16.** On the right side of the Print box, you can tell Word how many copies to print and whether or not you'd like them collated. In the Zoom section at bottom, you can choose to print more than one page per sheet of paper; Word automatically shrinks everything to fit. The "Scale to paper size" drop-down menu shrinks or enlarges your document to fit a different size of paper.

## Printing on Both Sides of the Page

Printing on both sides of the paper produces attractive, professional newsletters, reports, and brochures. Your subject matter can benefit from nice big two-page spreads. Or maybe you'd just like to cut down on the amount of paper you're using. Whatever the reason, you can print on both sides (also known as *duplex* printing).

Word gives you two ways to print both sides of the page—the easy way and the hard way. Unfortunately, the easy way is more expensive. It requires you to have a duplex printer that knows how to print both sides. Duplex printers vary, so you may need to explore your printer's Properties (Ctrl+P, Alt+P) to make sure it's ready for printing on both sides. If so, you'll also see some extra options in the Print dialog box to turn two-sided printing on.

If you don't have a duplex printer (most people don't), you can get the same result if you're willing to do a little paper juggling:

1. **Go to Office button → Print to open the Print dialog box. Turn on the "Manual duplex" checkbox.**

   the Manual duplex checkbox is on the right side, below the Properties button, as shown in Figure 7-17.

2. **Click OK to start printing.**

   Word prints all the odd-numbered pages on one side of the paper, and then it prompts you to remove the printed pages and place them back in the printer tray.

3. **Take the printed pages out of the tray, flip them over, and then click OK.**

   Word prints the even-numbered pages on the backs.

   You may want to experiment on five or six pages to get the routine down. The process is different for different printers. You need to watch for a couple of things with the second print run. First, you need to learn whether to place the pages face up or face down. You may also need to reorder the pages so they print properly. Hint: On the second run, page 2 prints first, so you want page 1 at the top of the pile.

**Figure 7-17.** Even if you don't have a fancy duplex printer for printing both sides of the paper, Word will help you out. Turn on "Manual duplex," and Word first prints the odd pages, and then prompts you when it's time to reload.

# Printing Envelopes

Computers have always been great for printing documents on standard-size paper, but envelopes present a little bit more of a challenge. Envelopes are oddly shaped and kind of thick. And on some machines, the text needs to print sideways. Fortunately, Word 2007 and most modern printers have overcome the hurdles presented by printing on envelopes.

The first step for successful envelope printing is to make sure that your return address info is stored in Word.

1.  **Go to Office button → Word Options and click Advanced.**

    The buttons on the left side of the Word Options box show you different panels of Word.

2.  **Scroll down to the General group.**

    Oddly, the General group is almost at the bottom of the Advanced options.

3.  **Enter your information in the "Mailing address" box. Click OK when you're done.**

With your vital details stored in Word, you're ready to print an envelope. Here are the steps:

1.  **On the ribbon, go to Mailings → Create → Envelopes (Alt+M, E).**

    Most of the tools on the Mailings tab are for mail merge and mass mailings. The Create group, with two buttons—Envelopes and Labels—is on the left side. Clicking Envelopes opens the Envelopes and Labels dialog box to the Envelopes tab, as shown in Figure 7-18.

2.  **At the top of the Envelopes tab, in the "Delivery address" text box, type a name and address.**

    Just type in the information on different lines as you'd put it on an envelope.

    The little book icon above and to the right of the Delivery address text box opens your Outlook address book. Click it to select an existing contact. (Look, ma—no retyping!)

---

**NOTE**

The first time you click the Address Book icon, the Choose Profile box opens. There you can select a source for addresses, including your Outlook address book.

---

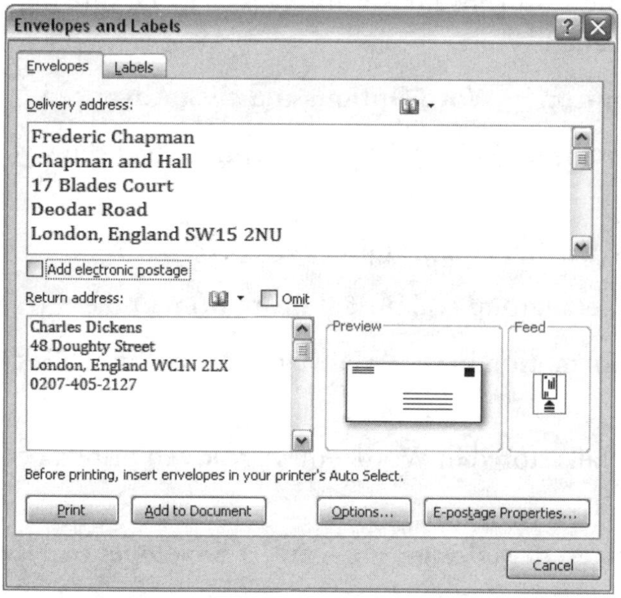

**Figure 7-18.** The Envelopes tab in the Envelopes and Labels dialog box provides a place to enter both a delivery and return address. The Preview and Feed icons in the lower-right corner show you how the envelope will look and the way to place your envelope in the printer.

3. **In the bottom text box, inspect your return address and edit if necessary.**

   If you provided an address in your Word Options, as described in the previous steps, that information appears in the Return address box. If you want, you can change the details now. Just delete the existing address and type the new information. (If your envelopes have a preprinted return address, turn on the Omit checkbox to prevent your stored return address from printing on the envelope.)

4. **Check the preview window and take notice of the feed direction for your envelope.**

   The Preview panel shows you how the envelope will look with the addresses printed on it. The Feed panel gives you guidance for placing envelopes in your printer.

The Options button leads to another dialog box where you can choose a different envelope size (assuming your printer can handle it). You can also change the font and font size.

# Printing Labels

Word comes ready and wiling to work with standard address labels. If you just want to print a single label, or if you want to print a bunch of the same label, then follow the steps in this section.

Word is prepared to handle labels from Avery and many other manufacturers. Take note of the maker and model number of the labels you've bought, and follow the manufacturer's instructions for loading them into your printer. Then follow these steps to print one or more of the same label:

1. **Go to Mailings → Create → Labels.**

   The Envelope and Labels dialog box opens to the Labels tab.

2. **In the Address box at top, type the address you want to put on the label.**

   If you want to print a batch of your own return address labels, click the box in the upper-right corner labeled "Use return address."

3. **Click the Label section. (It's not just a preview—it's a button!)**

   The Label Options dialog box opens, as shown in Figure 7-19. Choose your label manufacturer, and then choose your label's model number. This information tells Word how many labels are on a sheet and how they're spaced. Click OK when you're done.

4. **In the Print section, select "Full page of the same label" or "Single label."**

   If you want to print the same label a bunch of times on a sheet of labels, choose the first radio button, "Full page of the same label."

   You can print a single label from a sheet of labels, saving the rest of the sheet for another project. Click the "Single label" radio button, and then identify the row and column for Word, so it knows which label to print on.

5. **Click Print when you're ready to go.**

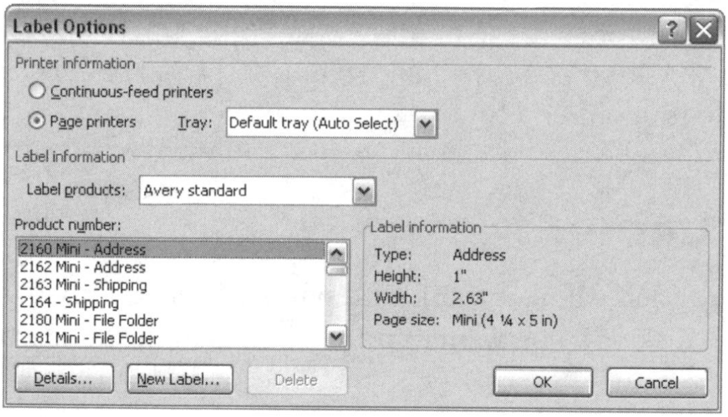

**Figure 7-19.** Word's label printing tool is all set to work with a mind-boggling variety of label types. It also gives you some ways to make the most of your label resources. For example, using the Single label button (not shown), you can print one label on a sheet and save the rest for another project.

# Setting Print Options

The Word Options window is where you tweak Word to make it behave the way you want. Some print settings worth knowing about are, somewhat oddly, tucked away on the Display panel. Go to Office button → Word Options → Display. The printing settings are at the bottom. A checkmark indicates the option is turned on. Here's what you find:

▶ **Print drawings created in Word.** The factory setting is to have this option turned on. Turn it off if you ever want to print a document without any graphics or floating text boxes.

▶ **Print background colors and images.** Page color and background images work better for Web pages than they do for printed documents. When you install Word, this option is turned off, but you can always toggle it back on.

▶ **Print document properties.** Turn this option on, and Word prints your document, and then prints the document properties—author, title, and so on—on a separate page at the end. (If you've never checked out your document properties, take a look by choosing Office button → Prepare → Properties.)

- ▶ **Print hidden text.** You can hide text in your document using a font style command (Alt+H, FN, Alt+H). With this box turned on, that text doesn't stay hidden when you print.

- ▶ **Update fields before printing.** Word fields include things like the date in a header (page 139) or a contact from your Outlook address book. It's usually a good idea to leave this box turned on because it makes sure you have the most up-to-date information before you print.

- ▶ **Update linked data before printing.** Like the fields option above, this option is turned on when you install Word, and it's good to leave it that way. If you link a table or chart from an Excel spreadsheet, this option makes sure it's using the most recent info.

# PART TWO: CREATING LONGER AND MORE COMPLEX DOCUMENTS

# PLANNING WITH OUTLINES

8

▶ Switching to Outline View

▶ Promoting and Demoting Headings

▶ Moving Outline Items

▶ Showing Parts of Your Outline

**IF YOUR TEACHERS** kept hammering you about how important outlining is and made you do elaborate outlines before you tackled writing assignments, forgive them. They were right. Nothing beats an outline for the planning stages of a document. When you're facing writer's block, you can start listing your main topics in a Word document, and then break your topics into smaller pieces with some subtopics underneath. Before your know it, you're filling out your ideas with some essential bits of body text. You've broken through the block.

Word's Outline view is a fabulous outlining tool. It lets you move large blocks of headings and text from one part of your document to another, and rank headings and their accompanied text higher or lower in relative importance. In Outline view, you can even show or hide different parts of your document, to focus your attention on what's important at the moment. Best of all, Outline view is just another document view, so you don't have to outline in a separate document.

# Switching to Outline View

Outline view is another way of looking at your document, like Draft view or Print Layout view. In other words, in Outline view, you're just looking at your document in outline form. When you switch into Outline view, your heading text (Heading 1, Heading 2, Heading 3, and so on) simply appears as different outline levels (Figure 8-1). Similarly, you can start a document as an outline—even do all your writing in outline form—and then switch to Print Layout view and have a perfectly normal looking document.

> **TIP**
>
> Jumping back and forth between Outline view and the other views can be very conducive to brainstorming. If you're working with your document in Print Layout view or Draft view and need to get a feeling for the way one topic flows into another, then pop into Outline view, collapse the body text, and examine your headings.

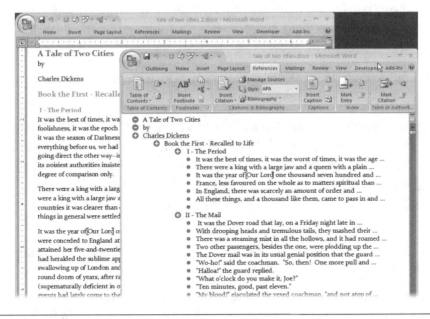

**Figure 8-1.** Outline view gives you a dramatically different look at your document. In back is A Tale of Two Cities in Print Layout view. In front is the same document in Outline view. The body text is collapsed and hidden, but you get a clear view of the major and minor headings. When you click one of the plus (+) buttons, the headings and text expand beneath.

To switch views in Word, go to View → Document Views and click the button you want, or use the keyboard shortcuts in the following list:

▶ Use **Outline view** (Alt+W, U) to develop headings, establish a sequence for presenting topics, establish a hierarchy between topics, and jump from one section to another in long documents.

▶ Use **Draft view** (Alt+W, E) for writing rapidly when you don't want to worry about anything except getting ideas down on the page. In Draft view you aren't hindered by too many formatting niceties.

▶ Use **Print Layout view** (Alt+W, P) when you're putting the finishing touches on your document. In this view, you get a feel for the way your document looks to your readers.

When you switch to Outline view, a new Outlining tab appears on the ribbon. The Outlining Tools group at left has two parts, separated by a vertical bar. You use the controls to move paragraphs around and change their outline levels for (more on that shortly). The tools on the right side don't actually affect the outline—they just control the way it looks.

When it comes to outlining, Word divides your document into two distinctly different elements:

- **Headings or topics.** You can tell headings are the most important element in outlines by the big + or – button at their left. With headings, it's all about rank. Every heading has a level, from 1 to 9. More important headings have lower-level numbers and are positioned closer to the left margin. Level 1 starts at far left, Level 2 comes below it and is indented slightly to the right, followed by Level 3, 4, and so on.

  Each heading is called a *subhead* of the one that came before. For example, Level 2 is a subhead of Level 1, Level 3 is a subhead of Level 2, and so on.

- **Body text.** For outlining, body text takes the back seat. It just gets that little dot, and if it's in the way, you can hide it entirely, or you can view only the first line—just enough to give you a hint of what's beneath. Body text doesn't really get assigned to a level; it stays glued to the heading above it.

## Promoting and Demoting Headings

Planning a document is a little bit like putting a puzzle together. You try a piece here and then over there. A topic you thought was minor suddenly looms larger in importance. When you're brainstorming and plotting, it's important to keep an open mind. Word's helpful because it's so easy to try things out, and you can Ctrl+Z to undo whenever you need to.

When you *promote* a topic, you move it toward the left margin. At the same time, it moves up a rank in the headings hierarchy; so, a Level 3 header becomes a Level 2 header, and so forth. For most documents that means the formatting changes too. Higher-level headers typically have larger or bolder type—something that distinguishes them from their less impressive brethren. To *demote* a heading is the opposite; you move a heading toward the right, usually making it a subordinate of another topic.

For you, these promotions and demotions are easy. In fact, you encounter a lot less complaining here than you'd find in promoting and demoting employees in your company. The easiest way to promote and demote is to click a header and move it to the left or to the right. When you move it a little bit, a vertical line appears, providing a marker to show you the change in rank, as shown in Figure 8-2.

> **NOTE**
>
> When you promote or demote a heading, the body text goes with it, but you have a choice whether or not the subheads move below it (page 245).

When you're brainstorming and pushing ideas around in your document, you don't want to get distracted by the mechanics. When it comes to outlines, you may be grateful that Word provides so many different ways to do the same thing. You get to choose the method that works best for you, and keep your focus on shaping your document. Word gives you three ways to manipulate the pieces of your outline:

▸ **Dragging.** For outlining, nothing's more intuitive and fun than clicking and dragging. You can put some words in a heading, and then just drag them to another location. As you drag topics and text, Word provides great visual clues to let you know the end result (Figure 8-2).

▸ **Ribbon.** The buttons on the Outlining → Outline Tools group give you quick, visual access to the commands for promoting and demoting headings and for showing and hiding the bits and pieces of your document. It's a bit more mechanical than just clicking and dragging the pieces where you want them (Figure 8-3).

One potentially confusing thing about the Outlining tab are those two drop-down menus showing levels. They look almost identical and both give you a choice among the nine topic levels that Outline has to offer. Here's the key: The menu on the left promotes or demotes the current item, while the menu on the right shows or hides levels.

▸ **Keyboard shortcuts.** Keyboard shortcuts are ideal when your hands are already on the keys and you're typing away. During the planning stages, speed isn't as much of an issue, but if you took your teachers' advice to heart and do lots of outlining, keyboard shortcuts can really streamline your work. Just remember that all these commands use Alt+Shift plus another key, as shown in the table.

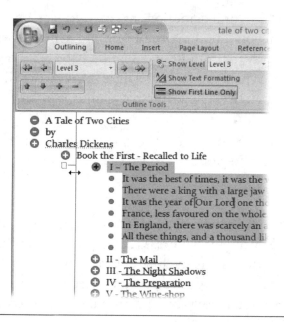

**Figure 8-2.** Dragging works well when you're brainstorming. It's satisfying to push, pull, and drag your document into shape as if it were clay and you're the sculptor. As you drag, your cursor changes to a double arrow. The long vertical line indicates the outline level you're currently dragging through.

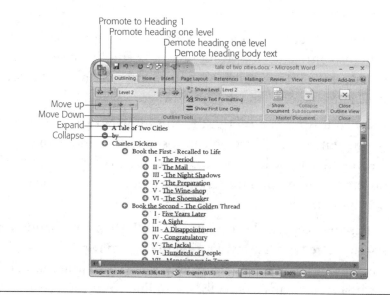

**Figure 8-3.** The buttons on the Outlining tab provide a command central for promoting and demoting topics and showing just the right part of your document. The up and down buttons move topics forward and backward in the document, providing a great way to move big chunks of text.

| Action | Keyboard Shortcut |
| --- | --- |
| Promote Heading Up a Level | Alt+Shift+Right arrow, or Tab |
| Demote Heading Down a Level | Alt+Shift+Left arrow, or Shift+Tab |
| Demote Heading to Body Text | Alt+Shift+5 (number pad), or Ctrl+Shift+N |
| Expand Outline Item | Alt+Shift++ |
| Collapse Outline Item | Alt+Shift+_ |
| Expand or Collapse Outline Item | Alt+Shift+A, * key (number pad) |
| Show n Level Heading | Alt+Shift+n, n=number key (top row, not the number pad) |
| Show Only First Line of Text | Alt+Shift+L |

___ TIP _____

Another keyboard shortcut helps with outlining: the / key on the number pad. That one little key conceals any fancy character formatting you've applied so you can focus on your outline. See page 249 for more on the Show/Hide Text Formatting command.

## Controlling Subheads During Promotion or Demotion

When you promote or demote an outline item, any subheads and subtopics below it move with that item, but only if you collapse the items below, so that they're hidden. In other words, when you move the header above, the subheads keep their relationships even though you can't see them. When you drag topics, the subheads go along, because when you select a topic, you automatically select the subtopics, too.

Word gives you a number of ways to move the header but leave everything else where it is. Here's a step-by-step description of the ways you can promote or demote a heading all by its lonesome:

1. **Click anywhere in the text of the header.**

   *Don't* select the entire header; just place the insertion point somewhere in the text.

2. **Change the header level using one of the ribbon buttons or by pressing a keyboard shortcut.**

   Use the shortcut keys Alt+Shift+Left arrow or Alt+Shift+Right arrow to promote or demote the header. As long as the subtopics below aren't highlighted, they won't move when you do the header promoting or demoting.

   You can use any of the ribbon controls that promote and demote headers in the same way. As long as the subtopics aren't selected, they won't change (Figure 8-4). The buttons that you can use include: Promote to Heading 1, Promote, Outline Level (drop-down menu), Demote to Body Text.

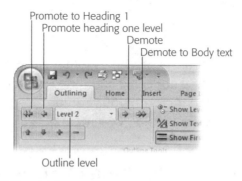

**Figure 8-4.** Use the various promotion and demotion buttons and the Level drop-down menu on the Outlining tab to organize your outline. If subheads are collapsed under a topic or they're selected, they maintain their relationships when you demote or promote the header. Otherwise, if only the header is selected, it moves and the subtopics stay put.

---

__ NOTE __

Working with outlines is actually a lot simpler to do than it sounds. Want to test drive Word's outline features? To check out the screencast—an online, animated tutorial—of the examples in this chapter, head over to the "Missing CD" page at *www.missingmanuals.com*.

---

# Moving Outline Items

Part of organizing your thoughts means moving them to an earlier or later position in the document, without changing their outline level. Say you decide a section you've typed in the middle of your document would make a great introduction. You can move it to the beginning of the document, without promoting or demoting it. Moving topics and items up and down in your document is very similar to moving them left and right. (Figure 8-5). If you want to take subtopics along with an item when you move it, make sure that they're selected (or collapsed) under the item that you're moving.

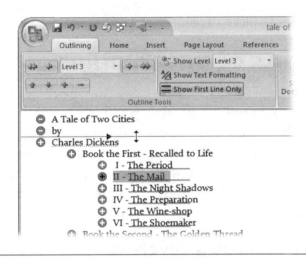

**Figure 8-5.** When you drag a header up and down, you see a horizontal line that acts as a marker to show you exactly where the heading (and connected text) will appear when you let go of the mouse button.

In addition to dragging, Word gives you two other ways to move topics up and down in your outline. Select the heading you want to move, and then click the Move Up or Move Down buttons on the Outlining tab (Figure 8-6). You can also use the shortcut keys Alt+Shift+up arrow or Alt+Shift+down arrow.

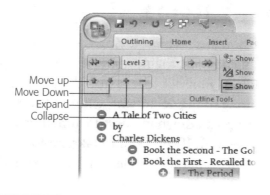

Move up
Move Down
Expand
Collapse

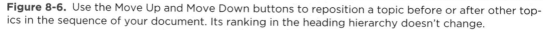

**Figure 8-6.** Use the Move Up and Move Down buttons to reposition a topic before or after other topics in the sequence of your document. Its ranking in the heading hierarchy doesn't change.

# Showing Parts of Your Outline

Outline view doesn't just let you see and organize the structure of your prose; it also helps you zero in on what's important while you make decisions about the shape and flow of your work. If you want, you can show your headings only so you can focus on their wording with all the other text out of the way. When you want to read inside a certain section, you can expand it while leaving everything else collapsed. (Or, if you're having trouble with a passage, you can collapse it so you don't have to look at it for a while.)

## Expanding and Collapsing Levels

You know that old saying about not being able to see the forest for the trees. On the Outlining tab, the Expand and Collapse buttons help you put things in perspective (Figure 8-6). Collapse a topic, and you can read through the major headers and get a feel for the way your document flows from one topic to another. When you need to explore the detail within a topic to make sure you've covered all the bases, expand the topic and dig in.

When you're mousing around, the easiest way to expand or collapse a topic is to double-click the + sign next to the words. It works as a toggle—a double-click expands it, and another double-click closes it. The topics with a minus sign next to them have no subtopics, so you can't expand or collapse them.

If you're interested in making grander, more global kinds of changes, turn to the Outlining → Outline Tools → Show Level menu; it's the drop-down menu on the right (Figure 8-7). Just choose a level, and your outline expands or collapses accordingly.

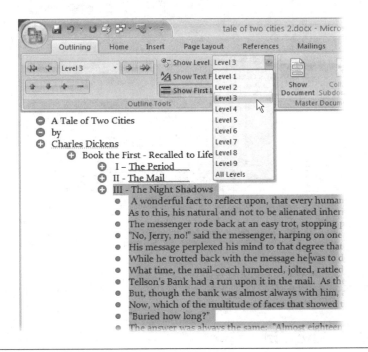

**Figure 8-7.** Use the drop-down menu on the right to show and hide levels in your outline. The smaller dots are next to body text. In this view, the body text is limited to showing just the first line.

## Showing and Hiding Text

Text takes a subordinate position when it comes to outlining and planning, so it's not surprising that Word provides a couple different ways for you to hide the body text (Figure 8-8). You can double-click the headings above the body text to expand and collapse the topic, just as you would with subheads. The + and – buttons on the Outlining tab work the same way. You can also use the keyboard shortcuts Alt++ to expand and Alt+_ to collapse body text under a heading.

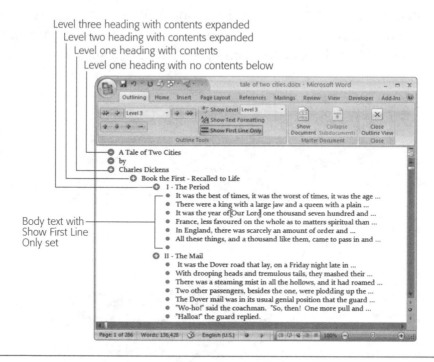

Level three heading with contents expanded
Level two heading with contents expanded
Level one heading with contents
Level one heading with no contents below

Body text with Show First Line Only set

**Figure 8-8.** Show and hide text by double-clicking the header just above the text. Click the Show First Line Only button on the Outlining ribbon to hide the paragraphs while leaving the first line to hint at the contents.

## Showing Only the First Line

Because each paragraph of body text is like a sub-subtopic, Word's outline view lets you work with them as such. Click the Show First Line Only button, and all you see is the first line of each paragraph. That should be enough to get a sense of the topic that's covered. It's just another way that Outline lets you drill down into your document while you're in a planning and plotting phase.

## Showing Text Formatting

Your document's character formatting—different fonts, font colors, and sizes that may bear no relation to the Level 1, Level 2 hierarchy—can be distracting in Outline view. The easiest thing is to turn the formatting off. You can click the Show Formatting button on the Outlining ribbon (Figure 8-9) to toggle formatting on or off, or you can use the shortcut key, which is the / (forward slash) on the number pad.

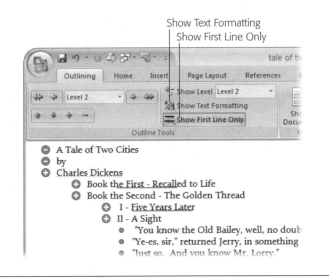

**Figure 8-9.** Use the Show Text Formatting checkbox (or the / key on the number pad) to hide text formatting, as shown here. This image also shows the result of clicking the Show First Line Only button or pressing Alt+Shift+L to show and hide all the paragraph text except the first line.

# ORGANIZING YOUR INFORMATION WITH TABLES

▶ Creating Tables

▶ Moving Around a Table

▶ Selecting Parts of a Table

▶ Merging and Splitting Cells

▶ Adjusting Column Width and Row Height

▶ Formatting Tables

▶ Doing Math in Tables

IF YOU THINK OF TABLES AS AN UGLY GRID for holding numbers in place, something more suited to a spreadsheet than a Word document, think again. Or, better yet, talk to someone who's done some Web design. Tables are incredible tools for page design, both the printed page as well as a Web page. With tables, you can group related text and pictures so that they stay together no matter how your document changes. You can use background and border colors to give your words a visual splash and to draw attention to important parts of your message. If you're presenting numbers to your readers, you need the rows and columns that tables offer to line everything up and provide totals. Once you're comfortable creating and modifying tables, you'll probably find all sorts of ways to use them.

Word's table feature has grown stronger and more versatile with each passing version. For example, you can choose from a few different ways to create tables and multiple ways to modify them by inserting or deleting rows, columns, and individual cells. You can also get really creative and add color and other formatting. If you're a number cruncher, you can use tables as a simplified spreadsheet right in your document. Word 2007 also offers Quick Tables, preformatted tables for things like calendars and other common uses.

# Creating Tables

If you've never created a table in a Word document before, don't worry—it's remarkably easy and even fun, especially if you use the drawing-with-the-mouse method.

You can create tables by:

▶ **Pointing at and clicking a mini table map.** Chose Insert → Table and click the grid that appears to size and create a table.

▶ **Filling in numbers and clicking button in a dialog box.** Choose Insert → Table → Insert Table or press Alt+N+TI to open the Insert Table dialog box.

▶ **Drawing your table on the page with your mouse.** Choose Insert → Table → Draw Table or press Alt+N+TD to turn your cursor into a table-drawing tool.

# Creating a Table from the Ribbon

As always, the ribbon approach to the job is very visual, and it may seem vaguely familiar. It's a variation on the way you'd create tables in the last few versions of Word, where you'd click a button and drag out a grid that represented the table. Word's new method is even a little easier for newcomers to grasp. The drop-down menu presents a 10×8 grid. You click to select the number of boxes you want in your table, as shown in Figure 9-1.

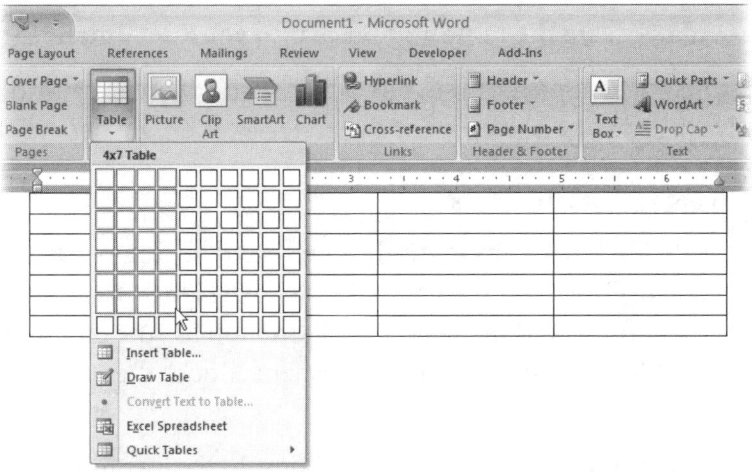

**Figure 9-1.** Click the Tables button (Insert → Tables → Table) to open this menu, and then click the grid to choose the number of columns and rows you want in the table. The message at the top shows that this table will have four columns and seven rows.

> **NOTE**
>
> A column is a group of cells running vertically, while a row is group of cells that run horizontally.

1. **On the ribbon, choose Insert → Tables → Table.**

   A menu appears with what looks sort of like a bunch of boxes or a piece of graph paper (Figure 9-1).

2. **Point to a box on the grid to create a table with the number of rows and columns you want.**

   As you move your mouse over the grid, the boxes in the grid are highlighted, and you see the table appear on your page. (Tables use Microsoft's Live Preview feature that shows you what will happen if you click the mouse button.) A message above the grid on the menu keeps tally of the number of columns and rows. You don't have to be exact; it's easy enough to create or delete columns and rows later.

3. **Click the grid to create the table and place it in your document for real.**

   The Tables menu disappears, and your table is right there in your document with evenly spaced columns and rows.

## Using the Insert Table Box

The Insert Table dialog box is a more traditional—and boring—way to create a table. Choose Alt+N, TI to open the Insert Table box (Figure 9-2). The box is a simple affair. Just type numbers in the text boxes at the top for the columns and rows you need in your table. This dialog box also lets you choose the AutoFit behavior, as explained below:

▶ **Fixed column width.** Use this option if you want to limit columns to a specific width. Enter a number in the box next to this option to set the width of the columns. Or, if you choose Auto instead, Word creates a table that fits in your current margins, with the number of columns specified above, each of equal width.

▶ **AutoFit to contents.** With this option, the column width adjusts automatically to accommodate the amount of text you type in the cells. Use this option if you're not sure how much space your text will take up until you type it.

▶ **AutoFit to window.** This option is more suited to Web pages than printed documents. It makes the table expand and contract to fit a browser window. Web pages are designed to work on all different types of computers, PDAs, cell phones, TV sets, and who-knows-what in the future. AutoFit tables like these help Web designers create pages that work for screens and browsers with dramatically different capabilities.

If you're going to create similar tables in the future, turn on the "Remember dimensions for new tables" checkbox, and Word keeps the settings in the Insert Table box for your next visit.

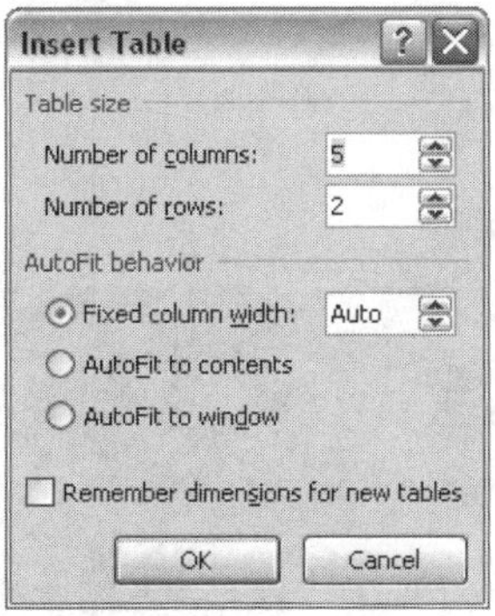

**Figure 9-2.** The Insert Table box gives you a more traditional but less artistic way to create tables. The advantage of using this box is that you can specify exact column widths for precise layout. The AutoFit to window option is helpful if your document is going to end up as a Web page.

## Drawing a Table

As you can guess, the least mechanical and most creative way to make a table is to draw your own. It's a great technique if you need an irregularly shaped table. With Word's table tools you can draw tables, and divide them into columns and rows in just about any configuration imaginable. As you can see from Figure 9-3, you can do just about anything except make a curve.

Here's how to use the table drawing tools to draw a fairly traditional table:

1. **Choose Insert → Tables → Table → Draw Table.**

   Your mouse cursor changes into a pencil, inviting you to start drawing.

2. **On an empty place on the page, drag diagonally to draw your first rectangle (Figure 9-4).**

   The rectangle that appears on your page marks the borders for your table. Soon you'll divvy it up, creating columns and rows inside. Word adds paragraphs, adjusts margins, and generally does whatever's necessary to place your table exactly where you draw it.

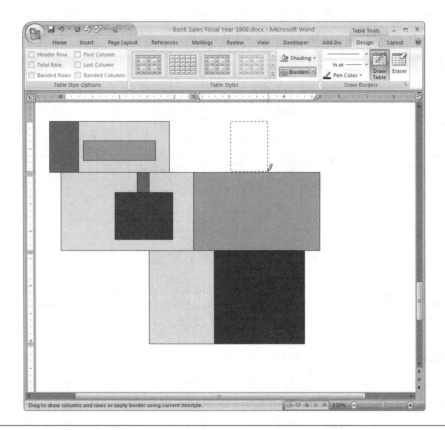

**Figure 9-3.** You may be surprised how flexible tables are, especially if you use the Draw Table option (Alt+N, TD). Using the cell shading and border tools, tables become strong graphic elements in your document.

The moment you release the mouse button, the Table Tools contextual tab appears on the right side of the ribbon. Two tabs appear in this contextual tab: Design and Layout. You're now on the Design tab, where you see tools for formatting your table. On the right side, the Draw Table button is highlighted, indicating that you're in Draw Table mode.

3. **Next, drag to draw a vertical line to divide your table in half.**

   Your line separates the table into two cells. You can draw lines wherever you want to divide your table into cells of just about any shape. When you drag diagonally, you create rectangles instead of lines. Rectangles turn into cells, or if they're far enough from the original table, they're new tables.

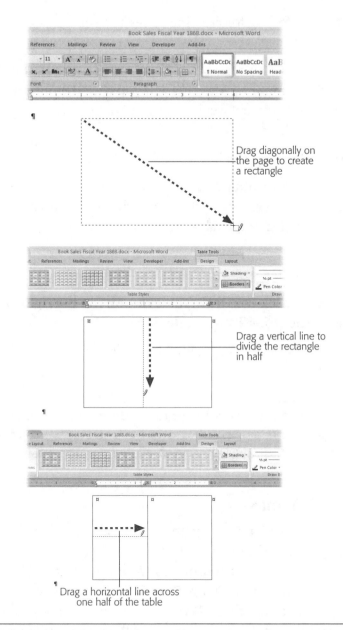

**Figure 9-4.** Top: First click and then drag the pencil cursor diagonally across the page to create the table.

Middle: Click at the top of your table, and then drag down to draw a line that divides the table into two cells.

Bottom: Draw another line from the left side to the center to create two rows on the left.

Experiment to get a feeling for creating tables and cells. If you make an error, undo it with Ctrl+Z.

Next to the Draw Table button you find an Eraser button (Table Tools | Design → Draw Borders → Eraser or Alt+JT, E). If you click the button to highlight the eraser, then your mouse cursor changes to an eraser icon. Dragging it over lines in your table erases them.

4. **Draw a horizontal line on the left half of your table.**

When you draw the horizontal line, you divide one of the cells into two cells, creating a new row. You can draw the line to the vertical divider or you can continue onto the right side of the table. This horizontal line creates two rows in your table.

You can continue to divvy up your table into additional cells.

5. **When you're done, click the Draw Table button (on the right side of the ribbon), to turn off the Draw Table mode.**

The Draw Table button loses its highlight glow, and the cursor changes from the pencil back to its familiar I-beam.

___ **NOTE** _____

Drawing a table is actually a lot simpler to do than it sounds; for a screencast—an online, animated tutorial—of the steps you've just read, head over to the "Missing CD" page at *www.missingmanuals.com*.

## Choosing Quick Tables

If three ways to create tables aren't enough, you can always choose from one of Word's predesigned tables. Choose Insert → Tables → Quick Tables to see a menu full of pre-rolled tables that you can drop into your documents. The choices range from calendars to periodic tables (Figure 9-5). Of course, you don't have to keep the content that Microsoft's put in there. If you like the look of one of the tables, you can always insert it and then delete the text and fill the space with your own words and graphics.

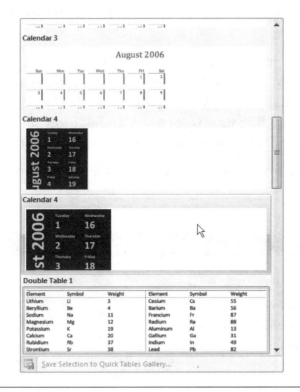

**Figure 9-5.** If you're in a hurry, you can choose one of the predesigned Quick Tables (Alt+N, TT). The large menu gives you a good view of the different tables available. Once it's in your document, you can edit it and alter it for your own purposes.

# Moving Around a Table

Working with tables, columns, rows, and cells is different from working with plain text. Still, you want to do the same things, such as select bits and pieces so that you can copy, move or delete them. And when you type in text and numbers, you want to be able to move around the table, preferably without taking your hands off the keyboard.

If you're rapidly entering text in an empty table, the best way to move from cell to cell is with the Tab key. Just hit Tab when you're finished typing in a cell. Word selects the next cell, and you can continue typing. It's important to note that the cursor doesn't just move to the next cell; everything in the cell is selected, so if text is already in there, Word deletes it when you start typing. If you want to move backward, use Shift+Tab.

The arrow keys work pretty much as you'd expect, moving the insertion point one character at a time through your document. When you get to the point between two columns, the insertion point hops over to the next cell. The up and down arrows behave in a similar way. The up arrow moves the insertion point to the next line of text above it; that line may be in the same cell, or it may be in the row above.

Here are some keyboard shortcuts you can use to move around and work in your table:

| Command | Keyboard Shortcut |
| --- | --- |
| Select next cell | Tab |
| Select previous cell | Shift+Tab |
| Move to first cell in a row | Alt+Home |
| Move to last cell in a row | Alt+End |
| Move to last cell in a column | Alt+PageDn |
| Move to first cell in a column | Alt+PageUp |
| Create new paragraphs in a cell | Enter |
| Insert tabs in a cell | Ctrl+Tab |

# Selecting Parts of a Table

Before you can copy, format, or delete something, you have to select it. That's just as true with tables as it is with any other text. When you're working with tables, it's often easiest to use your mouse to make selections. The keyboard commands are a little cumbersome, and the ribbon commands are best when you're just learning your way around.

▶ **Select table.** Hold your mouse over the table, and you see a button appear just off the upper-left corner. The Select Table button is a square, inside of which is a cross with arrows pointing in four directions. That's a hint that you can grab this button and drag the table wherever you want it. Clicking that button selects the entire table.

▶ **Select column.** Move the cursor to the top of a column, and the cursor changes to an arrow pointing down (Figure 9-6). One click and you select the column the arrow points to. Drag to select more than one column.

Select and drag to select multiple rows

Click button to select table

Selected Rows

Selection cursor

| Book Sales Fiscal Year 1868 | 1st Qtr | 2nd Qtr | 3rd Qtr | 4th Qtr |
|---|---|---|---|---|
| Pickwick Papers | 35 | 68 | 72 | 35 |
| Oliver Twist | 18 | 53 | 24 | 112 |
| David Copperfield | 56 | 49 | 256 | 148 |
| A Tale of Two Cities | 49 | 72 | 168 | 312 |
| Great Expectations | 78 | 119 | 84 | 354 |
| Total | 236 | 361 | 604 | 961 |

Sum column formula field

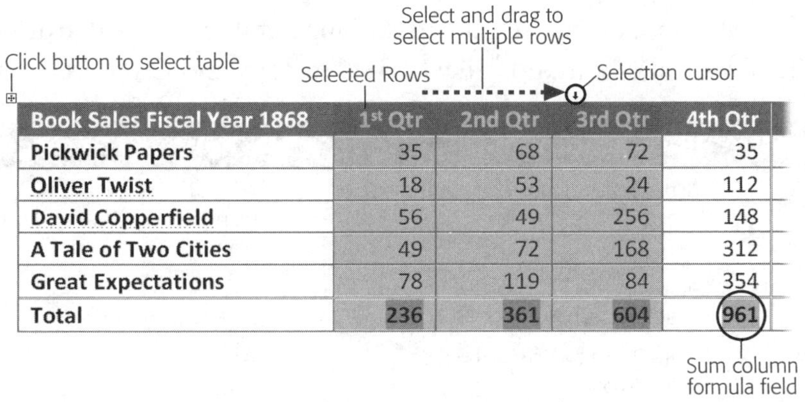

**Figure 9-6.** When you hold your mouse above a column in a table, the cursor changes to a small arrow pointing down. Click to select a single column, or drag to select more than one column. Row selection is similar: Just position your cursor in the left margin, and then click or double-click to select an entire row.

▶ **Select row.** When your cursor is at the left edge of the table, it changes to a small dark arrow, angled up slightly. (It's different from the hollow arrow you see if move your cursor into the left margin.) One click selects the first cell in the row. A double-click selects the entire row. If your table happens to be on the left margin, you can select a row just like you'd select a line of text, with a single click in the margin.

▶ **Select cell.** Move the cursor to the lower-left corner of any cell, and the cursor changes to a small dark arrow, angled up slightly. One click and you select the cell and any text, graphic, or other object in the cell. A highlight color fills selected cells. Drag to select more than one cell. If you want to select cells that aren't next to each other, select the first cell, and then press Ctrl while you click and select more cells.

A quick triple-click is another way to select a single cell. Keep your finger down on that last click, and you can drag to select multiple cells. Press Ctrl as you triple-click to select random cells that aren't next to each other.

If you're working on text that's inside a cell, the basic selection and editing commands work as always. You can select text and format it, or move it around using all your favorite tools and commands, like Ctrl+C to copy and Ctrl+V to paste.

| Command | Ribbon Command | Keyboard Shortcut |
|---|---|---|
| Select table | Table Tools \| Layout → Select → Select Table | Alt+JL, KT or Alt+5 (on the number pad, with NumLock off) |
| Select column | Table Tools \| Layout → Select → Select Column | Alt+JL, KC or Alt+Shift+PageDN |
| Select row | Table Tools \| Layout → Select → Select Row | Alt+JL, KR |
| Select cell | Table Tools \| Layout → Select → Select Cell | Alt+JL, KL |

# Merging and Splitting Cells

The cells in your table don't have to be a perfect grid, so don't be afraid to get creative with your table layouts. Maybe you want to have a single "1st Quarter" heading centered over three columns of sales figures. To merge cells, select two or more adjacent cells, and then use Table Tools | Layout → Merge → Merge Cells or the shortcut Alt+JL, M.

| Command | Ribbon Command | Keyboard Shortcut |
|---|---|---|
| Merge cells | Table Tools \| Layout → Merge → Merge Cells | Alt+JL, M |
| Split cells | Table Tools \| Layout → Merge → Split Cells | Alt+JL, P |
| Split table | Table Tools \| Layout → Merge → Split Table | Alt+JL, Q |

To split cells, make sure the insertion point is in the cell you want to divide, and then use either the command Table Tools → Layout → Merge → Split Cells or the shortcut Alt+JL, P. A dialog box appears, asking you to specify exactly how you want to divvy up the real estate (Figure 9-7).

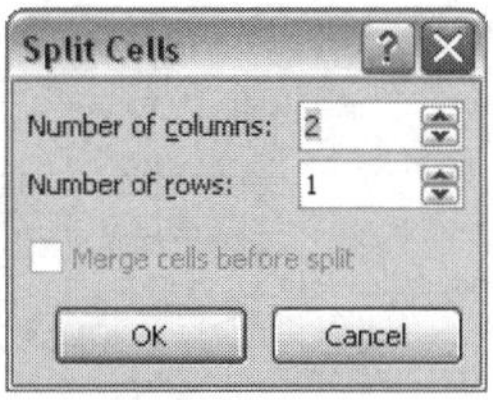

**Figure 9-7.** The Split Cells dialog box lets you be quite specific about how you want to divide the territory. Enter the number of columns and rows you want in the text boxes. If you select more than one cell before you give the Split Cell command, you have the option to merge the cells before you break them into smaller parts.

# Adjusting Column Width and Row Height

Once you have your table in place, you may want to make some adjustments. Tables can shape-shift in a number of ways to work with whatever you decide to toss into them. Even though tables can automatically change shape to accommodate the contents, it's still good to know how to adjust them manually. You can change the width of individual columns and the height of the rows in your table.

To adjust the width of a column, move your mouse cursor over one of the vertical lines in the table. The cursor changes to a two-headed arrow (Figure 9-8). Drag the line where you want it. The entire line from top to bottom of the table moves in one motion. If, for some reason, just one piece of the line moves, that means you selected a cell or two before you dragged the line. When a cell is selected, your modifications affect only the selected cell.

Changing the height of a row is similar. Just click to grab one of the lines, and then drag it where you want. You'll probably find that it's less necessary to change row height than it is column width, since rows automatically adjust to accommodate the lines of text. As you type into a cell and your words create a new line, the row height increases to make room.

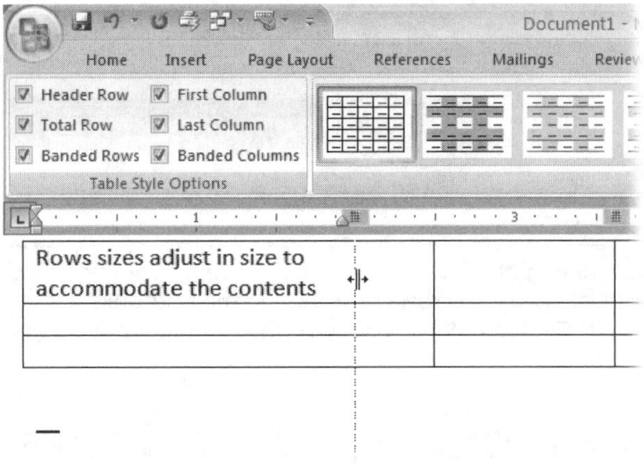

**Figure 9-8.** When you hold the cursor over a line, the cursor changes to a double-headed arrow. Drag one of the lines in your table to resize a row or column. The dotted line helps you line up the edges of the cell with other objects in the table or on the page.

## Inserting Columns and Rows

Often when you're first creating a table, it's difficult to know how many rows and columns you'll need. It's not a major issue, because it's easy enough to add and delete rows and columns. You can make these changes using buttons on the ribbon, with keyboard shortcuts or with the handy pop-up menu that appears when you right-click within the table.

When you're inserting rows or columns, the first step is to click somewhere in the table to position the insertion point. Clicking in the table does two important things. First, the Table Tools contextual tab doesn't make an appearance unless the insertion point is inside a table. Second, the insertion point serves as a reference point so you can tell Word to add the row or column before or after that spot.

With the insertion point in place, you can choose one of the commands from the Table Tools | Layout → Rows & Columns group. The menu commands and their icons present a clear picture of the options (Figure 9-9): You can delete individual cells, or rows, or columns, or the entire table.

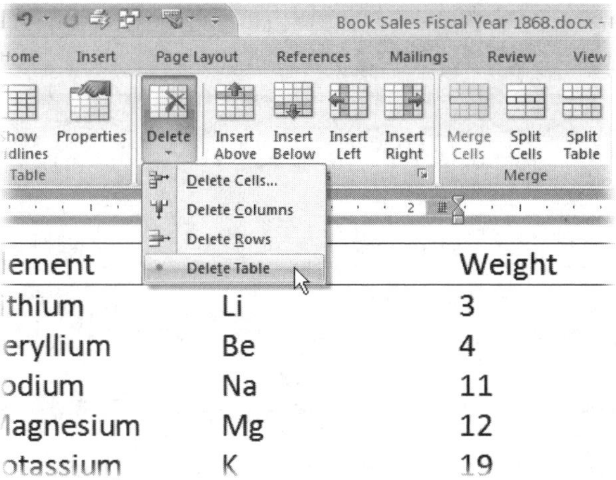

**Figure 9-9.** The commands to insert and delete rows and columns are neighbors in the Table Tools | Layout → Rows & Columns group. Make sure you click within a table, or you won't see the Table Tools contextual tabs.

All the options shown on the ribbon have keyboard equivalents. Here's a table of the commands and the ways to use them:

| Command | Ribbon Command | Keyboard Shortcut |
|---|---|---|
| Insert row above | Table Tools | Layout → Rows & Columns → Insert Above | Alt+JL, A |
| Insert row below | Table Tools | Layout → Rows & Columns → Insert Below | Alt+JL, E |
| Insert column left | Table Tools | Layout → Rows & Columns → Insert Left | Alt+JL, L |
| Insert column right | Table Tools | Layout → Rows & Columns → Insert Right | Alt+JL, R |

A right-click within a table makes a shortcut menu appear, and as usual Word's pretty smart when it comes to figuring out what you're trying to do. So, if you've selected an entire row before you right-click, then the shortcut menu gives you options to insert or delete rows, as shown in Figure 9-10. Just take your pick from the list.

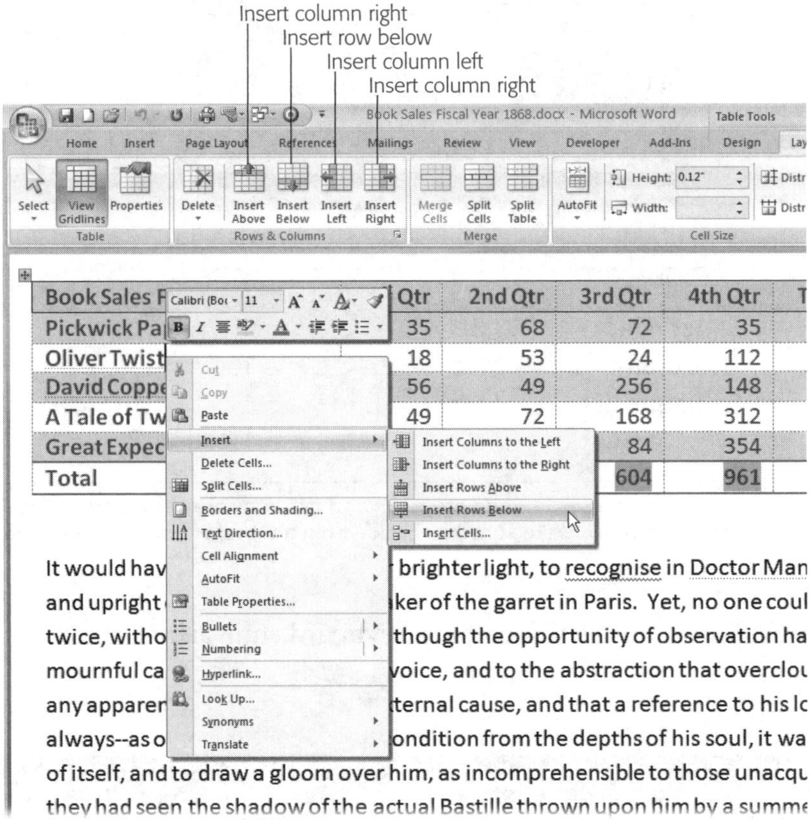

**Figure 9-10.** If you've already got your mouse in hand, here's an easy two-step way to add a row. Move the mouse into the left margin, and then click to select an entire row. Right-click to display the shortcut menu, and then choose Insert → Insert Rows Below or Insert Rows Above. You can create columns with a similar technique.

## Deleting Cells, Columns, Rows, and Tables

The techniques to delete columns and rows pretty much mirror the ways you insert them. Deleting individual cells is a little trickier, since plucking cells out of the middle of your table tends to shift things around. Easiest of all is deleting the entire table. As long as your insertion point is somewhere in the table, you can use Table Tools | Layout → Delete → Delete Table or the shortcut Alt+JL+DT.

Using the Delete menu (Table Tools | Layout → Rows & Columns; see Figure 9-9), you can delete any element of a table from the entire table down to groups of rows and columns on down to a single cell. Just select the bits and pieces you want to remove, and then choose the command. You can select several rows, and then delete them all at once. Keyboard shortcuts are also available for deleting table parts:

| Command | Ribbon Command | Keyboard Shortcut |
| --- | --- | --- |
| Delete table | Table Tools | Layout → Rows & Columns → Delete → Delete Table | Alt+JL, DT |
| Delete columns | Table Tools | Layout → Rows & Columns → Delete → Delete Columns | Alt+JL, DC |
| Delete rows | Table Tools | Layout → Rows & Columns → Delete → Delete Rows | Alt+JL, DR |
| Delete cells | Table Tools | Layout → Rows & Columns → Delete → Delete Cells | Alt+JL, DD |

### Deleting cells

Deleting cells is sort of like pulling a brick from the middle of a wall. Other bricks have to move in to take its place. But it doesn't happen at random: Word lets you choose how you want cells to fill in the space. When you give the command to delete a cell or a group of cells (Alt+JL, DD), Word shows a dialog box asking whether you want to pull cells up or bring them over to the left (Figure 9-11).

> **NOTE**
>
> Selecting a cell and then pressing Delete on the keyboard deletes the contents of the cell but not the cell itself. And that's just fine, because most of the time that's exactly what you want.

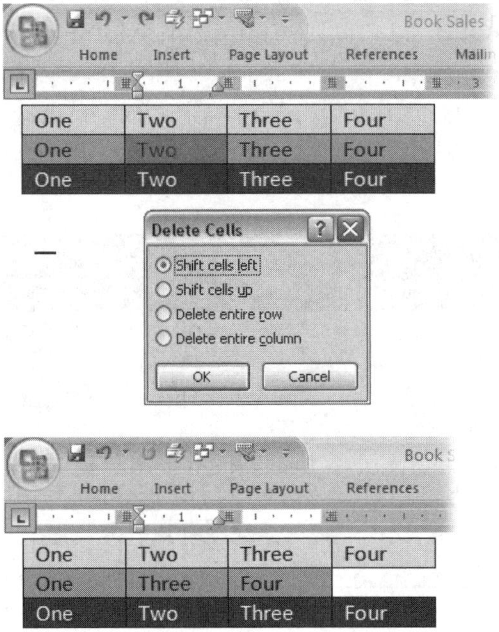

**Figure 9-11.** Top: The cell second from the left and second from the top is selected for deletion.

Middle: After invoking the Delete command, Word asks for advice on how to shift the rest of the cells.

Bottom: With the "Shift cells left" button selected, the cells in the second row shift over from the right.

# Formatting Tables

The Table Tools contextual tab has two tabs devoted to Design and Layout, indicating that formatting is a big part of working with tables. In fact, these two tabs are so close to each other in function that it's easy to forget which tab holds certain commands. The Design tab holds commands related to color and borders, while the Layout tab relates more to the structure of the table: inserting and deleting rows and columns, aligning text, and adjusting cell size.

## Using Table Styles

For a quick and easy way to add color to your table, nothing beats Table Styles (Table Tools | Design). Word provides dozens of styles using a variety of colors, fonts, and font styles. When you design tables, try to look at them from your readers' point of view. What information is most important to them? Do you want to emphasize headings on the top row or in the left column? Is it important for readers to compare numbers along a horizontal row? Answering these questions will help lead you to good table design decisions (Figure 9-12).

The Table Styles are on the Table Tools | Design tab. Use the two groups on the left side to modify and select a table style. The Table Style Options group (far left) is pretty nifty. As you make choices and check off options, the styles in the Table Styles menu change per your specs. Here are your options:

- **Header Row** puts an emphasis on the top row, either with a color or a strong border. This option works best when your top row contains headings.

- **Total Row** puts an emphasis on the bottom row. As the name implies, this style is ideal for emphasizing the totals at the bottom of columns when your table is a spreadsheet.

- **Banded Rows** uses alternating row colors to help readers track text and numbers horizontally. It's useful for wide spreadsheets, but you can also use it for design effect.

- **First Column** puts an emphasis on the first column, like when your left column holds a list of categories.

- **Last Column** puts an emphasis on the last or right-hand column. It's particularly useful when you sum up rows of numbers in the right column.

- **Banded Columns,** like banded rows, help guide your reader's eye, but you can also use them strictly for design purposes.

The toughest thing about applying table styles is choosing one from the many that the menu presents you (Alt+JT, S):

1. **Click within your table so that Word knows where to apply the style.**

   You don't have to select the entire table; it's enough to have the insertion point in the table you want to format.

2. **Choose Table Tools | Design to show the Design tab.**

   With the Design tab selected, on the left end of the ribbon you see the two groups that apply to Table Styles: Table Style Options and Table Styles. You want to tackle them in order from left to right.

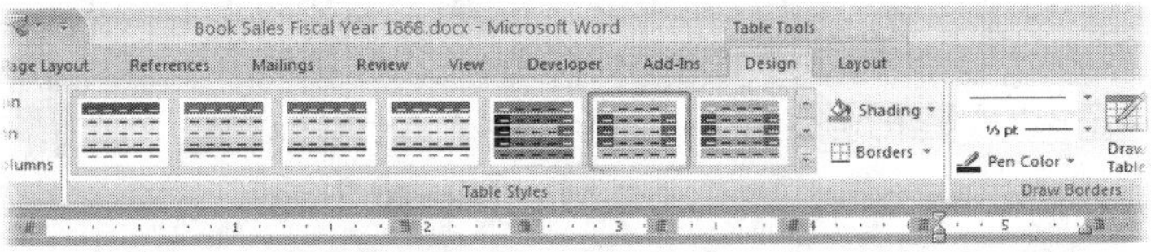


| Book Sales Fiscal Year 1868 | 1st Qtr | 2nd Qtr | 3rd Qtr | 4th Qtr | Total Sales |
|---|---|---|---|---|---|
| Pickwick Papers | 35 | 68 | 72 | 35 | 210 |
| Oliver Twist | 18 | 53 | 24 | 112 | 207 |
| David Copperfield | 56 | 49 | 256 | 148 | 509 |
| A Tale of Two Cities | 49 | 72 | 168 | 312 | 601 |
| Great Expectations | 78 | 119 | 84 | 354 | 635 |
| **Total** | **236** | **361** | **604** | **961** | **2162** |

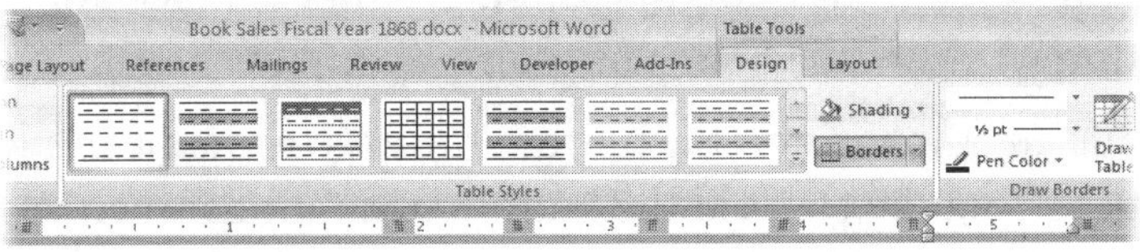


| Book Sales Fiscal Year 1868 | 1st Qtr | 2nd Qtr | 3rd Qtr | 4th Qtr | Total Sales |
|---|---|---|---|---|---|
| Pickwick Papers | 35 | 68 | 72 | 35 | 210 |
| Oliver Twist | 18 | 53 | 24 | 112 | 207 |
| David Copperfield | 56 | 49 | 256 | 148 | 509 |
| A Tale of Two Cities | 49 | 72 | 168 | 312 | 601 |
| Great Expectations | 78 | 119 | 84 | 354 | 635 |
| Total | 236 | 361 | 604 | 961 | 2162 |

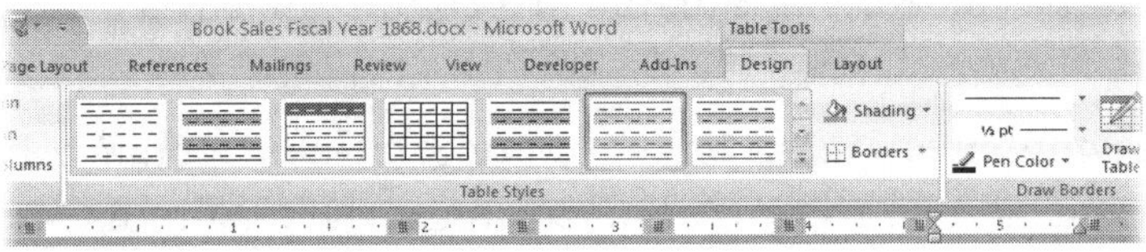


| Book Sales Fiscal Year 1868 | 1st Qtr | 2nd Qtr | 3rd Qtr | 4th Qtr | Total Sales |
|---|---|---|---|---|---|
| **Pickwick Papers** | 35 | 68 | 72 | 35 | **210** |
| **Oliver Twist** | 18 | 53 | 24 | 112 | **207** |
| **David Copperfield** | 56 | 49 | 256 | 148 | **509** |
| **A Tale of Two Cities** | 49 | 72 | 168 | 312 | **601** |
| **Great Expectations** | 78 | 119 | 84 | 354 | **635** |
| **Total** | **236** | **361** | **604** | **961** | **2162** |

**Figure 9-12.** Three different table styles give this one table a dramatically different look.

Top: This style, called Colorful Grid Accent 1, sets the numbers off from the headings and the totals at bottom and right.

Middle: This table, using the Basic style, looks more mundane, but if you're making multiple photocopies, it's best to avoid cell shading, which tends to get splotchy.

Bottom: The bottom table, Light Shading style, has alternating cell shading, making it easier for readers to track numbers across rows.

3. **Adjust the Table Style Options to match your needs.**

   As you turn the Table Style Options checkboxes on and off, you see the Table Styles on the right change to match your desires. (Everything in life should work like this.)

   Not all the Style Options work well together. For example, you may not need both Banded Rows and Banded Columns. So, it may be good to take a less-is-more approach. Try unchecking everything, and then, one by one, click the options you think are most important for your table.

4. **Preview the different styles on the Table Styles menu.**

   Move your cursor over one of the Table Styles to see how it fits your table. About a half-dozen styles appear on the ribbon. To see more, use the scroll button, or click the drop-down menu in the lower-right corner. With Live Preview, you see your table change as the cursor hovers over different styles. You can go back and forth between the Table Style Options and the preview until you come up with the perfect format.

5. **Select the style that works best for your table.**

   To choose a Table Style and modify your table, on the Table Styles menu (Table Tools | Design → Table Styles), click the style of your choice.

## Aligning Text, Numbers, and Data

Tables are in the high-maintenance category when it comes to formatting and other housekeeping chores. With all those different bits of text and numbers in different boxes, it seems you constantly need to realign something. Usually, you want text to align on the left and numbers to align on the right (especially if you're performing math on them). Or, when no math is involved, it may look better to center numbers in the columns. Also, usually you want your column headers to have the same alignment as the items below.

And that's just horizontal alignment. To add to the choices, you can also align text to the top, center, or bottom of a cell. All that's required is some decision making. Fortunately, applying this formatting is easy, so you can keep tweaking until everything looks right. It's one of those standard "first you select, and then you apply" formatting jobs. You can speed things up by selecting multiple items, and then applying a single alignment command to them all. (See page 280 for the selection techniques you can use with tables.) Here are the steps for changing text alignment inside table cells:

1.  **Select the cells you want to align.**

    Often you can apply alignment to a column or more at a time. To select a column, hold the cursor at the top of the column. The cursor changes to a dark arrow pointing down. Click to select the column, or drag to select multiple columns.

2.  **Choose Table Tools | Layout → Alignment and select the alignment option.**

    On the left side in the Alignment group, click one of the buttons to apply an alignment format to the selected cells (Figure 9-13).

    You have nine alignment options. You can choose to have text horizontally aligned left, center, or right. With each of those options, you can also choose the vertical alignment: top, center, or bottom.

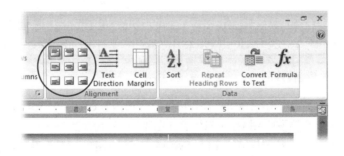

**Figure 9-13.** Nine buttons help you align text within your table cells. If you can't quite make out what the icon means, hold your mouse cursor over a button, and a screen tip appears, explaining the command.

## Applying Shading and Borders

Word's Table Styles primarily apply to a table's shading and borders. You can customize your table with these settings too. Or, better yet, you can apply one of Word's styles, and then make modifications to fit your needs.

Here's an example of manually changing the shading and border for the top row in a table. In this example, you'll highlight your table's top row with nice light blue shading and a double line along the bottom of the row. You'll also delineate the top of the table with a dark blue, 1.5-point line. Here are the steps:

1. **In the lower-left corner of the first cell of your table, double-click to select the entire top row.**

   Before you apply shading and border styles, you need to select the cells that you want to change. When you move your cursor to the lower-left corner of a cell, the cursor changes to a dark arrow angled upward. A single click selects the cell, and a double click selects the entire row.

2. **Choose Table Tools | Design → Shading, and then select a light blue color from the drop-down menu (Figure 9-14).**

   The Shading drop-down menu is in the Table Styles group of the Design tab. You see a menu with colors that match your theme at the top. Bold, standard colors are near the bottom, along with a button that removes colors from the selected cells.

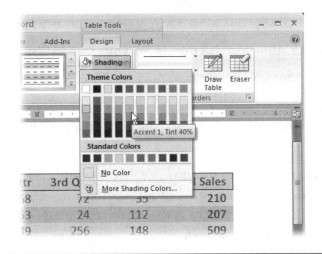

**Figure 9-14.** The Shading button in the Borders and Shading dialog box shows colors that match your document's theme. When you point to a color chip, a screen tip describes the color. Click the chip to apply the color to the selected cells.

3. **Choose Table Tools | Design → Table Styles → Borders, and then select the Borders and Shading option at the bottom of the menu.**

The Borders and Shading box opens to the Borders tab. At left are preformatted options. In the middle, you can choose different line styles, colors, and widths. On the right side is a preview box, but this box does more than just show you the results; you actually use it to format your borders.

4. **At left, click the None button to clear all borders from the selected cells.**

By clearing all the borders, you can start from scratch to create a new look.

5. **In the middle of the dialog box, scroll down through the Style box, and then select the double line from the list.**

You see a variety of solid and dotted lines, as well as different types of multiple line options. When you choose the double line, you see a double line in the Width box below.

6. **In the Color box, select a dark blue color.**

Click the button on the right side of the Color box to show the menu. The color chips at the top match your document's theme. Click one of the chips to select a color. The menu closes, and the color you selected shows in the box.

7. **In the Width box, choose 1-1/2 points for your line width.**

You can't enter your own number in the width box; you must select one of the preset line widths.

8. **In the Preview box on the right, click the border at the bottom of the preview example.**

At first, no borders appear in the example, because you cleared all the borders in step 4. When you click the bottom border, the thick double line appears along the bottom of the example. Clicking the border elements in the preview is how you tell Word where to apply borders.

9. **In the Style box, click the single line, and then choose "3 pt" on the Width menu. In the Preview box, click the top border to apply this line style.**

   When you've made your changes, the preview box looks like Figure 9-15. (You can, if you wish, continue to design border styles and apply them to different parts of the selected cells.)

10. **When you're done, click OK to close the Borders dialog box.**

   Using these tools and techniques, you can apply shading and borders to any of the cells in a table.

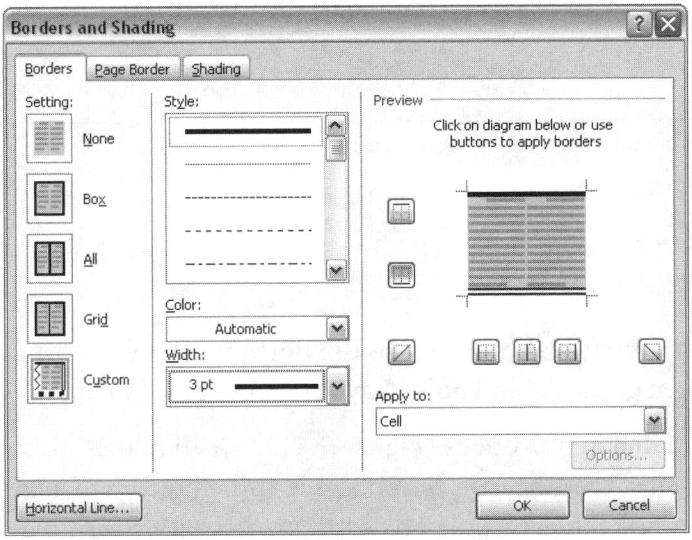

**Figure 9-15.** The Borders dialog box gives you the tools to format border styles for the cells in your table. This dialog box is Word's standard tool for applying borders to paragraphs, around pictures, and around text boxes.

# Doing Math in Tables

When presenting numbers in your document, whether it's a budget, or sales figures, or an inventory tally, you probably want to total some of the columns. Sure, you could add up the numbers on a calculator, and then type the totals into the cells. That's fine if you know the figures aren't going to change, and you're certain you won't transpose any figures between your calculator and the table. A better (though, admittedly, not necessarily easier) way is to insert one of Word's fields with instructions to sum the column above. Use the Formula button (Figure 9-16) on the Layout tab to insert the field into your table.

**Figure 9-16.** Use the Formula button (Table Tools | Layout → Data → Formula) to insert a math field into your table.

Here are the steps for adding a SUM field that totals the number in the column above:

1. **Click to place the insertion point in the bottom cell of a column with numbers, and then go to Table Tools | Layout → Data → Formula.**

   The Formula dialog box opens (Figure 9-17). Word makes some assumptions based on the fact that the insertion point is at the bottom of a column of numbers. For example, the Formula box is preloaded with a formula designed to total the column of numbers. It's almost as readable as plain English: =SUM(ABOVE). If your insertion point had been at the end of a row of numbers, the formula would have read: =SUM(LEFT).

2. **In the Formula box, check to make sure the formula does what you want, and then click OK.**

   Word inserts the field code in the cell, and then it runs the calculation—in this case, a sum, which then shows up in the cell.

It's not unusual to have several columns that you want to total. If that's the case, you can select the cell with the SUM field, and then press Ctrl+C to copy it. Then move the insertion point to the next cell, and then press Ctrl+V to paste it. At this point, you may notice that the numbers don't add up right. That's because you need to update the function field. Word tables may look a little like spreadsheets, but unlike Excel and most other spreadsheet programs, Word doesn't automatically recalculate formulas when you edit cells. If you change numbers in a row or a column that's summed with a field, you need to update the SUM fields just like any other Word field (page 139). Click to place the insertion point in the field, and then press F9. Word runs the math again, and then places the correct number in the cell. To update all the fields in a table, select the entire table (Alt+JL, KT), and then press F9.

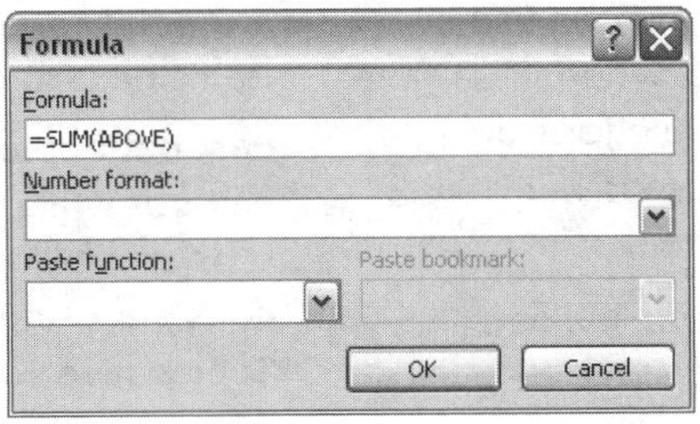

**Figure 9-17.** If all you're doing is summing a column of numbers, the Formula box is pretty easy to manage. In the top text box, you see the actual formula that Word uses to create the text it places in the cell. Use the "Number format" box if you want the total to show as currency. The Paste function box leads to other formulas such as average, round, and count.

# Other Table-like Options

When you need to organize parts of your document separate from the body text, you have a few different options. You can use either tables or text boxes to separate blocks of text from the body of your document. If you're working with numbers, you can use a table, or you can insert an Excel spreadsheet into your document. When you're working with columns of newspaper-style text, you can use Word's columns or you can use a table. So the question arises, when should you use tables for these jobs and when should you use an alternative? Here are some rules of thumb:

* For a pull quote or a sidebar, it's better to use a text box than a table to hold the text. The end result may look pretty much the same no matter which you use, but text boxes provide easier, quicker formatting options.

* However, if you need to do more complicated math formulas, it's easier to insert an Excel spreadsheet into your Word document. The printed page will look the same, but it's easier to create and update the formulas in a spreadsheet.

* Word's columns are fine for text that flows evenly and predictably from one column to another, but they're murder if you're trying to organize a page with irregularly shaped text. So, for example, if you're creating a newsletter with blocks of text of different shapes and sizes, it's probably easier to create a table with a few cells, and then place blocks of text inside the cells. Tables are great for accurately positioning items next to each other.

* Last but not least, if you're pulling your hair out while trying to align items with tabs and paragraph marks, it's time to consider using a table for the job. Tables give you much better control when you're aligning items. What's more, you can automatically turn that text with the tabs into a table with the command Insert → Tables → Table → Convert Text to Table or the keyboard shortcut Alt+N, TE.

# ADDING GRAPHICS TO YOUR DOCUMENTS

**10**

- ▶ Drop Caps, Text Boxes, and WordArt
- ▶ Working with Pictures and Clip Art
- ▶ Working with SmartArt
- ▶ Working with Shapes
- ▶ Customizing Color

**A STRIKING GRAPHIC** helps you capture your readers' attention and cement your message in their memories. A chart or graph helps clarify complex topics better than words can say. Even in text-heavy documents, graphic elements like pull quotes and drop caps help lure readers into your words.

Word's here to help. It lets you embellish your documents with photos, drawings, charts, clip art, and a new Word 2007 graphic type called SmartArt that combines text with graphic shapes. (See the box on page 283 for a full rundown on all the graphic types.) Word gives you a whole range of tools to place graphics in your document. You can use a slew of options for positioning them, applying borders and special 3-D effects. This chapter shows you the whole gamut of tools and techniques you can use with photos, drawings, and other graphics. It also shows you how to add video and audio files, so you can give your readers a multimedia presentation right there in your Word document.

---
**TIP**

Although graphics and other objects add pizzazz, it's important to understand your audience and keep the graphics appropriate. For example, you don't want to get too cutesy if you're presenting a budget to the Board of Directors.

---

# Drop Caps, Text Boxes, and WordArt

Drop caps, text boxes, and WordArt let you turn text into a design element. Although these elements lose their impact if you overdo them, putting a little pizzazz in your text can direct your audience's attention to important information. For example, you can use a text box to create a pull quote that highlights your company's stellar performance.

Drop caps, text boxes, and WordArt take color, font, and design cues from the theme you've selected for your document. When you see color choices, the theme colors are usually presented at the top of the menu. Later, if you decide to change the theme for your document, the accent colors and font styles in your graphics change to match.

# In Graphic Terms

People use the word *graphic* to mean any kind of visual representation or illustration, whether they're thinking of a photograph, a line drawing, a chart, or what-have-you. Word works with several types of graphics, each of which looks and acts a little differently in your document. Here's a guide to what all these graphic terms mean:

* **Pictures.** With the Insert Picture command, you can find photos and drawings you've created or saved on your computer and place them in a Word document. As long as it's in a computer graphic file format—like .jpg, .tif, or .emf—Word thinks of it as a picture. You insert pictures, along with the following four items, from the Insert → Illustrations group.

* **Clip art.** Word comes with a huge library of photos and pictures that you can add to your documents for free. Also, although they're not technically clip art, you can find media files like movies, music, and other sounds in the Clip Art task pane. Some of these files are on your computer and others are in libraries on the Internet. The task pane lets you search for just the right image, video, or audio out of the thousands available. (Obviously, you'll use the video and audio files in documents destined for the Web or email rather than print.)

* **SmartArt.** Part graphic and part text, SmartArt is a new type of graphic introduced in Word 2007. All you have to do is type text into a box and SmartArt handles all the formatting and placement chores, creating a great looking graphic image. When you make changes to the words, SmartArt is smart enough to make everything fit.

* **Shapes.** Word includes a library of simple shapes, lines, arrows, and common icons. They're easy to size, position, and format. You can use them to create your own charts and illustrations.

* **Chart.** Charts are different from other images in that data is behind the graphic. Charts take numbers and translate them into lines, bars, or pie charts. You tell Word what kind of a chart to create, and then you provide the labels and numbers.

* **Drop caps, text boxes, and WordArt (Insert → Text).** These graphic elements are a little different from the other items in this list because they're character-based, but when it comes to sizing and positioning them, they behave much like photos and drawings.

To work with pictures, drawings, and SmartArt, you need to be in Print Layout or Web Layout view. In Draft or Outline view, your graphics appear as placeholder boxes. In these views, you can position the placeholder boxes, but you can't modify the graphics. (If you don't see a placeholder box in your document, just click the empty space where the graphic should be. You then see a box that you can drag to a new location.)

## Adding a Drop Cap to a Paragraph

Drop caps are a decorative feature with a practical purpose. They give a paragraph an added sense of importance as the beginning of a chapter or document. Drop caps attract readers' attention and draw their eyes to the beginning of the text, inviting them to start reading (Figure 10-1). With Word you can easily add a drop cap to any paragraph, and if you're in the mood, you can fiddle around with it to create your own special effect.

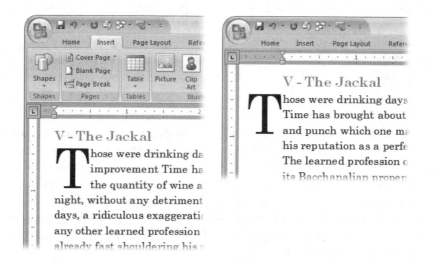

**Figure 10-1.** Word provides two styles of drop caps.

Left: Dropped is the most common style and fits within the body of the paragraph.

Right: The In Margin style places the drop cap by itself in the left margin.

Here are the two simple steps for creating a drop cap:

1. **Click within the paragraph you want to have a drop cap.**

   You don't have to select the letter. Word knows that a drop cap is going to be the first letter of the paragraph.

2. **Choose Insert → Text → Drop Cap, or use the shortcut Alt+N, RC, and then choose from the three styles on the menu.**

   The choices available are: None, Dropped, and In Margin. Dropped, as shown at the top of Figure 10-1, is the most familiar style. The In Margin style places the oversized initial in the left margin.

   When you click your choice, the menu disappears. Word changes the initial cap in the paragraph to about three lines tall and positions it according to the option you chose. That's all there is to it.

### Modifying a drop cap

When you create a drop cap, Word places the initial character in the paragraph in a frame of its own and positions it either in the paragraph or in the margin, but you can do lots of things to modify the design. Word provides a Drop Cap dialog box where you can make some changes (Figure 10-2), but it's just as easy to edit the drop cap right in the document.

Because the cap is in a frame, you can drag it anywhere you want. To resize the drop cap, simply drag on a corner or side of the frame. Click inside the frame, and then select the letter to format it. Use any of Word's font formats to modify the letter. The color, shadow, emboss, and engrave options are great for drop caps. You can even add letters to the Drop Cap frame, so you can create a drop word, as shown in Figure 10-3.

### Removing a drop cap

Use the same menu—Insert → Text → Drop Cap—to remove a drop cap from your paragraph. Just select the None option, and the drop cap and the frame disappear. The paragraph goes back to its regular shape, with the initial letter back in line and sized like its compatriots.

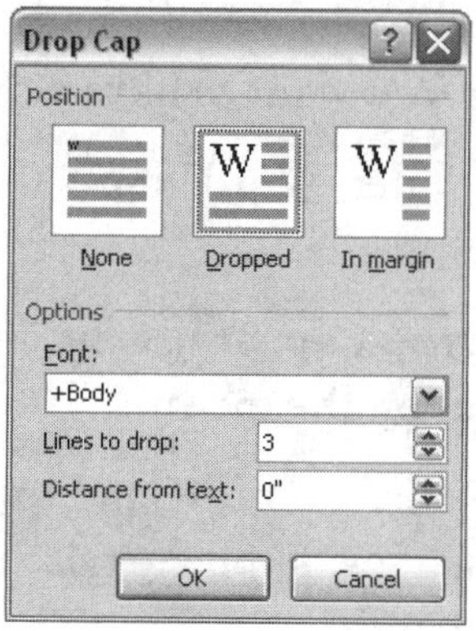

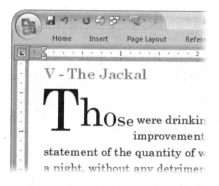

**Figure 10-2.** Using the Drop Cap box, you can choose one of the three styles and adjust the font, size, and position of the initial.

**Figure 10-3.** To create a drop word like this, first insert a drop cap, and then type the rest of the word. In this example, each letter was also selected individually and resized using the Home → Font → Font Size command. Then the drop word was positioned by dragging the frame.

## Bending Words with WordArt

WordArt is a lot more fun than it is useful. How often do you really need arched headlines in your documents? On top of that, you can waste a lot of time fiddling with all the options to see the cool effects you can produce (Figure 10-4).

To transform a word in your document into WordArt, double-click to select the word, and then choose Insert → Text → WordArt to see the menu of WordArt designs. If you click the one that suits your artistic purposes, you see your word transformed.

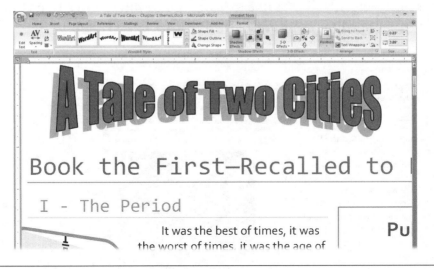

**Figure 10-4.** WordArt is way too much fun to be a serious business tool. You'll waste precious minutes trying out different bending, spacing, and twisting options when you should be working on that quarterly report for the VP.

### Modifying WordArt

When you click to select your WordArt creation, the WordArt Tools contextual tab appears on the right side of the ribbon. You can use this tab to make adjustments to 3-D effects (Alt+JW, U) and drop shadows (Alt+CW, V) and specify the text wrapping options (Alt+JW, TW).

In spite of the incredible ways you've transformed your word, it's still text to Microsoft. So if you catch a misspelling or need to make other changes, choose WordArt Tools | Format → Text → Edit Text to open the Edit WordArt Text box, where you can fix things up.

# Working with Pictures and Clip Art

When you insert a picture into your document, Word places it in a frame, similar to a text box or the frame around a drop cap. And as with those other objects, you can resize it, move it, and wrap text around it. As far as Word's concerned, if it's a graphic file—like a .JPG, .TIF, or EMF file—then it's a picture. The contents can be a photo or a drawing; it's all the same to Word. Once you've placed a picture in your document, you can edit it using any of the Picture Tools (Figure 10-5).

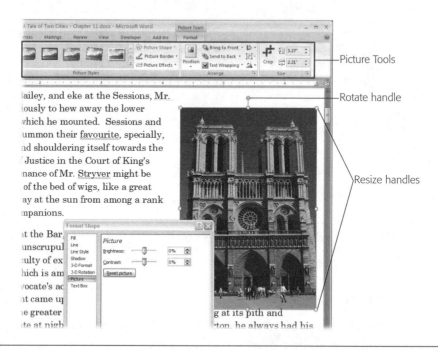

**Figure 10-5.** Click a picture to select it, and the Picture Tools contextual tab appears on the right end of the ribbon. Use these tools to size, position, and modify your photos, line art, and other graphic images.

---

**NOTE**

As explained on page 290, Word's clip art collection also includes photos and drawings. The main differences between clip art and pictures are the source of the images and how you insert them into your document. Use the Insert → Illustrations → Picture command to find pictures on your computer and place them in the document. Use the Insert → Illustrations → Clip Art command to search for photos in your clip art collection, including libraries of stock photos and artwork on the Internet.

---

## Inserting Pictures into Your Document

To get some practice with Word's picture tools, in these steps you'll insert a picture into your document and then adjust its formatting and positioning.

1. **Click to place the insertion point where you want to insert the picture.**

   Don't worry about putting the insertion point exactly where you want the photo. You'll be able to fine-tune the placement after it's on the page.

2. **Choose Insert → Illustrations → Picture or use Alt+N, P to open the Insert Picture dialog box.**

   The Insert Picture dialog box starts out showing you the contents of your My Pictures folder. You can use the tools along the left side and top of the box to navigate to any folder on your computer or network that contains image files. For example, if your computer is connected to a network, and you have a photo library on one of the other network computers, click the My Network Places button in the lower-left corner.

3. **When you find the picture you want to use, double-click it to place it in your document.**

   Double-clicking does the same thing as selecting the photo, and then clicking the Insert button in the lower-right corner. The Insert Picture box closes, and you see your photo in your document.

4. **To resize the picture, Shift-click, and then drag one of the corners.**

   When you close the Insert Picture box, your newly placed picture is selected, as you can see from the frame and sizing handles around the image. (If your picture isn't selected, click it.) You can resize your picture by dragging any of the sizing handles on the corners or edges of the picture. As you resize the picture, while you're still pressing the mouse button, you see both the full-sized image and a faint copy of the new size. Release the mouse button when the copy is the size you want.

   Usually, when you resize, one edge or corner of the image moves and the other edges remain in place. If you'd rather keep the center anchored while all the edges adjust to the new size, press Ctrl as you drag a sizing handle. Use the handle that's sticking out of the top to rotate your image (Figure 10-6).

To avoid squashing or stretching the image, press Shift as you drag, and your picture keeps its handsome proportions.

5. **On the right side of the Picture Tools | Format tab, click the Position menu, and then choose one of the positions for your photo.**

Generally, it's good design practice to place a picture in one of the corners or at one of the edges of your document. Occasionally, you'll want to place a picture smack dab in the middle. If one of these options works for you, you're in luck. Word's Position menu can place your picture in one of these typical locations, and automatically wraps the text around it.

**Figure 10-6.** Rotating a photo—or just about any other object in Word—is simple. A handle extends from the top center of the photo. Drag this handle around in a circle, and you see a ghost image of the photo rotating. When the image is in the position you want, let go of the mouse button.

## Finding and Using Clip Art

Once you insert clip art into your document, it's really no different from any other photo or drawing. The difference between pictures and clip art in Word is all in the finding and inserting. Any photo or image file you store on your computer and insert into a Word document is a *picture*. *Clip art* refers to the tens of thousands of graphics and other media files in online libraries on the Internet and in libraries Word installs on your computer.

Since you have such a wealth of images to sort through, you need a quick way to search those images and filter out the ones you don't want, so you can focus on a few good candidates for the job. Fortunately, that's exactly what the Clip Art task pane does (Figure 10-7).

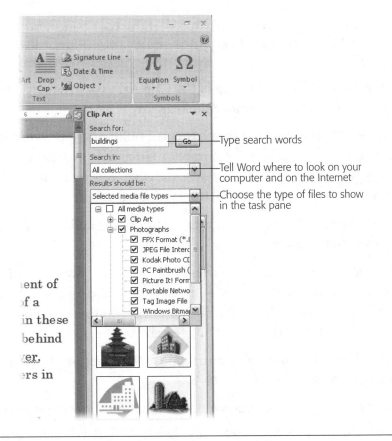

**Figure 10-7.** When you click the Clip Art button (Insert → Illustrations → Clip Art), the Clip Art task pane opens at your document's right. Answer three questions, and Word shows you clip art examples that meet your specifications. Word needs to know what to look for, where to look, and what type of files to show you (like JPEG, MP3, and AVI).

Here's how to find clip art and insert it into your document:

1. **Make sure you're on the page where you want to insert the clip art.**

   It's not important to position the insertion point carefully because you can always position your picture later.

2. **Choose Insert → Illustrations → Clip Art or use the shortcut Alt+N, F.**

   The Clip Art task pane opens at your screen's right.

   ___ TIP _____

   If you want to, you can click the top bar of the task pane, and then drag it out of the Word window, like a separate palette (Figure 10-8).

3. **In the "Search for" box at the top of the Clip Art task pane, type a word or phrase that describes what you're looking for.**

   For example, if you're looking for pictures of buildings, type *buildings* or *architecture*. If you want to reduce the number of images Word shows you, narrow it down by typing, say, *buildings France* or *buildings England*. The more specific you can be, the fewer images you'll have to look through.

4. **From the "Search in" drop-down menu, choose the collections and libraries you want Word to search.**

   Click the checkboxes to select libraries for the search. Some of the libraries have different subdirectories of images—you can tell by the square button with a + sign next to their names. Click the button to expand the list, and then you can choose specific subdirectories for your search.

5. **From the "Results should be" menu, choose the types of files you want to see in the Clip Art task pane (Figure 10-7).**

   Another way you can narrow down the search is by choosing the type of files you're looking for. Clip art includes photos, drawings, audio files, and video files. If you aren't interested in audio and video clips, open the "Results should be" menu, and then turn off checkmarks from the Movies and Sounds boxes.

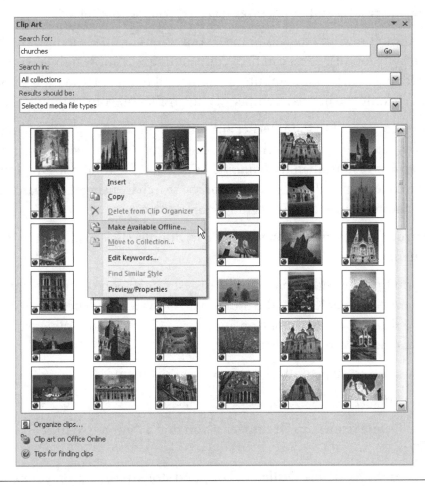

**Figure 10-8.** If you'd like a little more room to inspect all the pictures in your Clip Art task pane, drag it out of the Word window by the top bar. Then you can drag any of the borders to resize the Clip Art pane to give you a better view. Each thumbnail has a drop-down menu that lets you insert or copy the clip. (If you're connected to the Internet when you search for clip art, Word shows you results from online libraries, indicated by a tiny globe icon.)

6. **Click the Go button to start the search.**

   When you click Go, a message appears in the clip window to tell you that Word's searching for clip art. When it finds art that matches your search, the results of your clip art search appear as thumbnails in the main box in the Clip Art pane. (You see a small globe in the lower-left corner indicating art that's stored on the Internet.)

7. **Review the results and, if necessary, adjust your search terms.**

If Word can't find any images to meet your criteria, you see a message that says "(No results found)." You can do a couple things if your search fails. Double-check to make sure your computer is connected to the Internet. If it's not, Word can access only the limited number of clip art files on your computer.

If you're connected to the Internet and still get no results, try expanding your search by changing your search words. For example, if *cathedrals Paris* didn't bring up any results, then try *buildings France* and see what pops up. If you limited the collection and libraries used for the search by using the "Search in" box, try expanding your search to include more sources.

8. **When you find an image you want to use, double-click to place it in your document.**

Once you find the perfect picture, the easiest way to pop that image into your document is to double-click the thumbnail. Or, when you click once to select an image, a drop-down menu button appears on the right side. When you click to open this menu, you see several options:

▶Choose **Insert** to place the image in your document.

▶Choose **Copy** to place a copy of the image on Word's clipboard.

▶Click **Delete from Clip Organizer** if you don't want to see the clip in future searches.

▶Click **Make Available Offline** to copy and store the image on your computer.

Once the clip art image is inserted into your document, it's like any other picture or drawing. When you click to select the picture, the Picture Tools contextual tab appears on the right side of the ribbon. You can use all the usual formatting tools and commands to resize, position, and format your clip art, just as you would any other picture.

# Working with SmartArt

SmartArt is another new Word 2007 feature designed to help busy people create and format a strong, graphic message. It's a boon to non-artistic business types faced with the challenge of creating a sleek, professional looking PowerPoint presentation. Maybe the designers at Microsoft decided the world had seen enough white slides full of black, square bullet points. Still, take the "Art" in SmartArt with a grain of salt. SmartArt isn't Rembrandt, Gauguin, or even Andy Warhol. It's the kind of art that an MBA loves—relationship trees, pyramid charts, and matrices.

Say you have a list of bullet points: a few main topics, each with a few subtopics. Rather than just present them as bullet points, you want to create a graphic that helps tell the story with impact, so you peruse the SmartArt library (Figure 10-9). Once you choose your graphic, you simply type the text you want to add. Word does all the formatting, sizing, and arranging. If you don't like the finished product, you can choose another graphic. Word swaps in the new design and does all the reformatting—no need to retype the text. Word knows how to take your bullet points and fit them into any of the SmartArt graphics.

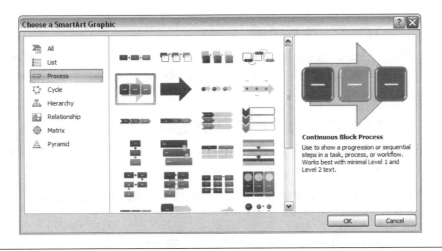

**Figure 10-9.** When you give the command to insert SmartArt, you see this box. Choose a category from the list on the left, and you see thumbnails of the options in the middle. Click a thumbnail to see a large preview on the right.

Like the other graphics in Word, SmartArt takes its cues for colors and fonts from your document's theme, so you don't have to worry about clashing. SmartArt and Themes are a natural fit. Here are the other elements that make SmartArt smart:

- **Layout templates.** Each of the images is a template just waiting for your text to deliver a message. The designs are contemporary and suitable for business and other organizations. You can transfer SmartArt graphics between the Office 2007 versions of Word, Excel, and PowerPoint, cutting and pasting artwork between programs.

- **A text pane for your message.** You get to focus on your message and let Word take care of the artsy design stuff. Because a consistency is present in the design of the templates, Smart-Art can reformat and reconfigure your text to work with many different graphics and layouts.

- **Automatic sizing and positioning of shapes and text.** One of the most time-consuming issues when it comes to developing graphics for business presentations is the endless tinkering you have to do every time you change a word. SmartArt removes this problem. Just edit your text on the text pane, and SmartArt takes care of the font size and the graphic's shape and size.

## Choosing a SmartArt Graphic

SmartArt graphics are divided into categories, each of which arranges information in a particular way. When deciding what kind of SmartArt to use, think of *how* you want to present your material:

- **Lists.** Great for individual facts, outlines, procedures, and other, well…lists.

- **Processes.** Used to track the changes in a project or goal, like harvest, production, distribution, sales, and consumption.

- **Cycles.** Suited to presenting processes that end back at the beginning. Think Winter, Spring, Summer, and Fall.

- **Hierarchies.** You've seen this type of organizational chart, where bosses proves they really *are* in charge.

- **Relationships.** The graphics in this group provide different ways to show the connections between items. For example, you find concentric circles, vertical tabs with arrows connecting them, and more.

- ▶ **Matrices.** This MBA favorite helps businesses make better decisions or at least understand why things aren't working.

- ▶ **Pyramids.** These graphics are good for illustrating proportions. For example, the U.S. Food and Drug Administration uses a pyramid chart to prove that you're not eating enough fruits and vegetables.

## Inserting SmartArt into Your Document

SmartArt is a little more complicated than your average drawing, so it takes a few more steps to insert it into your document.

1. **Click to position the insertion point on a page of your document.**

   You don't have to be exact when you position the insertion point. You'll be able to move SmartArt later, just like any picture.

2. **Choose Insert → Illustrations → SmartArt or press Alt+N, M.**

   The Choose a SmartArt Graphic box opens (Figure 10-9). It displays categories on the left side, thumbnails in the middle, and a preview panel on the right.

3. **On the left side, click to choose a category.**

   Choose from one of the general categories described earlier in this section. Or, if you want to see all your options, leave the category set to All. Thumbnails appear in the middle of the box. If you need to, use the scroll bar to check out all the possibilities. When you click a thumbnail, the image in the preview on the right shows a larger, color version of your selection.

   When you've made your selection, click OK to insert the SmartArt into your document.

   The dialog box closes, and the SmartArt of your choice appears in your document. A text pane opens next to the SmartArt, as shown in Figure 10-10.

4. **In the text box titled "Type your text here," do what it says.**

   The text box can vary depending on the SmartArt graphics you choose. Almost always, you see a bulleted list and prompts for you to start typing away.

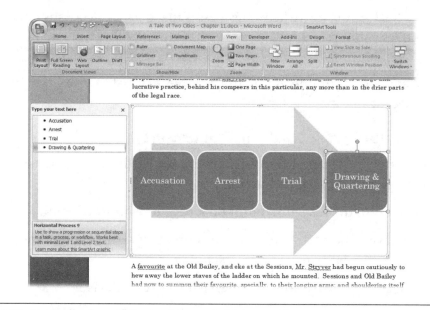

**Figure 10-10.** The large arrow in the background of this graphic suggests a process or sequence of events. As you type in the text pane, your words appear in the SmartArt graphic. To add elements to a SmartArt graphic, simply press Enter, and then keep typing. This SmartArt started with just three boxes. The fourth box was added by pressing Enter, and then typing Drawing & Quartering.

5. **Promote and demote items in your text pane.**

   You can promote and demote items in your bulleted list, just like you do with an outline. While you're working in the text pane, use the keyboard shortcut Alt+Shift, Left arrow to promote items, and Alt+Shift, Right arrow to demote them. The left side of the SmartArt Tools | Design tab (Figure 10-11) also has Promote and Demote buttons.

6. **Close the text pane to finish your graphic.**

   When you're finished, click the X button in the upper-right corner of the text pane to close it, or—faster still—just click within the text of your document. You see your SmartArt graphic formatted and in place.

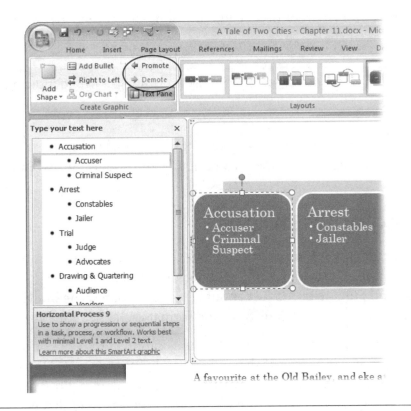

**Figure 10-11.** The SmartArt Promote and Demote buttons help you position and rank the bullet points in the graphic.

## Modifying SmartArt

When you click to select a SmartArt graphic, you don't see the usual Picture Tools contextual tab. Also, the frame around SmartArt looks different from the frame around other kinds of pictures. That's because you have a different set of SmartArt tools to use. Two tabs are located within the SmartArt contextual tab—Design and Format. Use the Design tab to fine-tune layouts and overall styles. Use the Format tab to apply specific colors and WordArt styles.

The frame around a SmartArt graphic, although it looks different, lets you move and resize the graphic just like any other picture. Hold the mouse over the edge of the frame. When you see a cross with four arrows, you can drag the art to a new place.

Hold the cursor over a corner or an edge, and you see a double-arrow that you can drag to resize the image.

---

**TIP**

The little dots on the edges of a SmartArt graphic's frame indicate a handle that you can drag with the mouse.

---

On the left side of the frame you see a tab with two triangle-shaped arrows. Click this tab to open the text pane, where you can edit and add to the text in your SmartArt.

# Working with Shapes

Word's Shapes don't have SmartArt's IQ, but they're much more flexible. SmartArt knows what it wants to do and can be stubborn if you try to change its ways. Shapes let you push and pull them into just about any size or shape. The drawback with shapes is that you must insert, position, and format each one individually.

To open the Shapes menu, choose Insert → Illustrations → Shapes or use the shortcut Alt+N, SH. You see dozens of shapes, arrows, lines, and icons. Down at the very bottom of the menu you find the New Drawing Canvas command. The drawing canvas is a rectangular work area where you can arrange several shapes, and then treat them like a single graphic. If you're inserting a single shape, you can simply insert it, format it, and then flow the text around it. If you're working with several shapes, it's better to place a drawing canvas in your document, and then work with your shapes on the canvas. That way, you can have your text flow around the entire canvas instead of fine-tuning it to flow around several individual shapes.

In the following tutorial, you'll place a canvas in your document and add shapes to it. In the process, you'll explore some of the myriad possibilities for positioning, sizing, and formatting shapes.

1. **Position the insertion point in your document where you want to place the canvas.**

   It works best if you have the insertion point on a blank line because Word initially creates a canvas that runs from margin to margin.

2. **Choose Insert → Illustrations → Shapes → New Drawing Canvas, or use the keyboard shortcut is Alt+N, SHN.**

   The drawing canvas appears in your document—a large rectangle bounded by a dashed line and solid black resize handles at the corners and the middle of each side. When you pass the mouse over the canvas, it turns into a clear arrow instead of an insertion point.

3. **If you wish, click a corner or edge to resize the drawing canvas.**

   If the edges of your canvas aren't visible, click anywhere on the colored area of the canvas to select it. When you hold the mouse cursor over one of the resize handles, the cursor changes shape, indicating that you can drag.

   If you hold the cursor over one of the canvas borders without resize controls, it turns into a cross with arrows pointing in four directions—so you can drag the entire canvas to move it.

4. **Open the Format Drawing Canvas dialog box.**

   You can open the Format Drawing Canvas box three different ways. Right-click the canvas, and then choose Format Drawing Canvas from the shortcut menu. Press the keyboard shortcut Alt+JD, FA, or go to Drawing Tools | Format → Shape Styles → Advanced Tools.

   The Format Drawing canvas box has tabs along the top, labeled Colors and Lines, Size, Layout, and Alt Text. For now, you use the first tab to change the canvas's color and transparency.

---

**TIP**

You can ignore the Alt Text tab unless your Word document is destined to become a Web page. (You can find more on this in *Word 2007: The Missing Manual*.) It lets you add some text describing the image. Folks who have images turned off in their Web browser see this text instead, and so get an idea of what the image shows. Alt text also benefits visually impaired people whose browsers read Web page text aloud.

---

5.  **On the Color and Lines tab, in the Fill section, choose a color for the canvas, and then set its transparency so that text or other objects show through the canvas.**

The Fill Effects button leads to yet another dialog box where you can adjust the shading and the gradations of color for your canvas (Figure 10-12).

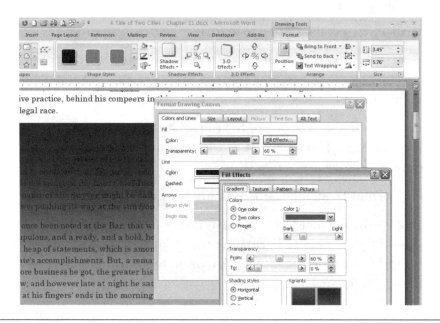

**Figure 10-12.** You use nearly identical tools to format the drawing canvas and the shapes that you insert into your documents. Once you're comfortable working with colors, borders, and transparency for the canvas, you can apply everything you know to the shapes and lines in your graphics. Other formatting tabs let you specify the canvas's size and position and the way that text wraps around the object.

6.  **When you're through, click OK to close the dialog box, and then return to your document.**

7.  **Go to Insert → Shapes and click to choose a shape (Figure 10-13).**

On the Drawing Tools ribbon, use the scroll buttons to see more shapes, or click the button at bottom to see them all at once on a menu.

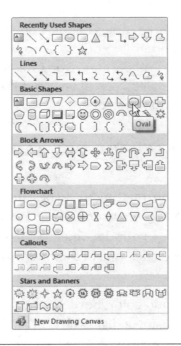

**Figure 10-13.** On the Shapes menu, click to choose one of the shapes, and then drag to create a drawing canvas. The selected shape appears on the drawing canvas in your document. You can add other shapes to the canvas. For example, you can create an organizational chart using a combination of boxes and arrows.

8. **Drag on the canvas to position and size the shape on the canvas.**

   After clicking one of the shapes, click somewhere on your canvas, and then press the mouse button as you drag diagonally across the canvas. You see an outline of the shape drawn on the canvas as you drag the mouse. When it's roughly the size and shape you want, release the mouse button.

   If you want to move or resize the shape, you need to click to select it. When the shape is selected, handles appear around the edges. The handles for different shapes can have slightly different functions, but controlling them is very similar. Drag the corner or edge handles to resize the shapes. The handle sprouting out from the top is used to rotate the shape; just drag to spin the shape around.

You may also see diamond-shaped handles on a shape. These handles have special functions depending on the shape. For example, on a rectangle, they let you round the corners. Don't be afraid to experiment and try out all the handles. You can always get back to square one with the wonderful Ctrl+Z undo keystroke.

9. **To add color to the shape, go to Drawing Tools | Format → Shape Styles and choose a style.**

   The quickest way to apply formatting to shapes, lines, and your drawing canvas is with one of the Shape Styles shown on the Drawing Tools ribbon. Seventy variations are available using your documents Theme colors with different borders and shades. When you click one of them, Word applies the formatting to the selected shape.

   As an alternative, you can add color, borders, and shades to your shapes just like you formatted the canvas using a dialog box. In fact, you can use the same command (Drawing Tools | Format → Shape Styles → Advanced Tools) or shortcut (Alt+JD, FA) to open the Format AutoShape box.

   Next, you'll add a second shape and shape-adjust its position with the Send to Back and Bring to Front commands.

10. **Choose a different shape from the Insert Shapes menu. Drag to place it on the canvas, making sure that it overlaps the first shape.**

    Notice that each shape exists on its own layer. It's like placing one piece of paper on top of another. Every time you add a shape or a line to your drawing, Word puts it on a layer above the existing shapes. You can change the layer order of your shapes using the commands in the Drawing Tools | Format → Arrange group. Under the Bring to Front and Send to Back drop-down menus, several variations let you move the selected shape one layer at a time or to the top or bottom of the heap.

    Next, you'll draw a line between the two shapes.

11. **Choose one of the lines from the Insert Shapes palette (it doesn't matter if it has arrows on the end or not).**

    The cursor changes to a cross, but when you hold it over one of the shapes, it changes, looking a little more like a crosshair, and the shape shows handles at the edges.

12. **Click one of the shape handles to attach one end of your line to that shape. Click a blank spot on the canvas to place the other end of the line anywhere that's not connected to one of the shapes.**

    Lines have some special talents. They can be independent, just like any of the shapes, or they can connect to a shape on either end. Word provides visual hints as you're drawing to let you know exactly how the line will behave.

    Now, if you move the shape, you see the line stays attached and moves along with the shape. The unattached end of the line moves freely.

    When you click to select the line, handles appear in the middle and on both ends. You can move the line by clicking just about anywhere except the ends and dragging it. You see the familiar move icon that looks like a cross with four arrows. Hold the cursor over one of the end handles, and the cursor changes to the cross without the arrows (Figure 10-14).

13. **Click the line's free end handle and drag it over to one of the handles on the other shape.**

    Word attaches the line to the shape. With the line attached to the two shapes, you can move the shapes around the canvas, and the line shrinks, grows, and repositions itself to remain attached to both shapes.

14. **Format the line using the tools of your choice.**

    Lines don't have to be dull black affairs. You can format lines using the same tools and commands that you use for the other shapes. You can apply Shape Styles (Drawing Tools | Format → Shape Styles), or you can fine-tune the formatting with the Format AutoShape box (Alt+JD, FA).

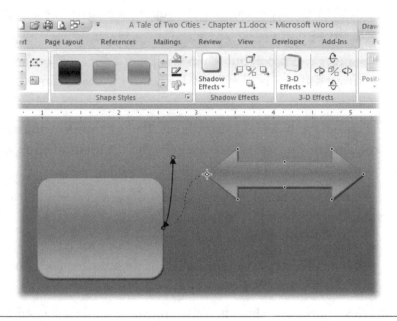

**Figure 10-14.** Lines have some pretty clever AutoShape behaviors. When you attach lines to the handles of shapes, they'll stay attached even when you move the objects around the drawing canvas. This makes it easy to create organizational charts and other graphics that show relationships.

At this point you have three objects, each on its own layer above or below the other objects. The line connects one shape to another and stays connected if you move either object. Sometimes when you're working on more complicated graphics, it's helpful to group several objects together as if they're a single object. Next, you'll group the drawings and the line.

15. **Click to select one of the shapes. In turn, Ctrl+click the line, and then Ctrl+click the second shape.**

With each click, selection handles appear on the shapes and the line.

16. **With all three objects selected, go to Drawing Tools | Format → Arrange → Group → Group.**

Now instead of lots of little handles, the trio of shapes and lines sport a simplified set of handles. You can position, size, and rotate the three objects as one. When you select the group as a unit, you can also apply formatting commands such as color to all the objects at once. If you want to apply formatting to just one of the objects, select the group first, and then click to select the object within the group.

17. **Go to Drawing Tools | Format → Arrange → Text Wrapping or Alt+JD, TW and set the text wrapping behavior for the canvas and drawings.**

Several options are available for wrapping text around your graphics or around the canvas. The different commands let you position the drawing above or below the text and choose how tightly the text wraps around the shapes or the canvas. Figure 10-15 explains how Word decides what to wrap the text around.

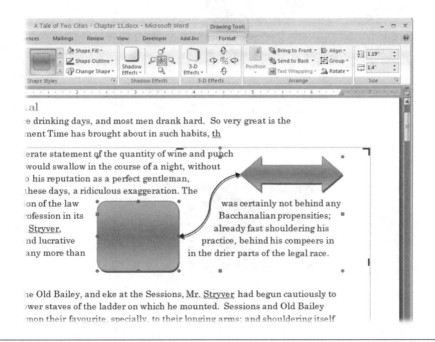

**Figure 10-15.** If your shape isn't on a canvas or if you didn't apply color to the canvas, you can choose to wrap the text tightly around the shapes. If your graphics are on a canvas with a color fill, the text wrap commands apply to the entire canvas.

# Customizing Color

Whenever you add color to a font, a border, or any of the shapes described in this chapter, Word shows you a palette of suggested colors from the document's theme to guide you in your choices.

But don't feel constrained if you don't like the colors on the menu. You can open the Colors box shown in Figure 10-16 and create just about any color you can imagine.

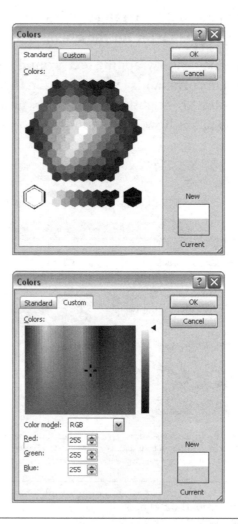

**Figure 10-16.** The Office 2007 Colors box lets you pick colors in two ways.

Top: The Standard tab is the easiest to use—just click a color swatch.

Bottom: The Custom tab gives you great color control, but requires a couple extra clicks. You don't need to know anything about these cryptic three-digit numbers in order to use the Custom tab, but if you're curious, see the box on page 309.

(This box is the same in all the Office programs, so you only have to learn how to use it once.) The Standard tab shows colors arranged as hexagons within a hexagon. Click a color or a gray shade (at the bottom) to make a selection. The Custom tab gives you more control over your color selection. To use it, click the rainbow-colored box on the left, and you get a crosshair cursor to choose a color with. Position the crosshairs on the color in the spectrum you want, and then click the slider on the right to adjust your chosen color's lightness or darkness. Using these two controls, you can select any color your computer can create. As you work with the Colors spectrum and the slider, the New and Current boxes show you a preview of how you're changing the color.

## Specifying Colors by Numbers

When graphic designers talk about color, they use a numerical system from 0 to 255, where any color imaginable can be described as a combination of red, green, and blue. A value of 0 means that the color contains none of that hue, with 255 being the maximum amount. These numbers let you describe color with great precision. For example, R197, G216, B255 specifies a particular shade of blue. To create this color in Word's Colors box, type 197 in the Red box, 216 in the Green box, and 255 in the Blue box. If you're company's logo specifies that shade of blue, you can type these numbers to get it exactly right every time.

Fortunately, you can forget everything you've read in this box and still create custom colors in Word. When you click a color and move the lightness/darkness slider in the Colors box, Word fills in the RGB numbers for you.

The other color model used in the Colors box is HSL, which stands for hue, saturation (intensity), and luminosity (brightness). Saturation refers to the amount of the actual color (hue) in the mix, and luminosity determines the amount of white or black mixed in to create degrees of lightness and darkness. Here, too, you can type numbers if you know them, or just use the color spectrum and slider until you've got the color you want.

# PART THREE: APPENDIX

**Appendix:**   Word Help and Beyond

# WORD HELP AND BEYOND

- ▶ Using Word's Built-in Help
- ▶ Using Microsoft's Office Web Site
- ▶ Third-Party Web Sites

**HELP WITH WORD 2007 IS NEVER FAR AWAY.** The first place to look is in the program itself. Word's built-in Help system includes information panels and tutorials stored both on your computer and online. In fact, to support its products, Microsoft has a whole sprawling network of Web sites where you'll find tips, updates, discussion groups, and downloads for templates, themes, and other Word tools.

There's lots of community support out there, too. About 11 years ago, Microsoft developed an MVP program to recognize the folks who freely give their time to help others with Windows, Word, and other Microsoft programs. MVPs aren't Microsoft employees, but they're very good at what they do. On the Internet, you can easily find Word MVPs from around the world—if you know where to look. This Appendix helps you explore all your help options, starting right there on your computer.

# Using Word's Built-in Help

When you're working in Word, the most convenient place to look for help is Word's built-in Help system. Press the F1 key, or click the little round button with the question mark in the upper-right corner of most Word windows to open Word Help, as shown in Figure A-1. The Word Help box conveniently opens in its own window, so it's not hard to drag it out of the way when you want to look at your work.

If Word Help doesn't automatically open to a page that's helpful, you'll have to do some searching. You can use two methods for finding the help you need: the Search tool in the upper-left corner or the Table of Contents.

▶ **Search.** Using the Search text box, type in a word or phrase, like *margins* or *hanging indent*. If you press Enter, or click the Search button, then Word hunts for help. When it's finished, articles that match your search words appear in the right panel. Look through the headings, and then click the one that's most likely to be helpful. If you need to come back and try another topic, click the back button.

Word can search in several different locations for help. To see a list of the locations, click the triangle to the right of the Search button to open the Search menu. Online resources are listed at the top of the menu, and content that's stored on your computer is listed at the bottom. You can fine-tune the search by directing Word Help to look in a specific location. Use the drop-down menu to the right of the Search text box to choose the locations for the search.

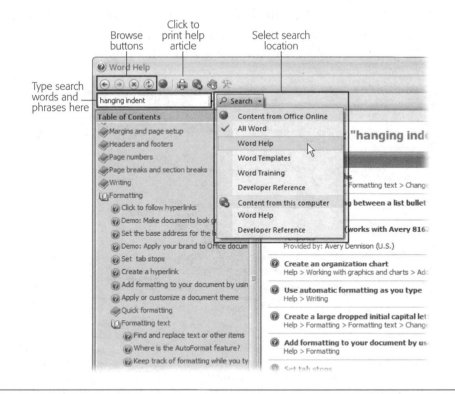

**Figure A-1.** Think of Word Help as a Web browser dedicated to articles about Word. Use the browser buttons in the upper-left corner to move back and forth through the articles you've viewed.

▶ **Table of Contents.** On the left side of Word Help, the Table of Contents works a lot like a Word outline. You can expand and contract the headings by clicking the little book icons to the left of the words. One click opens a heading and shows the contents. Another click closes the heading, hiding the subheads and articles inside. The icons with question marks are the actual help articles; click them to show the help articles in the pane on the right.

## Using Help Articles

For the most part, Word Help works a lot like a Web browser. You can use the buttons in the upper-left corner to browse forward and backward through the articles that you've read. There's even a button to stop and refresh the page, just like on your

Web browser. Click an article heading in the Help Window to read the article. Some of the help headings will open your browser and take you to Web pages where you can find resources like templates or view audiovisual demonstrations (Figure A-2).

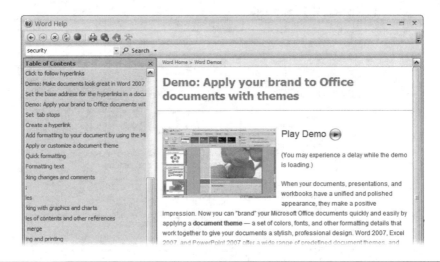

**Figure A-2.** Some help articles link to audiovisual demonstrations on the Internet. When you click the Play Demo button, your browser opens to a page on the Microsoft Web site. The demo begins playing as soon as it starts to download to your computer.

If you want to print one of the help articles, click the little printer button at the top of the Word Help window. The Print box opens, and you can choose a printer and make other printing adjustments before you send the article to the printer. For example, on the Margins topic, you may want to print a single page instead of all 10 pages.

The contents shown in Word Help can come from files stored on your computer or from Microsoft's Web site. Use the button in the lower-right corner of Word Help to choose your source (Figure A-3). The help content that resides on your computer is pretty comprehensive. The help content that comes from Microsoft's Web site is kind of a mixed bag that includes all the help articles found on your computer as well as audiovisual demos, templates provided by third parties, clip art, and access to

Microsoft's Knowledge Base of technical articles. One advantage of the online help content is that Microsoft continually updates and adds to it.

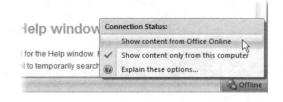

**Figure A-3.** A button in the lower-right corner of the Help window shows whether you're online or not. Click the button, and a pop-up menu appears, as shown here.

# Using Microsoft's Office Web Site

You'll find the main Web site that supports Microsoft office products at *http://office.microsoft.com*. The home page is slick—and about as helpful as a magazine ad. You need to dig deeper to get to the helpful features. To zero in on some more useful articles and links, click the Products tab at the top of the page. Along the left side, you find links to specific office products, including Word. Click the Word link, or go directly to the page that focuses on Word by typing *http://office.microsoft.com/en-us/word* into the address box of your browser. The Word page changes periodically, but it usually looks something like Figure A-4.

## Discussion Groups

Discussion groups are one of the great resources of the online world. You can post a question in a discussion group and come back in a couple hours or the next day and other people will be posting answers and debating the fine points of the issue. It's an excellent way to dig deep into a subject and make some online friends in the process. You can also search through the discussion group to see if someone else has asked the same question. Type a word or a phrase in the "Search for" box near the middle of the screen (Figure A-5). After some churning, topics related to your search words appear in the center list. Click a + button to expand the topic, and then click a name to read the contents of the post.

**Figure A-4.** The Microsoft Word Web page provides links to articles and other resources for the program. At the bottom of the left-hand column under Additional Resources, you find a link to Discussion Groups where you can ask questions and then later come back and read the responses.

---

**TIP**

Before you post your question, it's good online etiquette to check the group to see if a FAQ (frequently asked questions) posting is available. Sometimes experts get annoyed when newbies ask the same question over and over.

---

The posts in a discussion are listed in chronological order, with the first message at the top. So, start at the top to read the question, and then work your way down the list to read the answers and other responses. Some questions will be answered quickly, with one or two on-target responses. A hot topic can result in a lengthy debate, with a dozen or so responses.

Some of the experts who participate in these discussion groups are Microsoft MVPs. For a description of Microsoft MVPs, see the box on the following page. In general, you'll find the contributions from the Microsoft MVPs both accurate and concise.

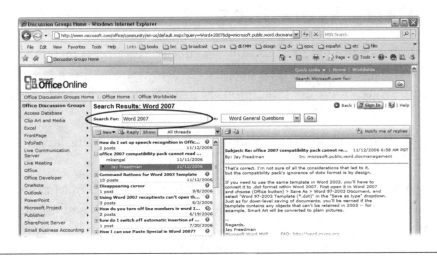

**Figure A-5.** The Office discussion groups are a great resource if you have a question about Word. You can use the two columns on the left to zero in on a topic, or you can type a word or a phrase in the "Search for" box near the middle of the screen.

## UP TO SPEED

# What's a Word MVP?

One of the smarter moves Microsoft ever made was to develop a way to recognize the people who voluntarily help others. Each year Microsoft singles out a few individuals who aren't Microsoft employees and dubs them MVPs (Most Valuable Professionals). There are MVPs for all the different Microsoft products, and of course, quite a few are Word MVPs. These folks know how to make Word jump through hoops. You find them offering free advice in computer forums, discussion groups, and newsgroups, and even publishing answers to frequently asked questions on their own Web sites.

Even better, these experts are often experts in other fields in addition to knowing the mysteries of Word. One expert may understand the financial world, while another may be knowledgeable about architecture and construction. Yet another may live in France and be able to answer Word questions particular to that language. This real-world experience along with a love of Word makes MVPs a valuable resource when you have a specific or sticky question.

# Third-Party Web Sites

You're certainly not limited to Microsoft-sanctioned resources when it comes to getting help with Word. Many Web sites are devoted to providing advice, services, and add-in software. Some are free, some are pricey, and you'll find everything in between.

If you type *Word help*, or *Word templates*, or *Word Add-in* in your favorite search engine, you'll see dozens of listings like the following:

▶ **The Word MVP site** (*http://word.mvps.org*). Run by a group of Microsoft MVPs, not Microsoft, this site sets out to tell the whole Word truth and nothing but the truth. As its home page declares: "Word rarely misses an opportunity to perplex." The site divides Word issues into a number of popular topics, and a handy search tool at the top of the home page makes it easy to quickly zero in on what you're looking for (Figure A-6).

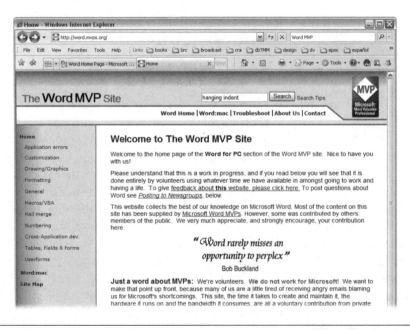

**Figure A-6.** The Word MVP site provides a wealth of expert advice. A simple, clean interface makes it easy to browse for a topic, or you can use the search tool at the top of the home page.

▶ **Woody's Office Portal** (*www.wopr.com*). For years, Woody Leonhard has provided the Word community with expert advice and his WOPR add-in. WOPR stands for Woody's Office Power Pack—a collection of Office-related add-ins. At the time of this writing, WOPR for Office 2007 was not yet on offer, but Woody's probably working on it. (There's been a WOPR for every version since Office 97.) The Web site is a little kitschy, but the information and tools are rock solid. Don't miss Woody's Lounge, an active online forum for Word and other Office programs (Figure A-7). You can read the posts without becoming a member, but to leave a message, you need to sign up. Membership is free, and the sign-up process simply involves agreeing to the rules of the message board. You can sign up for a free email newsletter.

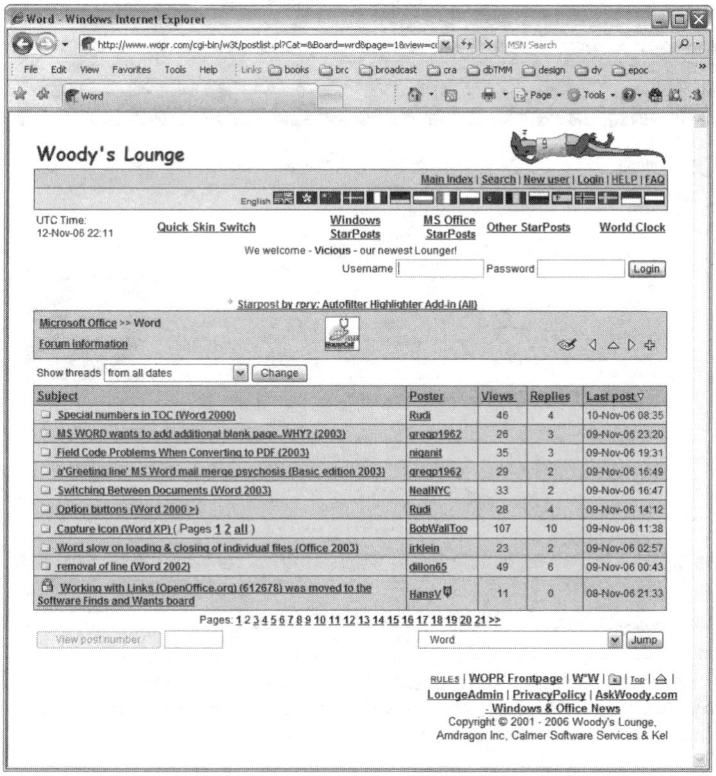

**Figure A-7.** Woody's Lounge is an active forum where visitors post questions about Word and other Office products.

▶ **Wordsite Office Automation** (*www.wordsite.com*). Founded by Microsoft MVP Bill Coan, Wordsite (Figure A-8) provides products and services related to Word and Office automation. Not interested in creating your own templates and macros? You can hire the folks at Wordsite to do it for you. They offer a free analysis of your needs. Wordsite also offers training tailored to individual business needs. On the Wordsite Web site, you find products like DataPrompter 2007, an off-the-shelf tool that enhances Word by automatically prompting people and updating documents. The site also offers free downloads with information about XML and utilities that are related to Word.

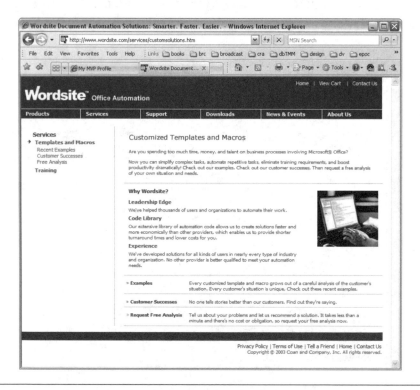

**Figure A-8.** If you need some Word expertise and don't have the time to do everything yourself, you can find a company like Wordsite to assist you. Wordsite provides training, sells add-in products, and creates custom macros and templates to customer specifications.

# INDEX

## Symbols

.doc extension, 45
.docm extension, 22, 44, 45
.docx extension, 19, 22, 44, 45
.dot extension, 45
.dotm extension, 45
.dotx extension, 45
.htm and .html extensions, 45
.mhtm and .mhtml extensions, 45
.pdf extension, 45
.rtf extension, 45
.txt extension, 45
.wps extension, 45
.xml extension, 45
.xps extension, 45

## Numbers

2 pages per sheet (booklets), 134

## A

Adobe Acrobat, 222
aligning text, 93
    in tables, 273, 280
Alt key (shortcuts), 39

animated type, 90
Arrange All (Window group), 35
arrows (what they mean in this
        book), 7
AutoCorrect, 186, 195–200
    adding entries, 197
    adjusting settings, 196
    deleting entries, 199
    formatting, 199
    Math, 199
    Replace text as you type box, 197
    Smart Tags, 200
    symbols, 199
    vs. AutoText, 196
AutoFit (tables), 256
AutoText, 80
    entries (templates), 173
    Quick Parts, 80

## B

backing up, 41
Backspace vs. Delete, 49
Bar tab, 109
bibliographies, 96
blank document (creating new), 16, 18
boilerplate text in templates, 173

**graphics** (*continued*)
  drop caps, 283–285
  inline (spacing for), 97
  pictures, 283, 289
  Print drawings created in Word, 234
  shapes, 283, 300–307
  SmartArt, 283, 295–300
  templates, 172
  views, 284
  WordArt, 286
**greeting cards (see stationery)**
**Gridlines box**, 30

# H

**headers and footers**, 138–145
  Building Blocks, 140–143
  custom, 143
  margins, 132
  removing, 145
  small caps for headers, 91
  tools, 139
**headings**, 242–246
  controlling subheads during
      promotion/demotion, 245
  promoting and demoting, 242–246
  subheads, 245
**height of page**, 128
**Help**, 5, 314–322
  Articles, 315
  button, 5
  discussion groups, 317

FAQs, 318
  Microsoft Office Web site, 317
  Search text box, 314
  Table of Contents, 315
  third party Web sites, 320
  Word MVPs, 319
**HighBeam Research**, 202
**highlighting text**
  **(see selecting text)**
**hyphenation**, 148–154
  automatic, 150
  guidelines, 151
  justified text, 151
  limit consecutive hyphens, 150
  manual, 153
  proper names, 151
  removing from document, 152
  styles (three to choose from), 149
  zone, 150

# I

**ignore**
  punctuation in find and replace, 79
  spell check, 188
  white space characters in find and
      replace, 79
**indenting paragraphs**, 95
  hanging indent, 96
  using Ruler, 113
  using Tab key, 96

insert mode vs. overtype mode, 49
insertion point, 48, 51
installed templates, 178–179
Internet connection
  clip art, 294
  research tools, 203
invitations (see stationery)
invoices (see business forms)

# J

justification, 94

# K

keyboard basics, 8
  clicking, 8
  ribbon, 8
  selecting text, 56
  shift-clicking, 8
  shortcuts, 9
keyboard shortcuts, 9, 21, 39, 69
  Alt key, 39
  Bold (Ctrl+B), 39
  C key, 39
  Copy (Ctrl+C), 69
  Cut (Ctrl+X), 69
  F key, 39
  formatting, 88
  new document (Ctrl+N), 39
  old vs. new version of Word, 39
  outlines, 243
  Paste (Ctrl+V), 69

References tab (S key), 39
saving, 40
spell checking (F7), 39
tables, 262–269
Undo, 69
keystrokes
  lessening, 80–82
  Quick Parts, 80–82

# L

labels (see stationery)
launcher (Clipboard), 75
launching Word, 14–16
  opening a Word document, 15
  Quick Launch toolbar, 15
  Start menu, 14
  your name and initials, 14
layout (see paper size and layout)
leaders, tab, 105
legal documents (and lists), 104
letters (see stationery)
line breaks (see page and line breaks)
lines, spacing, 97
  At least option, 97
  Exactly option, 97
  Multiple, 97
linked data, 235
lists, 100–104
  bulleted and numbered, 100–104
  multilevel, 104
Live Preview feature, 4, 165

# M

# COLOPHON

Philip Dangler was the production editor for *Word 2007 for Starters: The Missing Manual*. Mary Brady and Colleen Gorman provided quality control. Michele Filshie wrote the index.

The cover of this book is based on a series design originally created by David Freedman and modified by Mike Kohnke, Karen Montgomery, and Fitch (*www.fitch.com*). Back cover design, dog illustration, and color selection by Fitch.

Tom Ingalls designed the interior layout, which was modified by Ron Bilodeau. Robert Romano and Jessamyn Read produced the illustrations.

# Related Titles from O'Reilly

## Missing Manuals

*Access 2003 for Starters: The Missing Manual*

*Access 2007 for Starters: The Missing Manual*

*Access 2007: The Missing Manual*

*AppleScript: The Missing Manual*

*AppleWorks 6: The Missing Manual*

*CSS: The Missing Manual*

*Creating Web Sites: The Missing Manual*

*Digital Photography: The Missing Manual*

*Dreamweaver 8: The Missing Manual*

*eBay: The Missing Manual*

*Excel 2003 for Starters: The Missing Manual*

*Excel 2007 for Starters: The Missing Manual*

*Excel 2007: The Missing Manual*

*FileMaker Pro 8: The Missing Manual*

*Flash 8: The Missing Manual*

*FrontPage 2003: The Missing Manual*

*GarageBand 2: The Missing Manual*

*Google: The Missing Manual, 2nd Edition*

*Home Networking: The Missing Manual*

*iMovie HD 6: The Missing Manual*

*iPhoto 6: The Missing Manual*

*iPod: The Missing Manual, 5th Edition*

*Mac OS X: The Missing Manual, Tiger Edition*

*Office 2004 for Macintosh: The Missing Manual*

*PCs: The Missing Manual*

*Photoshop Elements 5: The Missing Manual*

*PowerPoint 2007 for Starters: The Missing Manual*

*PowerPoint 2007: The Missing Manual*

*QuickBooks 2006: The Missing Manual*

*Quicken 2006 for Starters: The Missing Manual*

*Switching to the Mac: The Missing Manual, Tiger Edition*

*The Internet: The Missing Manual*

*Windows 2000 Pro: The Missing Manual*

*Windows XP for Starters: The Missing Manual*

*Windows XP Home Edition: The Missing Manual, 2nd Edition*

*Windows XP Pro: The Missing Manual, 2nd Edition*

*Windows Vista: The Missing Manual*

*Windows Vista for Starters: The Missing Manual*

*Word 2007: The Missing Manual*

## Other O'Reilly Titles

*Excel 2007 Pocket Reference*

*Writing Excel Macros with VBA, 2nd edition*

*Excel Hacks*

*Analyzing Business Data with Excel*

*Excel Scientific and Engineering Cookbook*

# O'REILLY®

Our books are available at most retail and online bookstores.
To order direct: 1-800-998-9938 • *order@oreilly.com* • *www.oreilly.com*
Online editions of most O'Reilly titles are available by subscription at *safari.oreilly.com*

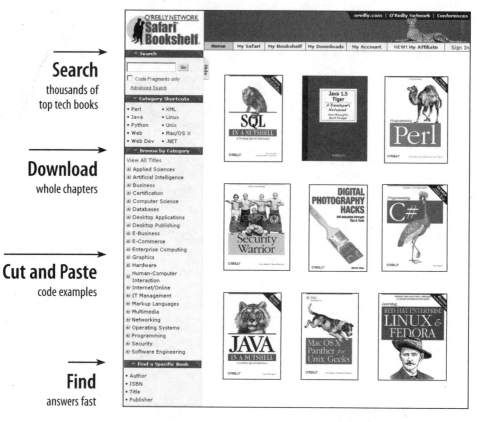